Counter-Reformation

Compilation of 1970-77 Newsletters

By
Rudolph M. Unger

Airleaf Publishing

airleaf.com

ISBN: 1-59453-849-2

Previous Books By
Rudolph M. Unger

The Chicago Tribune News Staff—1920s-1960s
(1991)

The Community of Fuller Park
Those Were The Days My Friends
(1997)

One Man's Journey
Faith—Family—Freedom
(2001)

Roses and Sunsets
Steeples and Stained Glass
Exploring God's World
Volume I
(2004)

Counter-Reformation

(Compilation of 1970-77 Newsletters)

Cover Photo by Author

The Author owes a great debt of gratitude to Inga Lasalle Stierwalt of Bookman for her superb editing of the book.

Dedication

This Compilation of the Counter-Reformation
Newsletters is Dedicated to:

Cardinal John O'Hara
Archbishop of Philadelphia

Cardinal Samuel Stritch
Archbishop of Chicago

Cardinal J. Francis McIntyre
Archbishop of Los Angeles

True Shepherds of Christ in the Catholic Church

Remembrances

Chapter 1

"These are times that try men's souls!"

Thomas Paine's immortal words certainly apply to our day.

As do those of William Yeats:

"Things fall apart. The center cannot hold. Mere anarchy is loosed upon the world…the best lack all conviction, while the worst are full of passionate intensity."

Even the Rock of Peter seems challenged and one is tempted to think if indeed the gates of hell will prevail. The devil has attained the respectability he always has sought.

Mary at Fatima (modernists shun those days of "Opiate Superstition") warned that she could no longer hold back the hand of her son and that if men did not repent, Russia would spread her errors throughout the world.

With the death of good Pope Pius XII, that conflict entered into a new advance phase. The struggle, which heretofore had been outside the church, now entered inside the church.

As St. Paul told his followers:

"Beloved, I charge thee in the sight of God and Christ Jesus, who will judge the living and dead…preach the word, be urgent in season, out of season, reprove, entreat, rebuke with all patience and teaching.

"For there will come a time when they will not endure sound doctrine, but having itching ears, will heap up to themselves teachers according to their own lusts, and they will turn away from the truth and turn aside rather to fables."

The bishops of the church, led by foolish John and weak Paul, have mounted the steeds of ecumenism and irenicism to do battle with the windmills of poverty, racism, war and difference; while Lucifer has infiltrated and is making a frontal assault on the bastion of faith and morals—the church—itself, in an attempt to devour the shepherd's lambs.

This is the age of "See no evil, hear no evil, and there will be no evil."

"Why all these recriminations?" asked John…And the church ceased to fight communism, Islamism and idolatry and ceased to pray for their victims.

This is the age of permissiveness, existentialism, subjectivism, the age of anything goes. You name it. You do it. Black is white, night is day. Up is down. In is out. Wrong is right...the God of change is in the driver's seat. The blind lead the blind. And the devil takes all.

The church is suppose to influence the world. But the world influences the church. The church is suppose to convert persons to the one, true faith. But the church instead is protestanized.

Truth, principle, morality. These give way to image and popularity. Christ never begged nor forced anyone. Church leaders today are reminiscent of salesmen on Maxwell street.

"What do you want? What's your price? Protestanize the liturgy? Make Saturday Sunday? De-emphasize Mary? Shun the angels and saints? Eliminate the sacramentals? Eliminate fasting and abstinence? Ease marriage and divorce? Wink at birth control? Go easy on criticism of abortion and sterilization? Minimize and don't harp on lust, theft, debts, sloth, greed, dishonesty, envy, jealousy.

"You want Christ but not sacrifice? You don't dig the crucified Christ but rather the Christ of 'Love' and to hell with good, truth, beauty and justice?

"Wait, wait. Don't go away. Let's have a dialogue about it. Strum your guitar, beat your bongo. Let's sing. Emote a little. Maybe we'll <u>feel</u> togetherness after all and evolve into one big homogeneous mass mess."

In a very finite attempt to counter this modern reformation of the church, <u>Counter-Reformation</u> will be published monthly. It will seek to recall what no longer is offered in the pulpit, school, press and seminary of a church intimidated, hypnotized and paralyzed in the face of Beelzebub.

I—September, 1970 Rudolph M. Unger

Chapter 2

To counter the "Reformed" and "Renewed" church, Counter-Reformation will seek to minimize the thoughts of the writer and offer impeccable sources to make its arguments against the folly and fallacy of the modernists, the pseudo-liberals, who control the church today.

In a church in which the only thing anathema is anathema itself, in which a representative of the Vatican itself calls "Great and good" the apostate and heretic, Martin Luther (who probably did as much damage to the cause of Christ as any man who ever lived), we propose to offer the healing balm of the scriptures and the tradition of the church.

In Rome in September, 1965, Pope Paul, while the Vatican II council was still in session, told the International Thomistic Council:

"There is no doubt that the return to the living sources of holy scripture and the study of the fathers, joined with the indispensable deep study of doctrine and light of the Magisterium's teachings, will spur an ardently desired renewal.

"We continue to recommend the work of St. Thomas as a sure norm for sacred teaching...the church's Magisterium making his teaching the basis of ecclesiastical teaching...Thomism, far from being a system sterilely closed upon itself, is capable of successfully applying its principles, its methods and its spirit to the new tasks that the problematic of our times proposes to the reflection of Christian thinkers."

The Pope went on to note, that in addition to Thomas;

"The church has never ceased to recognize the value of the great Christian thinkers of east and west, among whom the name of St. Augustine shines with particular brilliance."

The fundamental source Counter-Reformation will draw upon is "A Companion To The Summa" by the late Dominican, Father Walter Farrell.

The four volume series is a faithful chapter by chapter presentation of Thomas' "Summa Theologica" in modern layman's language. The brilliance of Father Farrell's clarity and simplicity in explaining the greatest work of Catholic theology is unmatched by any other writer.

Farrell is Thomas and Thomas is Christ. That in a nutshell is why Counter-Reformation will rely on the "Companion" as its primary source for light.

Contained in it is the refutation of every heresy that bedevils men inside and outside the church today. Though written 30 years ago, the "Companion" clearly foretold the fallacies that would plague the world today.

Once required reading in Catholic seminaries and colleges, the "Companion" is now out of print because Thomism, despite the Pope's admonition, has been pushed aside in seminaries and colleges. This fact, perhaps more clearly than any other, indicates the depth and duration of the crisis in the church and, consequently, the crisis of the world.

"There will come a time when they will not endure sound doctrine, but having itching ears, will heap up to themselves teachers according to their own lusts, and they will turn away from the truth and turn aside rather to fables." (St. Paul)

Among the others that Counter-Reformation will rely on in the tradition of the church to defend the orthodoxy of the church against the Modernist pseudo-liberals (for that is our purpose) will be:

Augustine (of course), Alphonsus, Ambrose, Anselm, Anthony, Athanasius, Basil, Bede, Bellarmine, Benedict, Bernard, Bonaventure, Catherine Siena; Francis (Assisi) (Desales) (Xavier), Gregory, Ignatius (Antioch) (Loyola), Irenaeus, Jerome; John (Evangelist) (Chrysostom) (The Cross), Leo (The Great) (XIII), St. Paul, Pius (X, XI, XII), Teresa, Therese, Thomas (More) (Kempis).

Also such others as—Belloc, Brownson, Chesterton, Gillis, Newman, Thompson, Sheen, Lunn, Derrick, Von Hildebrand, Molnar and Wilhelmsen.

II—October, 1970 Rudolph M. Unger

Chapter 3

What kind of man was Thomas Aquinas ...the man who will be our major mentor?

"By 20th century standards he could expect no rousing welcome," according to Father Walter Farrell, author of "A Companion To The Summa."

"He might be tolerated in an amused fashion but certainly no one would get chummy with him. He lived in the wrong place, his home was a cloister. He lived in the wrong age, long before the modern age of progress, in the very middle of the middle ages.

"He had nothing to say about earning more pay. He neither attacked God nor debunked man and society. His books had no scarlet pages, no profanity, no biological realism in perfumed words, no substitute for thinking, no escape from life.

"He had a good deal to say about truth, goodness, love and God. Far from rejecting the past, the man actually revered old things!"

Father Farrell went on to say:

"Thomas was a relentless searcher for reality, a ruthless enemy of falsehood. Thomas from the beginning was head over heels in love with God.

"From his first appearance in a professor's chair, Thomas was embroiled in intellectual battle. That battle continued all his life; nor is it finished yet. It was and is a battle in defense of God and man.

"Thomas would not stand by and see God torn down from his divine throne. He could not stand by and see the image of God defaced on, earth."

Why is Thomas important to us in our time?

"This is a man and a book providentially designed for the needs of the 20th Century," Father Farrell remarked. "Certainly no age has greater need for ultimate answers, for a plan of action, for an exemplar of human living. For no age has had less conception of the meaning of life.

"The men of our times have learned all but the important things. Forgetting God, our times have not recognized men and have yet to see the world. We are learned but far from wise."

Farrell goes on to say:

"In his book, Thomas offers the 20th Century love and truth. But the love cannot be reveled in until the truth has been mastered. This truth comes as a rather violent antidote to the two modern poisons of intellectual superficiality and naturalistic provincialism.

"This book looks to the last and adequate answer. Its aim is to develop the capacity to think for oneself. It is not an emphasis of facts to the neglect of wisdom. It will hit us between the eyes or it will not touch us at all. For the ultimate answers cannot be looked at without deep personal reverberations."

Farrell then notes:

"Thomas' study is of extreme pertinence to our times because we are victims of a constantly increasing confusion. We have become more and more timid about digging beneath the surface of life, more and more emphatic about a knowledge of facts, less and less concerned with the wisdom of beginnings and ends.

"We have concentrated more and more on the physical world and less and less on man and on God. The exclusive concentration on a study of the world does not unearth the important truths about the world. An exclusive consideration of man and the world results in a blurred, distorted vision of both.

"We have tried to know only the world and remained most ignorant of it, to know only man and the world and have become entangled in a mass of meaningless detail.

"The world is intelligible only in the terms of man and God. Man is intelligible only in terms of God. God is intelligible only in terms of himself."

Farrell notes:

"Such a study is not easy. But man was not made for easy things. He was made for hard things, almost insuperably hard things—a truth that intrudes itself on the mind of man in its every contact with the crucial things of life."

III—November, 1970 Rudolph M. Unger

Chapter 4

"Tell it like it is!" Is one of the favorite catch phrases of the Modernists.

Sounds good. Sounds fair. Sounds reasonable. Except that they don't mean it. It belies their intellectual and moral hypocrisy, which is their cardinal vice.

To tell it like it is, you have to see it like it is. And that's the last thing they want. That's precisely what they don't want. That's why they substitute emotional catch phrases for rational discussion. That's why they want action and not thought. That's why they insist on narcotics and acid rock and "Free" love.

To wipe out from their minds and memories and consciences that bright brilliant light called truth, called reality, called morality.

As Father Walter Farrell puts it in his "A Companion To The Summa":

"A truth that is at the heart of everything, a truth that must be seen if we are to see the meaning, the beauty, the full perfection that is in this world of ours, the truth, namely, that nothing exists alone, that everything has its place.

"That central truth of human life finds accurate expression in the phrase 'Man and his God'. For that is the truth of a man's place in the universe. If that truth is seen, then we have seen the place of God, the place of man and the place of the world.

"The attempt to deny this truth, to submerge it, escape from it, or despair in the face of it, makes up the history of much of the unidentified misery in the depths of the human soul.

"Seeing this truth of the proper place of man, we are presented with the singular spectacle of a dependently independent being. There precisely lies the beauty and marvel of man.

"There will be more than enough beauty, more than enough wonder in any human life to occupy the mind of man for a lifetime, if he sees man in his proper place—subject to his God—and above all the rest of the material universe."

Father Farrell continues;

"Man is gigantic, imposing compared to the level of life beneath him. Man is tiny, insignificant compared to the infinite perfection of divinity. Man, on his own level, is the combination of the lowest and highest in the universe—capable of great love, of unstinting sacrifice. But also, capable of great sin, of complete selfishness, of calamitous failure.

"To take any one of these as the whole story of humanity is to fall into absurdly tragic error…the truth is the whole view of human nature."

Farrell notes:

"Sometimes man's dream has been a distorted thing revolving around the absurd conceit that men were Gods because the human level was the peak of reality. Other times man's dream has been denied and he has only been allowed to look down, to search nauseated the depths from which he allegedly came.

"In our times, human nature is seen almost consistently from below, or, at best, from its own level.

"The naturalist today looks at man only from below And sees him as the peak of perfection. / The humanitarian sees man on his own horizontal level and is bewildered by the paradox of humiliation and inspiration with no key to the solution of the mystery. / Much of Protestantism has looked upon man from above and seen him only as insignificant, corrupted, utterly powerless, a fit victim for despair.

"It is the shame of our time to have shortened the horizons of man, step by step, until he is now blind for the want of something to see. By removing God and heaven from his heart and mind, our time has made it impossible to look up.

"Man's blindness must endure as long as he will not see his proper place, as long as men refuse to look at the God-man, at Christ's human and divine natures united in one divine person, the Incarnation."

IV—December, 1970 Rudolph M. Unger

Chapter 5

Perhaps the most fundamental illusion harbored by modern man which has led to the decay of his character and of his civilization is that figment called Christian Socialism.

Christian Socialism is a non-existent contradiction. It does not dwell in the real world. It dwells only in the minds and imaginations of men who refuse to see life, man and God as they really are.

It is the vain glorious child of arrogantly proud men who would be God, who delude themselves into believing they can make a heaven on earth, a materialistic, collectivistic paradise in this world. It is the damned lie called Utopia that irrational men are maddeningly committed to unceasingly pursue about the confines of their homemade insane asylums.

It is an enemy of the spirit. It is a direct attack on the dignity of man and on the providence of God. It is contrary to the nature of man and in direct opposition to the will of God, who made man in his own image. Meaning, an <u>independent</u> mind and a <u>free</u> will, capable of knowing truth and desiring good.

It is this sugar coated narcotic—Christian Socialism—that on one hand has corroded the Christian character of the people of the western nations, and, on the other hand has allowed the unchecked ascendancy in the east of Communism, which has consumed God's children with diabolical fire.

Socialists are philosophical brothers of communists. They are spewed from the same cancerous womb, and, it is for this very logical reason, that socialists are psychologically incapable of opposing communism.

Here, in this cowardliness, lies the real reason for the increasingly unchecked growth of communism, rather than in any great strength inherent in communism.

Thus we witness the ludicrous spectacle of Popes John and Paul, who after properly defining the dignity of the God imaged individual person as the truly sacred thing in this world, then proceed to suggest that his well being depends upon the development of power in materialistic, collectivistic groups and governments—those very entities which historically have proven anathema to man's spiritual and material welfare.

And the unspoken corollary of these two Popes is not really strange but follows rather logically—their all but total silence and effeminate inoffensiveness as to communism.

Likewise, not strange is the other corollary we see—the mutations of the church's liturgy and schooling, with the de-emphasis of religion as the relation between God and the individual person, and, the emphasis on the humanistic, collectivistic, secularistic socialization of men, with both God and man giving way to the group, the collective we.

Other Popes in other times, when the church was the militant, active agent and not the cowardly, passive one in its relations with the world, have written otherwise and have done so unequivocally.

"No one can be, at the same time, a sincere Catholic and a true socialist." Pope Pius XI.

"The main tenet of socialism, namely the community of good, must be rejected without qualification, for it would injure those it pretends to benefit. It would be contrary to the natural rights of man, and it would introduce confusion and disorder into the commonwealth." Pope Leo XIII.

"Socialism appears to be afraid of its own principles and of the conclusions drawn from them by the communists." Pope Pius XI.

"Socialists, communists and nihilists strive to uproot the fundamentals of civilized society." Pope Leo XIII.

Father Walter Farrell in his "A Companion To The Summa", drawing upon the Christ-like wisdom of St. Thomas Aquinas, remarks;

"Christian helplessness demands a recognition both of our limitations and our abilities. Pagan helplessness, with its basis of pride, makes a ruthless attempt to implant in others a sense of limitation without a sense of perfection, a knowledge of weakness with no courage or pride.

"For it is only in this way that these men who call themselves God can guarantee the service they demand. The inevitable conclusion is a denial of the personality of man, his humanity, substituting the mass for the person.

"For in this pagan world, man is not human in either his power or in his helplessness.

"Such an age, rather than insisting that man make room for divine things in themselves and fit themselves to be instruments of divine power, would ask men to narrow their minds down to the world of senses and the goals proper to the masses rather than men.

"No man would bc encouraged to look for enduring glory either within himself or within other men. For that would be completely fatal to the aims and ideals of mass movements since, in that case, all other things would have to serve the individual.

"A vision of glory men must have. So this age would speak movingly to him of the glory of the state, the race, the group, of humanity.

The strength of man can easily become a thing to be surrendered eagerly that men might feel the cowardly comfort and release from individual responsibility that are the rewards of incorporation into a mob.

"Man's primary work is to save his own soul, as against the social service idea which has been recently substituted for the kingdom of God. The things that pertain to the perfection of the individual soul come first. Then, and only then, the sacraments referring to the community.

"Man in the admission of his loneliness has insisted upon unity, even though, at times, he paid too high a price for quite the wrong kind of unity.

"The wisdom of the east advocated a unity of absorption. By it a man was united to the absolute, but to the complete destruction of his own individuality and personality. Its success in winning millions to the ideal of absorption into a process, a state, a group, or a race, is itself evidence of how thoroughly man has been calumniated by his champions of the last three centuries."

Farrell adds:

"The unity which has been the characteristic aim of the west insists upon a rigid safeguarding of the individuality and personality of man. Its claim has been, not to a destruction of man which might delight the heart of a coward, but to a perfection of man that would challenge the great heart of a saint.

"In the concrete, this unity is one of order and friendship, rather than one of physical absorption.

"The unity of order is accomplished by truth, a unity of the intellect in the recognition of man's place in the universe. This recognition is adequately expressed by sacrifice, which is a statement of man's dependence and God's superiority, bringing out at the same time, man's superiority to the material world in which he lives.

"The unity of friendship is accomplished by that unity of wills that lies at the root of unselfish love.

"Obviously, the unity of absorption ties men together by slavish bonds that destroy men themselves. The bonds of order and friendship, tying men to all the universe and the creator of that universe by truth and love, are altogether unintelligible without the enduring sovereignty of the individual mind and will.

"The supernatural medium of this latter unity is the Eucharist, both as a sacrament and a sacrifice. Here, in this 'Bond of Unity' as St. Augustine called it, here is man's road to peace and plenty, to the peace of order and the plenty of the fullness of love."

Farrell adds:

"Diluted Christianity has done much to further our modern American disregard of the supernatural. In this dilution there has been a kind of heartless mercy, the weakness of compromise, the kindness of a lie. When fundamentals are in question, this sweetly corruptive delicacy destroys all it touches.

"This half hearted Christianity is fundamentally destructive of man and of God, though the thing is advanced as a favor to man.

"Man wins heaven when he embraces God despite the alluring promises of all that is contrary to God."

V—January, 1971 Rudolph M. Unger

Chapter 6

A superb example of the stark sterility, the puritanical barrenness of the renewed, the reformed, the protestanized church is the renovated Holy Name cathedral, mother church of the Chicago Archdiocese.

Holy Name, whose feast, not incidentally but perhaps co-incidentally is no longer observed in the modern church.

That name, of which St. Paul said, “Every knee should bend of those in heaven, on earth and under the earth.”

That name of which St. Peter said, “This is the stone that was rejected by you…neither is there salvation in any other. For there is no other name under heaven given to men by which we must be saved.”

That name, of which the Palmist said, “All the Nations you have made shall come and worship you, O Lord, and glorify your name…You alone are God.”

Inside this once magnificent cathedral you will, today, find the superb stained glass windows, portraying the scenes from Christ’s life, replaced by colored formless windows. No food for meditation.

The paintings on the upper walls, depicting Christ’s life, have been replaced by black marble. No food for meditation.

Fortunately, the stations of the cross have not been eliminated, as they have been in the “Renewed” Sacred Heart church at the University of Notre Dame, where 14 crosses (not crucifixes) replaced them. But in Holy Name, the old stations have been supplanted by new ones, which portray persons in the modern caricature which passes for art, which perhaps does accurately portray the modernists’ grotesque distortion of man.

Gone, of course, is the altar rail. Modern man no longer kneels before God. Bold, emancipated, and intoxicated by the false dogma of the French Revolution—Egalitarianism—He stands!

Gone, of course, are the statues of the saints and angels. No exemplars here. Gone are St. John, St. Joseph, and the lovely Fred Miller family statue of Our Lady. The one before which, as a friend said, “You could fall on your knees, look up into her face, and cry, ‘Mother, help me.’”

Even the Sacred Heart has been escorted out. The great crucified Christ in the lobby, before which many a soul knelt to touch the nailed feet, has joined the scrap heap.

In the sanctuary, there is no altar. Only a table. Like any protestant church. When mass is not being said, there are no lights in the sanctuary. Which is appropriate. There, in the darkness, hangs the crucifix, but there is no living presence of God. As if the Christ crucified and the Eucharistic Lord were not one and the same.

There is only one thing, one essential substance, that keeps this place from being just another edifice like Rockefeller Chapel, the Fourth Presbyterian Church or Temple Sholom.

It is contained in a little gold ball over in the left front corner. If you look hard enough, you'll find it. That is, if you walk all the way up to the left front side.

Out in the courtyard, in the cold and snow, I found the Mother of God. I walked up to her, her hands outstretched, a finger missing. I looked up at her smudged face, her sorrowful eyes, and I asked, "What happened, my Lady?"

And she seemed to reply, "I don't know, my son."

Father Walter Farrell in his "A Companion To The Summa" wrote of: "The storm against images that swept Europe with the Reformation. The reformers' erroneous charge was that these images were being adored.

"The same error had been condemned in the councils of the Eighth century. In all its long history, the error has given way to vandalism, hatred, bloodshed, murder, general destruction.

"Why was all this argument about so simple a thing as images? Why was the church so stubborn about the whole thing? Would it not have been much simpler for the church to renew the old law prohibition against images and stop all this violence?

"<u>Well, there was first of all the matter of truth</u>.

"The church may surrender, in fact has surrendered territory, wealth, power, <u>but not truth</u>.

"For the last bit of truth is more important than all the safety, security, peace and beauty to be found in the world. (Laugh, modern man, laugh.)

"Then, too, there is the very purpose of images as a more than sufficient reason for the stubbornness of the church.

"These are the books of the little ones, the script that can be read by the most unlettered of men. And the souls of these little ones are worth any price that may have to be paid for them."

Father Farrell elaborates:

"Images are a memory lesson that continues to be repeated as long as a church stands. They are the seal by which the mystery and example of the lives of Christ, Mary, and the Saints are impressed on our minds.

"The world did not have to wait for modern psychology to discover that vision is an effective means for vivid, serious instruction, for the inflaming of affections and for indelible memory.

"In the ordinary course of human events, some things are going to strike our eyes, impress themselves on our memories and claim our affections.

"If among these are not the saints, the Mother of God, and her son, then we leave the field open to the undesirable things of the world to pay court to our hearts without rivals."

Such as the flow of pornography and obscenity—unparalleled in the history of the world—bearing the imprimatur of the nine anointed ones in Washington—challenged but whimperingly by our spiritual shepherds, the bishops, who "cleansed" our churches of "Pagan Idolatry".

That flow of lurid, vomitonegrous newspapers, magazines, books, art works, stage plays, and movies that would receive a 4 star rating from the critics from Sodom and Gomorrah, that defiles, "The souls of these little ones."

VI—February, 1971 Rudolph M. Unger

Chapter 7

A critical aspect of the crisis mankind finds itself in in our age is the lack of leadership.

The church, like America, like almost every nation on earth, lacks leaders. In all the important areas of life there is a painful paucity of leaders—in government, in all branches and on all levels; in business, in labor, in education, in communications, in religion.

And the crisis will not be surmounted and conquered until and unless these leaders are forthcoming, be that decades or generations. And it is highly questionable whether mankind has that much time to avert another plunge into the dark ages.

The difficulty lies in the fact that leaders must arise out of the people, and, that people get the leadership they want and deserve; be that to their growth and glory or their degradation and enslavement.

A leader is a standard bearer, an upholder of the truth; a witness, by his word and deed, to the goodness in reality. He advocates and protects what is right and condemns and opposes what is wrong. He does so against all who would line up on the other side, including, if need be, all men, including those he holds most dear.

The prime requisite of a leader is character. He must be able to withstand and bear loneliness which will result from his words and acts, an aloneness that will constitute the most piercing pain a man can know.

He may walk with his brethren until he reaches those bridges where he must walk over—leaving them if they do not follow—to truth, justice, goodness and beauty. For there dwells God and he knows salvation for man does not lie in men, himself included.

As Father James Gillis said in his "This Our Day":

"A really great man does not cajole the people. He corrects them. Tells them what they hate to hear, upbraids them, castigates them, challenges them to do their worst to him. I sometimes wonder if politicians who vociferate that they are 'Friends of the people' have ever read Isaiah, Ezekiel or Jeremiah.

"For that matter have they read St. Paul, who said such things to the people that he irritated them to the point of hatred, and then told them calmly:

'I love you the more even if you love me less.' That is the sign of a big man. They don't come that big nowadays.

"Did anyone ever hear a president who ran counter to the wishes of the people? Has there been one chief magistrate who said, 'Fellow citizens, the plan of action you have in mind would work to the detriment of the nation. In this I decline to do your bidding. You may vote me out if you will, but I cannot in conscience do what you demand."

As Father Walter Farrell said in his "A Companion To The Summa":

"The burial of a fundamental truth has all the bitterness of a buried civilization. The burial of a fundamental truth of leadership is a bitter blow to humanity. It strikes directly at the truth of man, his dignity, his freedom. And after that truth is buried, man must live on to submit to the despoilers of his humanity.

"The field most likely to contain more fundamental truths more deeply buried is precisely the field enclosed by the fences of 'Higher Civilizations'. The practice was never more common than in our own time.

"The fundamental truth of leadership proceeds from the fundamental fact that a man has someplace to go. In our own very high civilization, men are enthusiastically, fanatically following leaders who champion the denial of a goal for men.

"Some modern leaders have called forth goals that can have no meaning to the individual; goals of a race, a party, a class, which excludes the individual as such. Still others insist upon following the people as a mother follows a spoiled child's aimless wanderings.

"The burial of the perfection of leadership—Spiritual leadership—has left the soul of man bewildered, lost. From time immemorial, a leader has been a man who stood out in front between the people and their goal, so that they could be sure of the direction of their goal. Today, spiritual leaders, though seriously laying claim to leadership, insist that there is no God and consequently no purpose in leadership. Buried too are the related fundamental truths of sacrifice and priesthood."

Who, What is a leader?

It's Pope Leo The Great, who, while the Roman emperor hid in quivering fear, walked to the gates of Rome and met Attila the Hun, man to man, eye to eye. And turned his pillaging hordes away from the holy city. Why? To preserve the eternal city, the bastion of civilization in the dark ages, from destruction. To enable the city of God to continue to dwell in the hearts, minds and lives of mankind.

It's Pope Pius V and 24 year old Don Juan of Austria, who marshaled and led the fleet which destroyed the rampaging Turks at the battle of Lepanto. Why? To preserve Christian Europe from the unholy terror called Islamism.

It's St. Bernard, the eloquent hawk of God, taking on and mastering the greatest intellect in Europe, Peter Abelard, the giant of rationalism; leading to the church's condemnation of Abelard's errors. Why? So that the faith of God's children might not be eroded by brilliant, educated, learned, erudite intellectuals.

It's St. Thomas More, laying his head on the chopping block—giving up power, influence, wealth and life itself—to oppose almost single handedly the mighest monarch in Europe—Henry VIII. Why? So the sovereignty of God might be defended against a man who would be God.

It's St. Francis Xavier, who—while his brethren languished in the civilized comfort of Paris—set out into the unknown and, like St. Paul and St. Thomas before him, braved and suffered every fear, hardship and heartbreak that could befall a man. Why? So that the Pagan Asiatics might know, love and serve his glorious master.

It's St. Vincent De Paul, who trodded the slums of Paris to minister to the suffering and needy. Why? So that the least of God's children might know his mercy.

It's St. John Baptist De La Salle, who searched out and schooled the poor children of France. Why? So that they might also enjoy "Religion, morality and education." which are the foundations of civilization.

It's St. John Mary Vianney, the cure of ARS, the country Parish Priest who spend up to 16 hours a day in the confessional for 42 years. Why? To reconcile man with God. <u>That's relevancy!</u>

It's Cardinal O'Boyle, Cardinal Ottaviana, Cardinal Danielou, who, in contrast to so many of their brother princes of the church, refuse to bend, buckle or retreat in the face of the arrogant, hypocritical, demagogic intellectual faddists of the church, who preen themselves under the adulation of the secularistic academe and press. Why? To protect the prerogative of the one, holy, catholic and apostolic church against all pretenders.

It's Pope Paul in Humanae Vitae, the noblest hour of his vicariate, saying clearly and authoritatively "No" to the modernist, pseudo-liberals in the church; that one word they will not tolerate in their vocabulary. Why? To protect God's unquestionable title as "Lord of Life."

It's the priests, sisters and brothers who have withstood the blandishments, the rationalizations and the seductions of the roaring, ravaging lion called Lucifer; who have not forsaken their vows, who have stayed faithful to the bridegroom. Why? So that men may "Know, love and serve God on this earth and be happy with him for all eternity."

Not a cynic, not an anti-hero, not a nihilist, not a demagogue, not a heretic among them—these glorious leaders of the church.

Like St. John Baptist, who preceded Christ, they are the voices, the paths, the channels, the beacons that lead to Lumen Christi—the light of Christ.

And not infrequently, they felt, they feel, like the Baptist—"I am the voice of one crying in the wilderness, make straight the way of the lord."

That is the price of leadership, the price of sanctity, the price of the salvation of mankind.

VII—March, 1971 Rudolph M. Unger

Chapter 8

What is most repugnant to modern man? What repels him most? What does he push out of his mind, avoid, sidestep, retreat and flee from whenever and wherever possible? What is most inimical to his life style?

Is it not sacrifice? Known also as suffering, self denial, self restraint, self control, self discipline.

Whittaker Chambers, in the poignant forward to his children in his monumental "Witness", told them that in the book he was trying to lead them along that dangerous journey which ends at the foot of Calvary.

"When you understand what you see," he wrote, "You will no longer be children. You will know that life is pain, that each of us hangs always upon the cross of himself. And when you know that this is true of every man, woman and child on earth, you will be wise."

Pope Leo XIII wrote in "Rerum Novarum":

"The consequences of sin are bitter and hard to bear and they must accompany man as long as life lasts. To suffer and to endure, therefore, is the lot of humanity.

"Let them strive as they may, no strength and no artifice will ever succeed in banishing from human life the ills and troubles which beset it."

Our Lord himself told us:

"If anyone wishes to come after me, let him deny himself, and take up his cross and follow me. For he who would save his life will lose it. But he who loses his life for my sake will find it.

"He who does not carry his cross and follow me, cannot be my disciple."

Writing on this Central Truth of Christianity, Father Walter Farrell in his "A Companion To The Summa" stated:

"Surely there is no truth more thoroughly buried today than the fundamental truth of sacrifice.

"Christ came to remove the debris from buried fundamental truths as well as to give us new truths. Of the buried truths none received greater emphasis in his life than that of sacrifice."

Mary at Fatima said:

"Pray, pray a great deal, and make sacrifices for sinners, for many souls go to hell because they have no one to make sacrifices and pray for them."

Our Lord himself appeared to Lucy in 1943 and complained bitterly and sorrowfully that so few souls were fulfilling Our Lady's requests. He said, "The sacrifice required of every person is the fulfillment of his duties in life and the observance of my law. This is the penance I now seek and require."

Father Farrell commented;

"Sacrifice must pay man's debt to God, acknowledging God's sovereignty and man's dependence. It must fulfill man's need of dealing with sin and winning that divine life which is his peace.

"The wider sense of sacrifice includes all that is offered to God that the spirit of men might be lifted up to God. Surely, every act of Christ's life was directly aimed at that end. It is not lightly that we call him redeemer and savior.

"It is not without significance that the Catholic Church, alone of all the Christian churches, still has the sacrifice at a time when the Christian world is losing its hold on the truth of God, the truth of man and the truth of the universe."

Farrell goes on to explain;

"The large scale of man's life is—living, suffering, dying...Living is a preparation for suffering, it is a preparation for death. It is only a master in the art of living who knows how to suffer. In a sense, suffering is an intensified course in the perfection of living...suffering plunges us into the role of the master."

The Dominican then comments;

"Christ's way of living cannot, of course, be the mode of life in a world that has banned the spiritual to give itself wholly to the material. In such a world, there is no room for divine things, for the divine is not to be encompassed within the material.

"Here, indeed, there is nothing of glory for man. In such a world, human living is impossible. Man's nature is distorted, perverted, degraded. Growth can only be the crass material thing that, in any man, is a constant threat to the life and joys of every other man.

"It is only on the grounds of the spirit and its growth that men can live together as men… Man must live the way Christ lived or he must cease, slowly or quickly, to live as a man.

"He must hold fast to the vision of glory, even though the road be rough and long. For the loss of the vision will not make the road easier. It will, rather, make the whole necessity of the journey a thing of complete despair."

The priest goes on to say:

"To the superficial observer, suffering is obviously an interruption of the motion of life, while death is its end.

"Naturally, then, men have felt keenly about suffering and death. They have felt even more keenly about their inability to understand them.

"When the world is subject to a siege of severe suffering and violent death, philosophers of protest spring up like mushrooms. No doubt in the 1950s, a whole new crop of protest philosophies will rise up and set themselves against eternal truths because men by the millions have suffered and died."

Farrell then notes:

"Christ had come that all men might know by a glance at his life what they were to do at any moment of their own…He did not minimize the importance of a knowledge of the meaning and technique of suffering and dying.

"In one way or another, every man must meet these supremely hard facts of suffering and death. The way men meet them is an indication of what they have learned of the meaning of life.

"Men who see life, as above all, a spiritual race to a spiritual goal know it cannot be held up by a physical impediment. These men leave suffering and pain intact, not denying them, but ordering them to the soul's high purpose.

"In his death on the cross, Christ gave the full human meaning of suffering and added it to the rich flavor of the divine.

"God took the royal road of suffering himself. He gave it to the most perfect of his friends. His methods have not varied. The very special gift to the followers of Christ has always been a full cup of suffering.

"To them suffering was not a thing to be cringed from in terror. It was a share in and completion of the work of the master to be joyfully embraced, a vital help to others; a safe, sure, short way to heaven.

"Above all, it was an opportunity for the concrete expression of love—sacrifice."

Farrell added:

"This paradox of a suffering and dying God is not to be understood by the world. That he who had come that men's joy might be full, should leave a prescription of suffering.

"The most joyous people in the world are those who most eagerly embrace suffering for themselves yet are the most thoughtful towards suffering in others.

"The secret of this paradox is to be found in the union of the divine and human. In the participation of divine life by men through grace.

"That cross against the sky with its arms flung out to the world was a bold, challenging rebuke to the fears of men. This was the worst men could do and it could not stop the triumph of a man. What then is to be feared from men?

"To the Christian, the sufferer who dies, is in reality a sovereign master, wielding even such terrible weapons as his own pain and death for his own high purposes.

"...Always carrying within himself that spark (grace) that gives him independence of all that is less than the spirit."

"My grace is sufficient for thee"

VIII—April, 1971 Rudolph M. Unger

Chapter 9

Historians centuries hence will record as one of the great books of the 20th century—"Witness" by Whittaker Chambers.

They will record that it was so because it dealt with the great central conflict of the 20th century—the struggle between communism and freedom.

They will record that it was so because it was written by a man—who was intimately connected with that struggle on both sides of it, who clearly understood what the conflict was about. And who was able to lucidly and movingly explain the nature and meaning of the death duel to his fellow man.

The historians will likewise record that his fellow men accepted Chambers' leadership and advice and that the 20th century ended gloriously as an age of great faith—or—they will record that his fellows rejected Chambers' wisdom and courage and that the 20th century plunged into one of the deepest dark ages in history.

Today, no self respecting Las Vegas bookmaker would give you odds on the first possibility.

Chambers knew this when he broke from communism. He told his wife, "You know, we are leaving the winning world for the losing world."

Then he set out, in his "Lazarus like, impossible return", to spend the rest of his days, using the considerable intelligence and the enormous faith that God gave him, to prove his prediction wrong.

Following are excerpts from the soul stirring forward to this classic narrative of our age—"Witness".

As you read these excerpts, perhaps you would like to keep in mind, the witness of Pope Paul, meeting with Tito and Gromyko; that of Pope John, meeting with Khrushchev's son-in-law; that of Cardinal Mindszenty, exiled in Budapest. And think about whose witness bespeaks truth and whose witness betokens falsehood.

"Beloved children…I am writing a book. In it I am speaking you. But I am also speaking to the world. To both I owe an accounting. It is a terrible book. It is terrible in what it tells about men, about the world in which you live.

"It is about what the world calls the Hiss case. Much more than Alger Hiss or Whittaker Chambers was on trial. Two faiths were on trial. Human societies, like human beings, live by faith and die when faith dies.

"At issue in the Hiss case was the question whether this sick society, which we call western civilization, could still cast up a man whose faith in it was so great that he would voluntarily abandon those things which men hold good, including life, to defend it.

"At issue was the question whether this man's faith could prevail against a man whose equal faith was that this society is sick beyond saving.

"At issue was the question whether there still remained, in this desperately divided society, the will to recognize the issues in time to offset the immense rally of public power to distort and pervert the facts.

"At heart, the great case was this critical conflict of faiths, the two irreconcilable faiths of our time—communism and freedom. The history of our times can only end in the destruction of one or both of these forces.

"A witness is a man whose life and faith are so completely one that when the challenge comes to step out and testify for his faith, he does so, disregarding all risks, accepting all consequences.

"In nothing shall I be so much a witness as in trying to make clear to you and to the world, the true nature of communism and the source of its power, which is the historical ordeal of the world in the 20th century.

"For in this century, within the next decades, will be decided, for generations, whether the whole world is to become free, or whether, in the struggle, civilization as we know it is to be completely destroyed or completely changed. It is our fate to live upon that turning point in history.

"All the politics of our time, including the politics of war, will be the politics of this crisis.

"It is popular to call it a social crisis. It is in fact a total crisis—religious, moral, intellectual, social, political, economic. Communism, which claims to be a solution of the crisis, is itself a symptom and an irritant of the crisis.

"I see in communism the focus of the concentrated evil of our time. The revolutionary heart of communism is a simple statement of Karl Marx—'Philosophers have explained the world. It is necessary to change the world.'

"The tie that binds communists is this simple conviction—it is necessary to change the world. Their power, whose nature baffles the rest of the world, because in a large measure the rest of the world has lost that power, is the power to hold convictions and to act on them."

"Communists are that part of mankind which has recovered the power to live or die—to bear witness—for its faith. It is not new. It is, in fact, man's second oldest faith. Its promise was whispered in the first days of creation under the tree of the knowledge of good and evil—'Ye shall be as Gods.' It is the great alternative faith of mankind. The communist vision is the vision of man without God.

"It is the vision of man's mind displacing God as the creative intelligence of the world. It is the vision of man's liberated mind, by the sole force of its rational intelligence, redirecting man's destiny and reorganizing man's life and world.

"Communism grants man sovereignty by the simple method of denying God.

"It is the vision of materialism. Its tools are science and technology, whose traditional method—the rigorous exclusion of all supernatural factors—has contributed to the intellectual climate in which the vision flourishes, just as they have contributed to the crisis in which communism thrives. For the vision is shared by millions who are not communists. They are communism's secret strength.

"The communist party is quite justified in calling itself the most revolutionary party in history. It has posed, in practical form, the most revolutionary question in history—God or man?

"It has taken the logical next step which three hundred years of rationalism hesitated to take, and, said what millions of modern minds think, but do not dare or care to say—If man's mind is the decisive force in the world, what need is there for God?

"This vision is the communist revolution. Communism summons mankind to turn its vision into practical reality, to overcome the crisis of the world.

"It says to every man who joins it—the vision is a practical problem of history. The way to achieve it is a practical problem of politics. Have you the moral strength to take upon yourselves the crimes of history, so that man at last may close his chronicle of age-old, senseless suffering and replace it with purpose and a plan.

"The answer a man makes to this question is the difference between the communist and those miscellaneous socialists, liberals, fellow travelers, unclassified progressives and men of good will, all of whom share a similar vision, but do not share the faith because they will not take upon themselves the penalties of the faith.

"An educated man, peering from Harvard yard, or any college campus, finds in the vision the two certainties for which the mind of man tirelessly seeks—a reason to live and a reason to die.

"No other faith of our time presents them with the same practical intensity. That is why communism is the central experience of the first half of the century. And may be its final experience, will be, unless the free world in the agony of its struggle with communism, overcomes its crisis by discovering, in suffering and pain, a power of faith which will provide man's mind, at the same intensity, with the same two certainties—a reason to live and a reason to die.

"The crisis of communism exists to the degree in which it has failed to free the peoples it rules from God. The crisis of the western world exists to the degree in which it is indifferent to God, to the degree in which it actually shares communism's materialist vision. (Christian socialism)

"Economics is not the central problem of this century. Faith is the central problem of this age. The western world possesses the answer to this problem. But only provided that its faith in God, and the freedom he enjoins, is as great as communism's faith in man."

IX—May, 1971 Rudolph M. Unger

Chapter 10

"God writes straight with crooked lines" some Frenchman once wrote.

And that pretty well expresses the strange, enigmatic way that God's providence appears to our finite minds.

It really isn't strange, for as St. Paul explained it – "Oh, the depth of the riches of the wisdom and of the knowledge of God. How incomprehensible are his judgments and how unsearchable His ways. For who has known the mind of The Lord or who has been His counselor?"

St. Augustine put it this way—"O Lord, you who wait a thousand years to work one-thousandth part of thy vast plan."

And so, for example and by contrast, we note that St. Anthony de Padua was canonized within a year of his death, something almost unheard of in the annals of sainthood.

While it wasn't until 1935, exactly 400 years after an axe severed him from this life, that St. Thomas More was officially ushered into the Church Triumphant.

Then, in 1960, a brilliant, non-catholic, English playwright, Robert Bolt - disturbed by the rise of the collective, mass man and inspired by "This man, Thomas More, who had an adamantine sense of his own self, who knew where he began and where he left off"—proceeded to write a classic work of art which he called "A Man For All Seasons."

Thus did God thrust a man of the middle ages before the eyes of 20th century man as a model of Christian living for our season on earth, reassuring us that saints are never out of season.

The following excerpts from the prize winning play and film give us superb insights into this hair-shirt wearing chancellor of England who, in the crucible of living, matured from a youthful "Utopia" idealist of life to the rich realist of the "Dialogue Of Comfort Against Tribulation", which enabled him to meet the world and devil head-on and master both through "Our captain Christ"

Except where noted the speaker quoted is St. Thomas More.

"I believe when statesmen forsake their own private conscience for the sake of their public duties, they lead their country by a short route to chaos.

Common Man -- "From Sir Thomas' willful indifference to realities which were obvious to quite ordinary contemporaries, it seems all too probable that he possessed the quality of saintliness."

Henry VIII -- 'Because you are honest. What's more to the purpose, you're known to be honest. There are those who like Norfolk who follow me because I wear the crown. There are those who like master Cromwell who follow me because they are jackals with sharp teeth and I am their lion. And there is a mass that follows me because it follows anything that moves. And, there is you."

"I'm not God."

"Would you cut a great road through the law to get after the devil? And when the last law was down, and the devil turned round on you, where would you hide, Roper, the laws all being flat? Do you really think you could stand upright in the winds that would blow then?"

Cromwell - "Who has a strong head for success?"

Cromwell - "Our job as administrators, Rich, is to make it as convenient as we can...There are no rules, with rewards and penalties...Are you sure you're not religious?

"You're absolutely right, Rich. It must be done by law. It's just a matter of finding the right law, or making one."

Common Man - "Only an unhappy few were found to set themselves against the current of their times and in so doing to court disaster."

"Because I am afraid."

"This is not the stuff of which martyrs are made."

Chapuys - "Goodness can be a difficulty."

Chapuys - "Ah, Sir Thomas, in a better state, this threadbare stuff will metamorphose into shining garments, these dank walls to walls of pearl, this cold light to perpetual sunshine."

"Cromwell? He's a Pragmatist. That's the resemblance he has to the devil."

Cromwell - "If you could bring yourself, Sir Thomas, to agree with the universities, the bishops and the parliament of this realm."

Common Man - "You know the old adage? 'Better a live rat than a dead lion?'"

Jailer - "I'm a plain, simple man and just want to keep out of trouble."

"Oh, sweet Jesus! These plain simple men!"

"And when we stand before God, Norfolk, and you are sent to paradise for doing according to your conscience, and I am damned for not doing according to mine, will you come with me, for fellowship?"

"If the world is flat, will the king's command make it round? And if it is round, will the king's command flatten it?"

Cromwell - "Oh, justice is what you're threatened with."

"Then, I'm not threatened."

Cromwell - "Remove the prisoner's books."

Cromwell - "While More's alive the king's conscience breaks into fresh stinking flowers every time he gets from bed."

"What is an oath then but words we say to God?…When a man takes an oath, Meg, he's holding his own self in his own hands. Like water, and if he opens his fingers then—he needn't hope to find himself again."

(The following is More's own mature answer to his youthful 'Utopia'.)

"If we lived in a state where virtue was profitable, common sense would make us good, and, we'd live in the happy land that needs no heroes.

"But since, in fact, we see—that avarice, anger, envy, pride, sloth, lust and stupidity commonly profit far beyond humility, chastity, fortitude, justice and thought…Why, then we must stand fast a little—even at the risk of being heroes."

"Finally, it isn't a matter of reason. Finally, it is a matter of love."

"May almighty God keep me in my honest mind to the last hour that I shall live."

"Death comes for us all, my lords. Yes, even for kings he comes."

"For our own deaths, my lords, yours and mine, dare we for shame enter the kingdom with ease, when Our Lord himself entered with so much pain?"

"The world must construe according to its wits. This court must construe according to the law.

"The law is a causeway upon which, so long as he keeps to it, a citizen may walk safely."

"In matters of conscience, the loyal subject, is more bounden to be loyal to his conscience than to any other thing."

"A man's soul is his self!

"Is it my place to say 'good' to the state's sickness? Can I help my king by giving him lies when he asks for the truth?"

"What you have hunted me for is not for my actions, but the thoughts of my heart...It is a long road you have opened. For first men will disclaim their hearts and presently they will have no hearts. God help the people whose statesmen walk in your road."

"The indictment is grounded in an act of parliament which is directly repugnant to the law of God. The king in parliament cannot bestow the supremacy of the church, because it is a spiritual supremacy."

"I am the king's true subject and pray for him and all the realm. I do none harm, I say none harm, I think none harm. And if this be not enough to keep a man alive, in good faith, I long not to live."

"Death comes for us all, even at our birth. It is the law of nature and the will of God."

"Friend, be not afraid of your office. You send me to God."

Common Man –"I'm breathing. Are you breathing too? It's nice isn't it? It isn't difficult to keep alive, friends. Just don't make trouble."

X—June, 1971 Rudolph M. Unger

Chapter 11

They, you know, the famous, ever present, never seen they...say that the new church—the church of John, Paul and the second Vatican council—is a church of love and tolerance.

I say—nay, not so.

You see tolerance? I see tyranny. You see an easing? I see a hardening. You see a more democratic spirit? I see a more authoritarian spirit. You see renewal? I see decay.

You see growth? I see contraction. You see responsibility? I see dereliction. You see candor? I see duplicity. You see considerateness? I see cold, harsh indifference. You see a lamb? I see a wolf.

You see greater freedom of speech and thought? I see brainwashing and thought control. You see a gentle hand? I see an iron fist. You see greater wisdom? I see arrogant stupidity. You see the Holy Spirit? I see a spirit dark and sinister.

And nowhere is this dichotomy in the church more bitter, more harsh, more painful than in what has been done to the liturgy.

Not important, you say? I say it is eminently important. That is why it was changed! The people of my generation have been robbed. Our children and their children have been cheated.

The following excerpts from "Pavane, For A Dead Liturgy" by Christopher Derrick, in the Christmas issue of Triumph, I think states the truth of it well.

"For western Christianity and for the whole traditional culture that stems from Europe, the outward forms of the Latin Liturgy—and of the mass in particular—have for many centuries constituted a womb, a cradle, a nourishment, a home.

"We now see demolition men moving in cheerfully to start their work. The intellectuals stand by, ready with exhortation, commanding a positive attitude and a docile acceptance of their own view point.

"They arranged it all. It was by their standards and through their activities that the plan has been made to appear necessary, the old house anachronistic and absurd past any further toleration. And so, as the wreckers move in, these men tell us to rejoice.

"Their plan, we are told, is a beneficent one. We ought to be grateful. We have no right, they say, to demand in the liturgy any richness that might also comfort and sustain us at the human and psychological and cultural level.

"The new Missa Normativa that is replacing the home of our own and Christendom's childhood, will embody one fashion of mind, the outlook of one generation. At an old style Latin mass, all the Christian centuries seemed present, as though in eternity. In the new liturgy we shall emphatically be doing a thing of the late 20th century.

"This appears to be desired. People speak of contemporary relevance, of adaption to the present age. But nothing dates like contemporaneity, nothing looks more absurd than last year's hat. Within a very short time it will become apparent that in attempting to renew and revitalize our worship, we only succeeded in narrowing it, in tying it down to the dominant mood of a passing moment.

"Perhaps further adaptation will then be put in hand and, in a changing world, it will need to be continuous, thus inflicting turmoil and distraction upon us forever. Perhaps saner counsels will prevail and a refusal to run endlessly and tiringly after the rainbow's end of adaptation.

"Meanwhile, we are saddled with a new liturgy which will not possess the charm of novelty for very long. To our grandchildren, it will seem to embody an eccentric, one sided, and thoroughly dated kind of Catholicism.

"Relatively speaking, it will seem that our religion was centered upon man rather than upon God, not liking a situation in which priest and people faced in the same direction, united in their confrontation with God.

"Placing the second great commandment first, we preferred to confront man. And it will seem very symbolic that when we first put the old Roman canon into English, the translated text began with "We" where the Latin had begun with "TE" (God)

"Men centered we shall seem in retrospect, but curiously unconcerned with the individual man. To an almost neurotic degree, we concerned ourselves with the group or the collective. One-sidedly, we therefore tended to see the mass as a purely social thing, a group activity, and we often spoke as though experienced human solidarity was its desired end product, though the gospel hinted at nothing of the sort.

"From motives presumably egalitarian, we energetically played down the role of the priest and urged the laity to participate. But to an astonishing degree, we saw their participation in formalistic terms, with great emphasis upon word and posture and movement, and a correspondingly reduced emphasis upon inwardness and the private soul.

"Our grandchildren will marvel and be astonished at our willingness to submit the liturgy to pressures that were sociological and political in nature and at our relative indifference to the sacred. They will then address themselves to rebalancing the work done by our somewhat hysterical generation of Catholics.

"Our grandchildren will remember our generation as a pathologically oedipal and Jacobin generation, breathtakingly confident in our sense of superiority over the past.

"Did we think it was really so simple? Did we suppose that bare lucidity held all the answers, that the mass could ever lie within anybody's power of comprehension? Did we hate the idea of God's unsearchable richness? Did we see total depravity in the perennial instinct, which has driven men to seek mystery and splendor in the service of God, and to seek an escape from the obsessive now and therefore a hint of eternity?

"In rejecting Tridentine Catholicism we slap down a great deal besides Latin and incense—the whole tradition of orthodox worship.

"Such arrogance is hardly suitable for a generation that desires to be ecumenical.

"Very meekly, one can make a plea for toleration. When Pope St. Pius V reformed the liturgy, imposing the Roman missal we now remember, he made kindly exceptions. In our day, the church is supposed to be less authoritarian and monolithic than in the past, more tolerant, more flexible.

"The Second Vatican council said, 'Even in the liturgy, the church has no wish to impose a rigid uniformity in matters which do not implicate faith or the good of the whole community.'

"Can these words be taken seriously? Are we going too far if we suggest that a certain practical toleration might be extended—even at some cost in uniformity—to those Catholics who love and revere the old liturgy. Are their 'pietas' to be simply slapped down by authority?

"If in the changes accomplished, they see a great deal of obvious loss and a small amount of highly questionable gain, are they so plainly wrong as to deserve no consideration at all?

"It seems that the old liturgy is to be stamped out completely and everywhere, just as though it were some remarkably pernicious kind of heresy. As things stand now, it seems that a priest who preaches frank heresy will be treated far more gently than a priest who has the sinful temerity to begin his mass with "Introibo" and end it with "plenum Gratiae Et Veritatis.'

"If the good of the church 'genuinely and certainly' requires that the old liturgy has got to be abolished, the fact still needs to be demonstrated.

"Until sound reasons are offered, we can hardly be blamed if we suspect mere Jacobinism of a notably destructive kind. Some Catholic hierarchy and clergy now propose to destroy finally one of the great cultural monuments of western Christian civilization. In this age that claims to be so tolerant, may we hope for something less than 100 percent remorselessness?"

XI—July, 1971 Rudolph M. Unger

Chapter 12

Two years ago next month, Cardinal Alfredo Ottaviani, prefect-emeritus of the Sacred Congregation For The Faith, send a letter to Pope Paul, warning of dangers in the "Novus Ordo Missae" (The new order of the mass), and fervently urging the continuing use of the "Missale Romanum" (The Tridentine Mass), i.e., based on the doctrinal definitions of the Council of Trent.

Ottaviani enclosed a study of the new order made in Rome—by theologians and liturgists of different nationalities and differing tendencies which was a scathing indictment of "The Novus Ordo."

Three weeks later, Pope Paul delayed the extinction of the Tridentine mass and the mandatory imposition of the new order until November, 1971. Whether after November, Catholics will still have a choice between orthodoxy and the new order or whether the new order will dominate completely, only God knows.

In his letter to the Pope, Ottaviani stated that:

"The 'Novus Ordo' represents a striking departure from the Catholic Theology of the mass as it was formulated in the Council of Trent. The 'Canons' of the rite definitely fixed at that time provided an insurmountable barrier to any heresy directed against the integrity of the mystery. The innovations in the 'Novus Ordo' and the fact that all that is of perennial value finds only a minor place, if it subsists at all, could well turn into a certainty the suspicion, already prevalent, alas, in many circles, that Truths which have always been believed by Christian People, can be changed or ignored without infidelity to that sacred deposit of doctrine to which the Catholic faith is bound forever.

"Recent reforms have amply demonstrated that fresh changes in the liturgy could lead to nothing but complete bewilderment on the part of the faithful who already are showing signs of restiveness and of an indubitable lessening of faith. Among the best of the clergy, the practical result is an agonizing crisis of conscience of which innumerable instances come to our notice daily.

"It has always been the case that when a law meant for the good of subjects proves to be on the contrary harmful, those subjects have the right, nay the duty of asking with filial trust for the abrogation of that law.

"Therefore, we most earnestly beseech your holiness, at a time of such painful division and of ever increasing perils for the purity of the faith and the unity of the church, lamented by you, our common father, not to deprive us of the possibility of continuing to have recourse to the fruitful integrity of that "Missale Romanum" of St. Pius V, so highly praised by your holiness and so deeply loved and venerated by the whole Catholic world."

Following are excerpts from the theologians' critical analysis of the new order containing some of their general criticisms of it. Next month, Counter-Reformation will present some of their specific criticisms.

"Since the 'Normative Mass' now reintroduced and imposed as the 'Novus Ordo Missae' was in substance rejected by the synod of bishops, was never submitted to the collegial judgment of the Episcopal conference, nor have the people ever asked for any reform of the holy mass, whatsoever, one fails to comprehend the motives behind the new legislation which overthrows a tradition unchanged in the church since the fourth and fifth centuries.

"As no popular demands exists to support this reform, it appears devoid of any logical grounds to justify it and make it acceptable to the Catholic people.

"For if the desire of the people was expressed – thanks to St. Pius X— they began to discover the true and everlasting treasures of the liturgy, they never, on any account, asked for the liturgy to be changed or mutilated as to understand it better. They asked for a better understanding of a changeless liturgy, and one which they would never want changed.

"The Roman missal of St. Pius V was religiously venerated and most dear to Catholics, both priests and laity. One fails to see how its use, together with suitable catechesis, could have hindered a fuller participation in, and greater knowledge of the liturgy.

"An attentive examination of the 'Novus Ordo' reveals changes of such magnitude which in many points have every possibility of satisfying the most modernistic of Protestants.

"We have limited ourselves to a summary evaluation of 'The New Ordo' where it deviates most seriously from the theology of the Catholic mass. A complete evaluation of all the pitfalls, the dangers, the spiritually and psychologically destructive elements contained in the document—whether in text, rubrics or instructions—would be a vast undertaking.

"No more than a passing glance has been taken at the three canons, since these already have come in for repeated and authoritative criticism, both as to form and substance.

"Of Canon II, it has been well said that it could be recited with perfect tranquility of consciences by a priest who no longer believes either in transubstantiation or in the sacrificial character of the mass—hence even by a Protestant minister.

"The apostolic constitution itself gives the 'Coup De Grace' to the church's universal language of Latin—contrary to the express will of Vatican II. The demise of Latin may therefore be taken for granted, and, that of the Gregorian chant will logically follow.

"From the outset therefore, the new rite is launched as pluralistic and experimental, bound to time and place. Unity of worship, thus swept away for good and all, what will now become of the unity of faith that went with it, and which, we were always told, was to be defended without compromise?

"It is evident that 'The Novus Ordo' has no intention of presenting the faith as taught by the Council of Trent, to which nevertheless, the Catholic conscience is bound forever. With the promulgation of 'The Novus Ordo' the loyal Catholic is thus faced with a most tragic alternative.

"The eastern church will, by these changes, be ever more alienated. The new liturgy, however, will be the delight of those, who, hovering on the verge of apostasy, are wreaking havoc in the church of God, undermining her unity of doctrine, worship, morals and discipline in a spiritual crisis without precedent.

"St. Pius V had the Roman Missal drawn up so that it might be an instrument of unity among Catholics. In conformity with the injunctions of the Council of Trent, it

"Was to exclude all danger, in liturgical worship, of errors against faith, then threatened by the Protestant Reformation.

"The gravity of the situation fully justified and even rendered prophetic the saintly pontiff's solemn warning given at the end of the bull promulgating his missal – 'Should anyone presume to tamper with this, let him know that he shall incur the wrath of almighty God and of His blessed apostles Peter and Paul.' (Who no longer are mentioned in 'The new order'.)

"When 'The Novus Ordo' was presented, it was asserted, with great audacity, that the reasons which prompted the Tridentine decrees are no longer valid. Not only do they still apply, but there also exist, as we do not hesitate to affirm, very much more serious ones today.

"It was precisely in order to ward off the dangers, which in every century threaten the purity of the deposit of faith, that the church has had to erect, under the inspiration of the Holy Spirit, the defense of her dogmatic definitions and doctrinal pronouncements. These were immediately reflected in her worship, which became the most complete monument of her faith.

"As we see today only too clearly, the endeavor is to dismantle all the theological ramparts erected for the protection of the rite and to take away all the beauty by which it was enriched over the centuries.

"And all this at one of the most critical—If not the most critical moment—of the church's history. Today, division and schism are officially acknowledged to exist not only outside but within the church. Her unity is not only threatened, but already tragically compromised. Errors against the faith are not merely insinuated, but positively imposed by means of liturgical abuses and aberrations which have been equally acknowledged.

"To abandon a liturgical tradition which for centuries was both the sign and the pledge of unity of worship (and to replace it with another, which cannot but be a sign of division, and which teems with insinuations or manifest errors against the integrity of the Catholic religion) is, we feel in conscience bound to proclaim an incalculable error."

XII—August, 1971 Rudolph M. Unger

Chapter 13

This month we present some of the specific criticisms of the 'Novus Ordo Missae', The New Order of the mass, which were made in Rome in 1969 by theologians and liturgists of varying lands. The critical study was presented to Pope Paul for his consideration and he was urged to retain the Tridentine or Roman mass.

"Let us begin with The Definition Of The Mass given in the 'Novus Ordo'—'The Lord's supper or mass is a sacred meeting or assembly of the people of God, met together under the presidency of the priest, to celebrate the memorial of the Lord.'

"The definition is limited to that of a 'Supper' and this term is constantly repeated. None of this in the very least implies either the real presence or the reality of the sacrifice, or the sacramental function of the consecrating priest, or the intrinsic value of the eucharistic sacrifice independently of the people's presence.

"The deliberate omission of these dogmatic values amounts to their having been superseded and therefore to their denial.

"As is only too evident, the emphasis is obsessively placed upon the supper and the memorial instead of upon the unbloody renewal of The Sacrifice of Calvary.

"As the Council of Trent makes clear, the sacrifice of the mass is a true propitiatory sacrifice and not a bare commemoration of the sacrifice accomplished on the cross.

"The council also made clear that the celebrant, the offerer, the sacrificer is the priest, consecrated for this, not the people of God, the assembly.

"We now come to the Ends Of The Mass.

"Ultimate End -- This is that of the sacrifice of praise to the most Holy Trinity. This end has disappeared from the offertory of the 'Novus Ordo' with the disappearance of the prayer 'Receive, o Holy Trinity, this offering…'; from the end of the mass with the omission of 'May the homage of my service be pleasing to you, o Holy Trinity…'

"And from the preface, which on Sunday will no longer be that of the most Holy Trinity, as this preface will be reserved only to the feast of the Trinity, and so in the future will be heard but once a year.

"Ordinary End -- this is the propitiatory sacrifice. It too has been deviated from. For instead of putting the stress on the remission of sins of the living and dead, it lays emphasis on the nourishment and sanctification of those present.

"This shift of emphasis is met with also in the surprising elimination in the new canons of the momento of the dead and of any mention of the sufferings of the souls in purgatory, to whom the propitiatory sacrifice was applied.

"Immanent End -- whatever the nature of the sacrifice, it is absolutely necessary that it be pleasing and acceptable to God. After the fall, no sacrifice can claim to be acceptable in its own right other than The Sacrifice of Christ.

"The 'Novus Ordo' changes the nature of the offering, turning it into a sort of exchange of gifts between man and God. By suppressing the continual reference to God in the Eucharistic prayers, there is no longer any clear distinction between divine and human sacrifice.

"There is a danger that the uniqueness of this offering will become blurred, so that participation in the immolation of the victim comes to resemble a philanthropical meeting or a charity banquet.

"We now pass on to the essence of the sacrifice.

"The mystery of the cross is no longer explicitly expressed. It is only there obscurely, veiled, imperceptible for the people.

"The reason for this non-explicitness concerning the sacrifice is quite simply that the real presence has been removed from the central position which it occupied so resplendently in the former eucharistic liturgy. There is but a single reference to the real presence.

"The real and permanent presence of Christ—body, blood, soul and divinity—in the transubstantiated species is never alluded to. The very word transubstantiation is totally ignored.

"The suppression of the invocation to the third person of the most Holy Trinity, 'Come, O Sanctifier, Almighty and Eternal God, and bless this sacrifice prepared for the glory of your Holy Name' is yet one more instance of the systematic and tacit negation of the real presence.

"Note too, the eliminations of—genuflections, purification of the Priest's fingers in the chalice; purification of the vessels, of the consecration of movable altars, of thanksgiving kneeling, of ancient prescriptions in the case of the consecrated host falling…All these things only serve to emphasize how outrageously faith in the dogma of the real presence is implicitly repudiated.

"It is recommended in the 'Novus Ordo' that the Blessed Sacrament be kept in a place apart for the private devotion of the people, that the reservation of the Blessed Sacrament on the altar be excluded.

"So that, on going into a church, attention will no longer be focused upon the tabernacle but upon a stripped bare table. Once again the contrast is made between private and liturgical piety. Altar is set up against altar.

"This will mark an irreparable dichotomy between the presence, in the celebrant, of the eternal high priest and that same presence brought about sacramentally. Before they were one and the same presence.

"Pope Pius XII said—'To separate the tabernacle from the altar is tantamount to separating two things which, of their very nature, must remain together… It would be wrong to want the altar restored to its ancient form of table. Likewise, it would be wrong to want black eliminated from liturgical colors, to require crucifixes that do not represent the bitter sufferings of the Divine Redeemer, to exclude pictures and statues from churches…this attitude seeks to reintroduce many pernicious errors which the church has rightly condemned.'

"We find stressed the 'Sacerdotal Office' of the people, making it appear that the people, rather than the priest, are the indispensable element in the celebration. The priest's position is minimized, changed, and falsified. Instead of the consecrated minister celebrating in persona Christi, the invocations are attributed anonymously to the church, the part of the priest has vanished.

"In the Confiteor which has now become collective, the priest is no longer judge, witness and intercessor with God. So it is logical that he is no long empowered to give the absolution which has been suppressed.

"Not a word do we now find as to the priest's power to sacrifice or about his act of consecration, the bringing about through him of the eucharistic presence. He now appears as nothing more than a Protestant minister.

"The church—one, holy, catholic and apostolic—is diminished. The 'orthodox believers of the catholic and apostolic faith' are now no more than 'all who seek you with a sincere heart.'

"Desacralizing Omissions everywhere debase the mystery of the church. She is not presented above all as a sacred hierarchy. Angels and saints are reduced to anonymity in the second part of the Confiteor. They have disappeared as witnesses and judges in the person of St. Michael from the first.

"The various hierarchies of angels have also disappeared from the preface. In the communicantes, the reminder of the pontiffs and holy martyrs on whom the church of Rome is founded, the transmitters of apostolic traditions, has been suppressed.

"In the 'Liber Nos' following the 'Pater Noster', the Blessed Virgin, the apostles and all the saints are no longer mentioned. Her and their intercession is thus no longer asked, even in the time of peril.

"The unity of the church is gravely compromised by the wholly intolerable omission from the entire 'Ordo' of the names of the apostles Peter and Paul, founders of the church of Rome, and the names of the other apostles, foundation and mark of the one and universal church."

XIII—September, 1971 Rudolph M. Unger

Chapter 14

Having in recent issues presented criticisms of the liturgy of the new mass by a prominent catholic layman, by a member of the highest ranks of the church's hierarchy and by a group of theologians and liturgists from various lands, Counter-Reformation this month would like to present its own critical analysis of the new order.

Some of this analysis will cover some of the same points covered by these other persons, while some of it will refer to points not mentioned by them.

Thanks to the "enlightened", "tolerant", "democratic", "broadminded" modernist pseudo-liberals, who have seized hold of the reins of God's one true church and are imposing their narrow minds and arrogant wills on the members of the household…You and I will no longer—

"Go unto the altar of God, to God who gives joy to my being" to ask Him. "To fight my fight against a faithless people, to rescue me from the wicked and deceitful man who is within me."

No longer can I ask you Lord God "To send forth your light and your truth to lead me on, to bring me to your holy mountain, to your dwelling place" as Glorious King David had taught me to do.

No longer may I say "I will go unto the altar of God, to God who gives joy to my being" or to say "I will praise you on the harp, o God, my God!" or pray "Why are you so downcast, o my soul? Why do you sigh within me? Hope in God! For I shall again praise him, my own saviour and my God."

No longer will I sing "Glory be to the Father and to the Son and to the Holy Ghost. As it was in the beginning, is now and ever shall be, world without end. Amen."

No longer will I call upon "Blessed Mary ever virgin, Blessed Michael the Archangel, Blessed John the Baptist, the Holy Apostles Peter and Paul, and all the saints and you father (as God's representative)" to be witness to my sins and to intercede for me with the Almighty. No longer will I ask you father, as God's representative, to "Grant me pardon, absolution and remission of my sins."

Now they would have me confess my sins to my brethren. Like hell I will!

The angels of God announcing the birth of Emmanuel in Judea in the town of Bethlehem did not sing to certain poor shepherds, "Glory to God in the highest and peace to his people on earth."

They sang, as Catholicism has taught us for 2,000 years, "Glory to God in the highest and on earth peace to men of good will."

It may be the teaching of Protestantism that you can live as you will, sin as you like, as long as you have faith in God, you will be saved. It may be by that same illusion that "Liberated" modern man lives.

But it is not the truth. It is error. It is falsehood. It is heresy. It is not the teaching of the one true church.

"Men cry peace, peace, peace, but there is no peace." and there will be no peace on earth, until men turn from evil, from the adoration of themselves; until they once again make the second great commandment subservient to the first great commandment.

For like all things in God's creation, God's love has a condition, a price—submission to his will! Its reward is eternal peace, joy, life. Defiance of his will also has its just reward—hell. And what we see in the world today, as men have so often throughout history, is but a foretaste of hell

----

The readings that constitute the proper of the mass have of course, been changed. For, if the all but unrecognizable overhaul of the ordinary was not sufficient to shake Catholics loose from their missals, the change of the proper was designed to guarantee the missal useless. For there must be no permanent record of anything.

Of course, running the scriptural readings over a three year period instead of one, makes it impracticable to combine them all into one missal, for it would be too bulky. This aside, of course, from the fact that further changes will have to be made in the ordinary.

As for encouraging Catholics to be familiar with all of the scriptures through the reading of the whole of scripture, the bible; why, of course, that will never do. Because "We" know they would never, of their own volition, read the bible. That is why they must be forced to do it as "We" "Benevolently' arrange It.

No longer will I, in the spirit of Isaiah the prophet, ask God "To cleanse my heart and my lips that I may worthily proclaim His holy gospel" asking Him "To be in my heart and on my lips". Nor will I any longer add afterwards "By the words of the holy gospel may our sins be forgiven."

No longer will I profess that "I believe in one God…" For faith is no longer personal, for God is no longer a personal God, for the individual person and what he thinks and what he believes is no longer important. Now the Mod Credo is "We" and in "We".

No longer will I pray—"Receive O Holy Father, almighty and eternal God, this spotless host which I, your unworthy servant, offer to you, my living and true God, for my own countless sins, offenses and negligence, for all here present as well as for all faithful Christians, both living and dead, that it may profit me and them as a means of reaching salvation in the eternal life. Amen.

"You God, who wondrously ennobled human life in creating it and even more wondrously restored it, grant that through the mystery of this water and wine we may be made partakers of His Divinity, who condescended to partake of our humanity, Jesus Christ, your Son, Our Lord, who lives and rules with you in the unity of the Holy Ghost, One God, forever and ever. Amen."

No longer will I say "We offer to you, O Lord, the chalice of salvation, humbly begging your mercy... For our salvation and for that of the whole world." nor will I pray "Come, O Sanctifier, Almighty and Eternal God, and bless this sacrifice prepared for the glory of your Holy Name."

Of course, the intercession of Blessed Michael, of incense to God, of solemn mass, why we all know that belongs to "An outdated era of superstition".

No longer will I sing "...I go around your altar, listening to the sound of your praises, recounting all your wondrous deeds. O Lord, I love the beauty of your house, the dwelling place of your glory...teach me to walk in integrity and innocence. Redeem me. Have pity on me so that my foot might stand in the right path."

No longer will I pray, "Receive, O Holy Trinity, this offering which we make in remembrance of the passion, resurrection and ascension of Jesus Christ, Our Lord; and in honor of Blessed Mary, ever virgin; John the Baptist, the Apostles, Peter and Paul, and all the saints."

No longer will I recite the preface in honor of the Holy Trinity, "The distinction of persons, oneness in being and equality in majesty, which the Angels and Archangels, the Cherubim and Seraphim praise."

No longer will I pray for "The peace, protection, unity and direction of your holy Catholic church...And all the faithful guardians of the Catholic and apostolic faith."

No longer will I mention the names of the apostles and martyrs, Nor will I beg God to "Spare us from eternal damnation and help us to be numbered in the fold of your chosen." Neither will I ask God to make the mystery of the transubstantiation "reasonable and acceptable" to my finite mind and will. Nor will it be a chalice which the priest holds in his hands. How long will it remain "The mystery of faith."

Nor will I recall my link and bond with all men in God's creation and in God's love through "Abel, Abraham and Melchisedech." nor will I again ask my offering "Be carried by the hands of Your holy angel to Your altar on high, before your divine majesty."

They couldn't find a way to change "The Our Father" so they added something to it, compliments of the Protestant version of the bible. We no longer need the aid of Mary, Peter, Paul and Andrew "To deliver us from every evil, past, present and to come."

No longer can I ask God "To enter under my roof" to "Make me always obedient to Your commandments", to have His body be "A safeguard and healing remedy of mind and body", to possess it "With a pure heart" and have it "Cleave to my very soul."

No longer will I kneel to receive my God, nor in thanksgiving, nor in receiving His blessing through His Priest. Nor will I pray that "The homage of my service might be pleasing to The Holy Trinity. Deo Gratias."

XIV—October, 1971 Rudolph M. Unger

Chapter 15

In recent issues we have dwelt upon the reformation of the mass by the social engineers who are in the driver's seat in the Johannian-Pauline-Vatican II church.

But the changes in the mass, which is the heart of the church's worship, is but part of the wholesale, basement-to-the roof revamping of the liturgy which has been perpetrated.

There are many, many other embellishments in the rich fabric of the liturgical worship which have been affected by the overhaul. They have been partially or totally eliminated. Not necessarily by any announced orders, but more generally through the tacit ignoring of them, as is the manner of "the sophisticated" ones who have the run of the church today.

The quiet ushering out of some of these beautiful, meaningful forms of the worship of God—All designed with but one purpose in mind, bringing men closer to God—is discussed in the following conversation by two imaginary fellows.

And while they are fictitious, the mentality they portray, unfortunately, is all too real in the church today. And while this thinking may be generally couched in less plebeian, more sophisticated language, it is the dull, Dunder-Headed mentality that is stifling the growth of holiness in the wise and the simple among God's Children, by choking off the rich, varied avenues, and the multitude of intercessors that God has granted us to approach him.

Charley, they did quite a job not only in the rewriting of the mass but also in the new translation of the bible. Yes, Willie, they sure did. But there's no great magic to it. They just flip-flopped all the phrases and sentences and substituted some words for others. Not that they improved the meaning but they sure did change things. You know, they crossed all the Is and dotted all the Ts. Not exactly with a scalpel, more like with a butcher knife.

Well, I know, Charley, they sure eliminated or minimized a lot of those outdated words and concepts like hell, sin, the devil and punishment. After all, most modern, educated folks don't believe in that stuff anymore.

Yeah, Willie, you take all those special things, like nuptial vows and mass. They got rid of all that gruff stuff by that old hard head, Paul, about women being subject to their husbands and emulating those Old Testament women like Rebecca, Rachel and Sara. And that bit about being fruitful vines and seeing their kids' offspring to a couple of generations. Heck, the modern gals want to wear pants, smoke and have careers and not have to mess with kids.

You're right, Charley, same goes for the funeral mass. They sure got rid of all those morbid black vestments. And that "Dies Irae" dirge about death, suffering, judgment and the wages of sin. Man, that's enough to give anyone the willies. No pun intended, you know.

Yeah, Willie, I gotcha. That's why its good they're starting to minimize the crucifixes in the sanctuaries. Or at least showing the risen Christ and not all that gore, and replacing the stations with plain crosses. I mean, gee, people got enough troubles without thinking about suffering.

You know, Charley, I'm also glad in the Easter Vigil service they updated the book of Genesis. After all that bit about creation in seven days and then God taking a breather. After all, you got to admit it, it's a little far-fetched. Those scientists, like Darwin and lawyers like Darrow make pretty good sense and, you know, you can't rule out that swinger, the Chimp.

They were smart in that vigil rite to get rid of that canticle by Moses and his complaining about how he knew the Levites were going to turn into a bunch of rebels, Willie. That don't exactly fit in with today's thinking, anymore than those stone tablets Moses carried around.

I'm glad you mentioned that, Charley. Boy, I tell you, along that same line, I sure am glad they got rid of all that nonsense about fasting and abstaining. I mean, I can understand if someone wants to diet, but a guy can discipline himself if he feels like he wants to. He don't have to have someone else telling him what to do. After all, we got too many people telling us what to do. It's a free country you know.

Same thing, Willie, with that first Friday and first Saturday stuff you don't hear much about anyone.

All that harping on penance, reparation, sins, sacrifice and praying for the conversion of sinners and the communists. Heck my view is "Live and let live". And hell, those commies aren't so bad. They're going to sit down and talk with our boys and work our a deal, aren't they? What's so bad about that?

Same thing, Charley, with those prayers after the low mass they finally got rid of . Leo XIII started all that jazz. You think Pius XII was bad? You should have seen old Leo. He sure belonged in the 19th century. All that talk about Mary, Joseph, Peter and Paul, and sinners and the freedom and exaltation of holy mother church. And on top of that, that stuff about Michael and the malice and snares of the devil and other evil spirits running around the world. For cry Pete! That may have been alright for the peasants. But this is the 20th century!

Boy, you said it, Willie. And now you really got me going. Talking about peasants and superstition. Am I glad we don't hear much anymore about the rosary and that Mary cult. Sure, maybe it sounded good back in Old Dominic's Spain with that heresy jazz. But today's Catholics are scientific and educated. You remember that Father Peyton? Boy, talk about simple characters!

No really, Charley, you're right. All that talk about Mary's 15 promises, like "The rosary shall be a powerful armor against hell, it will destroy vice, decrease sin, and defeat heresies." What were they doing, selling Hadacol or holy water at Lourdes and beads at Fatima? Or miracles?

That's why it makes good sense, Willie, that they're throwing out all those statues, paintings and stained glass windows with the angels and saints. Today's rational folks don't need that stuff.

You're right, Charley, and the same smart thinking is shoving tabernacles over in a corner somewhere. No more benediction, Latin songs and divine praises. Yeah, sure glad they got rid of 40 hours devotion with the candles, roses and incense. And that Corpus Christi procession with the canopies, vestments, surplices and singing. That's okay for sentimental old ladies, but not for us.

Ha, ha! Remember, Willie, how they use to go to seven churches on Holy Thursday? What a drag. And yeah, the indulgences. Heck, Luther put the pin in that stuff way back when. Only they weren't smart enough to listen to him.

And wow, recall the missions and novenas and all those fancy talking preachers. And all those pilgrimages to Holy Hill, Mayslake, Notre Dame, Our Lady Of The Snows. Remember those silly May devotions. How did that song go? "Bring flowers of the fairest, bring flowers of the rarest."

Yeah, Charley, remember that stupid Father Lord song we had to sing in school with "God Bless America" and the Pledge of Allegiance. Something about, "On earth's battlefield never a vantage we will yield…Catholic action is our cry!" Man, I'm a flower child. I don't want to fight. I'm a lover.

Gee, and do you remember all those dumb litanies we had to say. They had a hundred of them—To the Holy Name, Sacred Heart, Blessed Virgin, St. Joe, and that real long one about the saints. My knees used to get sore.

They got rid of a lot of those guys, Willie. Remember old soldier boy George on his horse fighting the dragon. And that muscle man, Christopher. And that Barbara. Remember they tried to make us believe Lawrence being cooked on a grill, John being boiled in oil and Perpetua and Felicitas being gored by bulls. Wow, wild, man!

Well at least, Charley, they got the calendar straightened out now. They leave half of them saints off now. And no more of that feasts stuff, like they're not dead. Now they got it straight, they call them memorials. You know, ashes to ashes and dust to dust.

Talking about that, Willie, I'm glad they don't go out to graves at funerals anymore. I mean, after all, you got to have sensitivity, some feeling.

Thank goodness. They got some sharp boys running the show now. There's a lot of other stuff, all those prayers and devotions, most of it was all wrapped up in those missals. I'm glad they got rid of those. I felt like a holy roller carrying one.

But cool it, Willie, I got to buzz off. Right on, Charley, right on.

XV—November, 1971 Rudolph M. Unger

Chapter 16

Two thoughts keep sounding and resounding from the depths of the mind.

One, that we who are Catholics tend to take for granted the privileges of our belief. Two, that we who are Americans tend to take for granted the privileges of our land.

Perhaps that is why we are threatened with the loss of these two most precious things in our lives—our church and our country. Precisely because we assume they must always be there to serve us, to guide us, to protect us; because we do not fully appreciate what they mean to us, for time, for eternity.

Have you ever listened to Rimsky-Korsakov's "Russian Eastern Overture?" The soaring sounds of the almost unrestrainable jubilation at the awareness of, the knowledge of, the possession of—the source, the sustenance of being.

In the past half century, Russian Easter has come to be a contradiction. For Russian perforce has come to be communistic and communistic Easter is a contradiction, a mutual denial of the other, for one speaks of heaven, the other of hell; one speaks of salvation, the other of damnation.

To illustrate what faith and freedom mean to men who are forbidden them let us witness an Easter in Siberia.

The following excerpt, which describes it, is taken from "With God In Russia" by the Rev. Walter J. Ciszek, an American Jesuit of Polish extraction from Pennsylvania, who was given the vocation by God to serve his children in atheistic Russia. And who, to fulfill that vocation, spent 23 years in captivity (1940-63)—5 years in Moscow prisons, 10 in Siberian labor camps and 8 in enforced exile in Siberia.

"The Lent of 1958 in Norilsk saw some of the busiest weeks I've ever spent as a priest. In previous years, there had been three of us priests, and every year the congregation had grown steadily. Now I was alone and there was more work than ever. For Easter is the biggest feast in Oriental liturgy, and even today the people celebrate it at home with as much pomp and ceremony as they can. On this feast, they say, nature itself takes on a festive air.

"During Lent there were no marriages, but I was asked to make frequent visits to the cemetery to chant the Panikhida, or requiem, over the graves and I spent all my free time hearing confessions and baptizing.

"Of five baptisms one Saturday, three were in different parts of Norilsk but two were far up into the mountains at Medvierskaya. After work I therefore finished two of the baptisms, then caught a taxi for Medvierskaya. It was starting to snow heavily, but I made it on time. After the baptisms there, another family asked me to baptize their child. I apologized, saying I still had an appointment in Norilsk. They pleaded with me to come back that night, told me they would pay the cab fare both ways, and begged until I agreed.

"On the way down from Medvierskaya, however, the taxi got stuck in the snow storm and I was two hours late for my appointment in Norilsk. Afterward, I started back to Medvierskaya. The taxi driver thought I was crazy and would take me only part way up the mountain. I had to climb the rest of the way on foot. I arrived at the house at 2 a.m., but the family was still waiting for me. It was 5 a.m. Before I made it back to Norilsk on foot, just in time to begin hearing confessions for the Sunday masses.

"In addition to the Russians, there were in the area—Ukrainians, Poles and Lithuanians. The Ukrainians were almost militantly religious. They clung to religion tenaciously as a part of their national heritage and tradition. Out in their camp, they held huge weddings and christenings, openly religious.

"When one of their leaders died, they organized a mammoth funeral, a choir of more than 200 and a big cross with flowers and crepe to lead the funeral procession. From the camp they walked right through the main streets of town on the way to the cemetery, singing 'Sviati Bozie' (Holy God) at the top of their lungs. The cortege walked straight down the boulevard, stopping traffic, with the cross and choir leading the procession. Then the men bearing the coffin on their shoulders, followed by huge crowds of mourners. People on the streets, astounded at the religious demonstration, crossed themselves.

"On Palm Sunday, I said three masses with a sermon at each, and announced that the full Holy Week services would be held in the chapel (a shanty). The people began to make arrangements for the blessing of the Easter food. We had to form a committee to organize the blessings. I calculated that I would have to begin at 5 p.m. on Friday, work around the clock, and hope to finish, with luck, in time for Easter mass.

"I made arrangements at the factory to be excused from Thursday until the following Wednesday. A friendly doctor signed a certificate stating that I should 'Rest' and Anastasia, my boss, who knew what was going on, was happy to accept it. Thursday, I said mass in Kayerkahn, blessed food, and heard confession for hours as I had every night that week after work. Friday evening I set out after the Good Friday services to begin my tour of the city for the food blessings. Every place I went, people were waiting, even in the middle of the night and long cold hours of early morning.

"I got back to the chapel for 6 a.m. services. Many of the people had been there overnight in order to get a place before the altar for this long Easter vigil service. Many of them, too, stayed in the chapel after the Saturday services until it was time for Easter midnight mass. With nothing to eat all day, so they could be close to the altar. After vigil services I made the home rounds again. By 11:30 p.m. Saturday, I was back to the chapel but I couldn't get anywhere near it. Crowds of people swarmed outside in the midnight cold. The militia were there too but I ignored them.

"By midnight it was so crowded I couldn't lift my arms, so someone had to pull the vestments over my head. The altar was covered with flowers and candles and there was a choir of trained voices.

"As I began the solemn intonation of the Easter mass, I thought the chapel would explode with sound. The Easter mass is a joyous one to begin with, but the enthusiasm of the people that night I shall never forget.

"Tired as I was after 48 hours without sleep, hurrying from place to place, I felt suddenly elated and swept along. I forgot about everything but the mass and the joy of Easter.

"The MVD stayed for the whole service. I paid no attention to them. I was practically carried out of myself with joy. I gave a little sermon on the Joy of Easter, but it was impossible to distribute communion because no one could move. It had to be distributed after mass.

"The services ended at 3 a.m., but at 9 a.m. I was still distributing communion to a constant stream of people. I could hear the crowds outside, going home through the Easter dawn, shouting the traditional Easter greeting—'Khristos Voskres' (Christ is risen!). And the joyous answer, 'Voistinu Voskres' (Indeed, He is risen!)

"Afterwards, I was completely exhausted. Yet I was deeply satisfied. I knew a joy that day I have rarely known. I felt that at last, in God's own good providence, I was beginning to live my dream of serving His flock in Russia. 'And all this' was the thought that kept flashing through my mind, 'all this took place in Russia'. The next thing I knew I was shaken awake. The room was full of happy people, repeating over and over "Khristos Voskres', 'Voistinu Voskres'. Everyone was shouting, laughing and I was made to go along for Easter dinner and its joyous celebration.

"On Wednesday, I was summoned to KGB headquarters. The official kept staring at me coldly. Then finally said abruptly, 'Your missionary work is not needed here. Do you understand? You have 10 days to leave Norilsk and never think of coming back. If you do, you will be arrested and put back into prison. You are to go to Krasnoyarsk and report to the MVD there and you are to do nothing in the way of religious work among the people.'

"I said mass every day until I left, heard confessions, baptized, visited the sick. The people were bitter, lamenting, 'They would take our last priest away from us.'

"As I left the city, I looked around for the last time. This had been my country since 1946, as prisoner and priest, and I was tremendously sorry to be leaving. I thought again of the people, knowing I could do nothing more for them but commend them to God. I repeated over and over—'Thy will be done, Thy will be done.'"

XVI—December, 1971 Rudolph M. Unger

Chapter 17

In 1966 a Lutheran minister and former representative of The World Council Of Churches, the Rev. Richard Wurmbrand, came to the United States after spending 14 years in communist prisons in Romania.

When he had the temerity to speak before congressional committees, at anti-Vietnam war rallies, and in other places about the evils of communism and the need to fight this diabolical power, he found himself as popular with the World Council of Churches, as Cardinals Mindszenty of Hungary and Slipyj of Ukraine found themselves with some persons in the Vatican.

The essence of Pastor Wurmbrand's unpleasant message is captured in the following excerpts from an article which appeared in 'The National Review' in 1968. (The author of the article first saw Wurmbrand in a London church pulpit in 1965.)

"I bring you greetings from the suffering Church of Christ behind the iron curtain.

"First I must tell you what happened with me. I was kidnapped in the street by the communist secret police in 1948. My family and friends were told I had fled the country. I was kept for the first three years in solitary confinement. My cell was 35 feet underground, three paces by three, with only a tube for air.

"I saw neither sun nor stars. I didn't know if it was night or day, or even what month or year it was. I survived torture, drugging and brainwashing in one jail after another for a decade. I was offered as a bribe by my communist captors the leadership of the Lutheran church in Romania, provided I led it their way.

"I was tempted alone in my cell by the devil. He was very near. He laughed at me. He said, 'Where's Jesus? Why doesn't he save you and the others who believed in Him? He's a false messiah!'

"I recall the screams of a woman being beaten in the next cell. Male prisoners were promised their wives would visit. No one came. 'You fools!' the guards said. 'They don't want you. They've found other men long ago. Your children are all communists. If they saw you, they would spit.'

"Loudspeakers filled the cells 24 hours a day with taped messages—'Communism is good. Christianity is finished. God is dead.'

"And in the end, I believed this, when they said nobody was Christian. I am not a hero. I believed. Then I said to myself, 'But if Christianity is dead. I will sit at its tomb and weep until it arises again.'

"In prison I found another parish. I converted prisoners by tapping Morse code through the walls, converting even wardens and secret police interrogators.

"I had grown up as a Jew. As a youth, I became a sharp businessman, made money, lived a wild life and despised others and hated myself. I landed in a hospital with TB where I was left alone to think. I had called myself an Atheist and a Marxist. In that hospital an inner struggle within me was resolved. I became a Christian. I was ordained in the Lutheran church, although I think that if I had met Christianity in any other form I would have accepted it.

"During World War II, the fanatical fascists in Romania persecuted religious minorities. I was arrested three times and at least once escaped assassination. My wife's family died in the slaughter of the Jews.

"When the communists took over in 1945, delegates from all the churches were summoned to a Congress in parliament. They were promised pay and protection from the state. In return, they were expected to mount the rostrum under Stalin's portrait and pledge support for the new regime.

"When my time came, I spoke against communism, telling the 4,000 delegates that their task was to praise God, not earthly powers. Applause, cheering broke out. The microphone was taken from me. The meeting ended in an uproar.

"But here is the irony. After I went to prison I met all those priests and pastors who had collaborated with and praised and worked for the communists—in the end they were treated just like me.

"The regime wanted a confession from me that The World Council of Churches was a facade for an international spy net. This would have led to a Mindszenty type show trial to blacken religious leaders around the world. No pain was spared to break me.

"It was an image of hell in which the suffering is eternal but you cannot die.

"I was not the worst tortured, for here I am alive. Nearly all our Catholic bishops have been so handled that they died.

"I was flogged, forcibly filled with water until my stomach swelled, then kicked around the room, bastinadoed while trussed like a chicken on a spit and submitted to other old and new devices in the interrogator's armory. A doctor was present at each session so that I, as a valuable prisoner, did not die.

"Spells of drugging blacked out my memory but I had vowed to kill myself before I betrayed friends. I named no names. There was no witness at my eventual trial, which lasted 10 minutes. I was sentenced to 20 years in prison.

"Silence in the underground cell was total. The guards never spoke and padded about in felt shoes. I had nothing to read, no writing materials, a plate of thin gruel once a day. To pass the time I did various things. I danced for one thing. I recalled that those who suffered 'on account of The Son Of Man' were blessed and should rejoice and dance for joy.

"When the guard spotted me leaping about the cell he brought me food to distract 'the madman.' I often felt such overwhelming joy that I thought I would burst if it did not find expression. I composed sermons and preached them aloud. I prayed, meditated and sang. I spent hours writing letters in my mind to my wife and son.

"Later, in mass cells, my wish to be a priest in prison was fulfilled. I preached in cells containing a hundred men packed to the ceilings. Later many of us prisoners went through a 're-education'. Not by means of books but by beatings. Criminal prisoners were promised early release if they beat up others systematically over weeks and months, until they not only said they were communists but really believed it. Pain and indoctrination can do this. But the mockery was worse than the pain.

"One man was tied for five days to a cross. Twice a day the cross was laid on the floor of the cell and all his cellmates were made to fulfill their necessities on his face and body. Then the cross was raised again and a 're-educator' said, 'Look now at your Christ.'—another priest was forced to say mass over excrement and urine. He said, 'Don't reproach me. I have suffered more than Christ.'

"My wife was arrested and put to work on the Danube Canal where thousands of prisoners died of cold or starvation. They ate rats, snakes, crows, dogs. But let me tell you a beautiful story. At the canal a gang of 400 religious prisoners shoveled earth for 16 hours a day in 20 below zero weather.

"A young Catholic priest was asked provocatively if he still believed in God. He knew it might be his last hour if he said yes. Everyone looked at him as he stood for a moment silent. Then he said to the officer, 'When I joined the church I knew that thousands had already died for their faith. And when I went to the altar in my fine robes I promised God that if they became prison rags, I would still serve Him. Prison is no argument against religion. I love Christ with all my heart.'

"'And do you believe in the Pope?" the officer went on. The priest replied, 'Ever since St. Peter there has a been a Pope of Rome and never will a Pope be friends with the communists. Yes, I believe in the Pope!' The priest was marched off. We never saw him again. It was not long afterwards Gromyko was calling at the Vatican.

"In my 14th year in prison the jails were almost emptied of political prisoners to clear the way for a series of major trade deals between Romania and the west. Our camp commandant made a last speech. 'You fools! You have sat for years in prison, expecting the Americans to come and free you. Now I will give you the news. The Americans are coming—not to free you, but to help us. They come to make business and build the industries we need. The Americans if you beg, give nothing. If you insult and mock them, you get everything. You fools, we have been more clever than you.'

"After being freed, I found most people I met did not know what communism is and they did not want to hear that it was a threat to their way of life.

"When I was released the communists told me I could preach about Christ but not against communism. In the free world, many clergymen gave me the same advice.

"I am very sad. The church can never have peaceful coexistence with atheism. How can a man preach God is good and not preach communism is evil?"

XVII—January, 1972 Rudolph M. Unger

Chapter 18

In August, 1960, a week-long Christian anti-communism crusade meeting was held at Glenview Naval Air Station.

The speakers included Protestants, Catholics, Jews, clergymen, military men, psychiatrists, intelligence agents, men from all walks of life who had firsthand experience or expert knowledge about Lucifier's 20th century play toy, designed to confuse, delude, seduce, enslave and destroy God's children.

Evident in the audience were large numbers of Catholic priests and nuns with their students.

Shortly, thereafter, the New York Times, the pseudo-liberal bible of humanistic secularism in the United States, did a hatchet job on the persons who were engaged in the work of the crusade. Following that, the Chicago Sun-Times, the local champion of amoral, immoral secularism, including abortion and birth control, which is so proudly read and quoted by so many Catholic hierarchy, religious and laymen, followed with its smear job on the persons engaged in the work of the crusade.

Sometime thereafter, Cardinal Albert Meyer, that great proponent of liberality at the Vatican II Council, and his chancery officials passed the word that Catholic religious, students and laymen were not to be encouraged, were to refrain from participating in or attending any sessions sponsored by the crusade.

Of all the superb speakers who had appeared at that week long session at Glenview, perhaps the most outstanding was a young Maryknoll priest by the name of Father Frederick J. Becka.

Father Becka, unlike Cardinal Meyer and the other ivory tower, arm chair experts in the archdiocese chancery office, knew what he was talking about. On Jan. 9, 1952, he was one of nine Maryknoll missioners who walked out of Red China at Hong Kong after seven years there, including 2 1/2 years in prison.

Cardinal Francis Spellman, who was on hand to meet the emaciated 121 pound, 33 year old priest and his companions, remarked—"<u>This is a repetition of the worst persecution and martyrdom in the ancient history of</u>

<u>the church</u>."

In his talk at Glenview, as at hundreds of others which he gave while stationed in Chicago, Father Becka opened with a Chinese sing-song and when he finished it 30 seconds later, the eyes, ears and mind of every person in the audience were right on him.

"This is probably the first time you've met a priest with a prison record," he remarked. Then he proceeded—"The communism of Russia is world communism. The communism of China is world communism. Their objective is world domination. The organization and propaganda of communism has never been beaten.

"An example of communist organization? I was stationed in a small village in China, 1,500 families. You won't find it on the map. One village street had 15 houses on the north side and 15 houses on the south side. There was a communist spy for every 5 houses. It was his job to find out everything about the lives of those five families. And for every five of those spies, there was another spy whose duty was to spy on the spies. In this way, the village was completely covered. It's the same in every village, city, province in China...a perfect hierarchy of spies completely blanketing the country. And they control 669 million people. That's organization!

"An example of communist propaganda? In the beginning, before communism took control, Johnny Wong from this village...which never saw an electric light bulb, ice cube, or water flowing from a faucet...Would buy a paper from the junk that came down the river from the larger city and would take it to the tea house where he would have his breakfast.

"Then the communists took over the newspaper and filled it with propaganda. It didn't take Johnny Wong long to realize it wasn't a newspaper anymore. So he stopped buying it.

"When the communist magistrate came to inspect the area and noticed unopened stacks of days old papers on the wharves, he knew the propaganda wasn't reaching the people. He went back to headquarters and had a meeting. The communists never have a situation they cannot cope with. They just take out of the little black book...how did we do it in East Germany, in Poland, in Latvia, in Czechoslovakia? The propaganda must reach the people.

"So a soldier set up a stand in the village at night and by a peanut oil lamp read the paper from cover to cover in a loud voice. Every single family in the village had to have a representative at that reading. If they failed to come, the family was fined five pounds of rice. That feeds a family for one day. Johnny Wong went to listen to the reading.

"In my 2 1/2 years in a Chinese communist prison, I was brainwashed sometimes two, sometimes six, sometimes nine hours a day. Sometimes I didn't know how long. I was brought back unconscious. I was strung up by the thumbs when I refused to tell the communists the names of the Catholics in the village. I went from 185 to 121 pounds on a diet of two bowls of rice a day.

"Every single day (900 days) I saw at least one prisoner executed. One day I counted 16. The execution yard was just outside my window. Mao TseTung himself has boasted, '20 million people have died in China for the glory of the hammer and sickle.'

"At my trial I heard myself accused of rape, murder, perversion, of distributing propaganda literature, of being not a priest at all, but a spy. I was sentenced to death. But later it was commuted to banishment from China. Was I thankful to get out of China? I cried like a baby to be leaving. I had loved the country. I had loved the Chinese. It was hard to leave them to their fate.

"I can't tell you too often—the communism of China is the communism of Russia. It is a way of life, almost a religion. When I was under house arrest, I could watch the Chinese soldiers receive their 'catechism' each morning from their commander.

"'Who gives you your clothes to wear?, he would ask, and they would answer, 'Mao Tse-Tung'. 'Who gives you your rice to eat?' 'Mao-Tse-Tung' 'Who is the creator of the world?' 'Mao-Tse-Tung' Who is the savior of the world?' 'Mao-Tse-Tung.'

"This is their plan for China. They have others—more sophisticated—for us. World domination is their objective. America is on their schedule.

"They know if they are going to conquer America, they must first break up the American family. If you are over 35, communism is not interested in you, unless it leads to your extermination. Communists are interested in the young, in the teen-ager.

"Let the teen-ager have 'freedom', license to do as he pleases. To see sex movies without control, to read any and all smutty magazines. Tease him with doped cigarettes by pushers hanging around his school. Break down parental control, respect for all authority. And when the American family bursts asunder, America is ripe for communism.

"Here is page 23 of a Russian text book for spies:—'Make alcohol easily available to the teenager, make dope available, encourage his wildness, stimulate him with sex literature, educate him to perversion. Then the psycho-political operators can create a mass confusion and then step in with a solution—communism. When we can break up national pride and patriotism, we will have won!'

"Back in 1911, Lenin said—'First Europe, then Asia, then Latin America, then that last bastion of capitalism, the United States. It will fall as an over ripe plum right into the hands of communism. Corruption from within will bring the downfall of America.'

"In China, 669 million people enslaved. How many in Poland, Latvia, Russia, Czechoslovakia, Hungary, Estonia, Romania, Bulgaria, Albania, eastern Germany, north Korea, indo-China, Vietnam, Cuba?

"Three out of seven people in the world today are living under communism.

"See how fortunate you are? Pray that you will never have to undergo that fate. Appreciate your liberty. Respect your freedom.

"But above all, accept your responsibility as Americans, whose country is dedicated under God. There can be no freedom without responsibility. We cannot get something for nothing. And nothing worthwhile comes easily."

XVIII—February, 1972 Rudolph M. Unger

Chapter 19

In 1960, the American bishops issued a landmark statement which ran counter to many of their pronouncements in the past 40 years. Particularly in the last 10 years.

It cut through the superficial solutions suggested in so many of their other messages for the problems of our nation and mankind generally and went to the substantial nature of man. And in defining it, they recommended the course that man must follow if he is to fight his way out of the quagmire of modern decadence.

The next two issues of this newsletter will be devoted to that 1960 statement which was entitled "Need for Personal Responsibility". The first portion follows.

"The history and achievements of America stand as a monument to the personal responsibility of free men.

"Our institutions and our industry, the fruit of the American sense of responsibility, have in the past inspired, guided and helped many other nations of the world.

"If our future is to be worthy of our past, if the fruit of America's promise is not to wither before it has reached full maturity, our present pre-eminent need is to reaffirm the sense of individual obligation, to place clearly before ourselves the foundation on which personal responsibility rests, to determine the causes of its decay and to seek the means by which it can be revived.

"The foremost signs of the decline of personal responsibility are to be found in the family. Marriage, a sacred contract, all too often is considered merely as an arbitrary arrangement to satisfy the instinct of pleasure. The failure of parents to fulfill their responsibilities, as revealed in the frequency of divorce, desertion and broken homes is a national disgrace.

"Any delinquency of parents may well be reflected in the delinquency of youth, which is now commonly considered our greatest national domestic problem.

"Equally conspicuous is the evidence of decline in the sense of responsibility within our industrial organization and in our general economic life.

"At a time when so much depends upon the soundness of our economy and upon our ability to produce to meet the needs of rapid growth, we have been faced by a lack of truly responsible leadership, both on the part of management and labor.

"Although personal responsibility and initiative have been our national characteristics, explaining in large measure our country's progress in human welfare, yet pressures are growing for a constantly greater reliance on the collectivity rather than on the individual.

"An inordinate demand for benefits, most easily secured by the pressure of organization, has led an ever growing number of our people to relinquish their rights and to abdicate their responsibilities. This concession creates a widening spiral of increasing demands and pressures with a further infringement on personal freedom and responsibility.

"The result is the condition recently noted by our Holy Father—'modern man sees that the sphere in which he can think for himself, act on his own initiative, exercise his responsibilities and affirm and enrich his personality is in many cases restricted to an excessive degree.'

"However varied the above mentioned evils, ranging from the single act of wrongdoing to the moral laxity of the mass mind, the root cause is the same—the rejection of personal responsibility. This is a moral evil as are all the major ills that beset the present world.

"As such their cure is largely within the power of individual persons. A Godly society is the work of Godly men. Even the most universal evil and the threatened mechanization of man can be made to yield before the just and determined wills of individual persons.

"America's progress has been achieved according to the measure of individual commitment to responsibility. The heroes of history have not been blind forces but stout hearted persons.

"Our national goals have been achieved not as a result of environment but by men who made their environment. A strong responsible nation is fashioned by responsible persons, not group pressures.

"As Pope Pius XII stated—'The people live from the fullness of the life of the men who make it up. Each of them in his place and in the manner proper to him is a person conscious of his responsibilities and of his own convictions.'

"What is a personal responsibility in the context of man's relation to the world? It presupposes the acceptance of one's dignity as a son of God in whatever environment he may be placed and the acknowledgment of binding moral law.

"It requires the free and deliberate acceptance of one's obligations in the position he occupies—in the family, in the church, in the corporation, in the labor union, in the community, in the nation, in the family of nations.

"It demands the rule of conscience, not of self-satisfaction. It recognizes that every deliberate action of the human person has a relationship with his creator and his purpose in creating the world. It affirms that every human action a man performs derives its significance from that relationship and makes him a cooperator with his creator in forwarding the kingdom of God.

"It is the solemn profession that consequently every product of his mind and his hand, every bounty wrung from the earth is to serve that high purpose. As man, bearing the image of his creator, is the brother of every other human being, his noblest work is to bring to his fellow man the blessings of the destiny intended for him by God.

"It must be emphasized, especially in these times, that the freedom innate in man, as well as the social nature he enjoys, demands as correlative the fullest personal responsibility. As St. Paul said, 'Therefore every one of us will render an account for himself to God.'

"The marvelous inventiveness of the human mind, conquering space and making each man a neighbor of every other human being on earth, gives urgency to this twofold need—to maintain one's freedom by using it according to the limits and norms of rightful authority. To use it according to his social nature and the needs of his fellow man.

"As St. Paul wrote, 'For you have been called to liberty, brethren. Only do not use liberty as an occasion for sensuality but by charity serve one another.

'For the whole law is fulfilled in one word, thou shall love thy neighbor as thyself.'

"The social pressures of today's complex life do not excuse from, but rather create a demand for, a greater exercise of personal responsibility. No man can be neutral in a moral cause. By his creation he is born to be committed to the cause of God. The more difficult the situation, the more imperative the need for such a commitment.

"If we are to restore man to his sense of personal responsibility and to the acceptance of life as a mission, we must understand more clearly the moral causes which undermined men's sense of responsibility.

"First among these causes has been the marked decline in the force of religious convictions. Washington warned the American people that they should indulge with caution the supposition that national morality could exist without religion. It cannot be doubted that for a long time religious influences have been losing their vigor among the American people, with a debilitating effect in consequence of both the public and private life.

"As a result of this decline of religious convictions, the grasp on moral principles has been greatly weakened. Through a faulty concept of morality modern man has come to imagine that sudden and drastic changes in situations changes principles. That principles no longer control situations but rather that situations shape principles.

"Inevitably this type of 'situational ethics' denies all unchanging principles and makes futile all moral judgments on which the sense of responsibility rests. The need which the world faces is the acceptance of an objective norm of morality, and hence of conduct.

"This decline in religious belief and moral conviction leaves modern man blind to his immutable spiritual nature. Thus, wittingly, and unwittingly, he aligns himself with the forces of materialism, among whose tenets there is no room for the concept of personal responsibility."

XIX—March, 1972 Rudolph M. Unger

Chapter 20

This is the conclusion of the American bishops' landmark statement in 1960 on the "Need For Personal Responsibility."

"The social ideals and purposes of modern man, due to the declining influence of religious and moral convictions and to the triumph of the material, tend in many subtle ways to efface the sense of responsibility.

"As a people we seem to be moving more deeply into a sensate culture. There is an excessive preoccupation with material security at the expense of spiritual well being.

"Uniformity of thought and supine loyalty to the organization, whether it be the industrial corporation, the labor union or the political party, are too often encouraged and rewarded.

"The organization man, cloaked in a sort of anonymity, rather than the responsible individual, is favored and advanced.

"The preparation for this condition is found even in the field of education, where emphasis is placed on adapting oneself to the thinking of the group. This pattern is so prevalent that some psychologists consider juvenile delinquency as a revolt, just for the sake of rebellion, against a stifling uniformity that fails to challenge the individuality of the student.

"The correction of these basically moral evils and the restoration of a vigorous sense of personal responsibility belong primarily to the field of religion.

"The development of a truly Christian character is primarily the task of religion, although its inculcation is of vital concern to the state. It is the function of religion to teach man his unique dignity as a son of God and brother of Christ.

"Pope Pius XII stated—'Always and everywhere, by unceasingly adapting herself to the circumstances of time and place, the church seeks to model persons. Individuals, and, as far as possible, all individuals, according to the laws of Christ, thus attaining the moral bases of social life.

'The object of the church is man, naturally good, imbued, ennobled and strengthened by the truth and grace of Christ.'

"Deepened religious convictions will bolster and reactivate the sense of personal responsibility. We must seek to enlarge the areas of personal autonomy to protect the human personality from a greater encroachment on its freedom and responsibility.

"The individual person must assume as his proud right the accomplishment of whatever he can for himself and for others, especially those of his family and herein lies the importance of the Christian home.

"Pope Pius XI in 'Quadragesimo Anno' stated—'Just as one cannot take away from individuals and transfer to the community the tasks they are capable of accomplishing by themselves, thus it would also be an injustice if one were to remove from groups of lower rank, functions they can exercise themselves and entrust them to a wider collectivity of higher rank. The natural objective of any intervention in social matters is to assist the members of the social body and not to destroy or absorb them.'

"Even when man enters into associations, as he must to achieve the goals which lie beyond his individual capacity, he should remember their purpose is in relation to his freedom and responsibility. In this respect, the Holy Father stated—'But this is to be done on the condition that each of these institutions remains within its own sphere of responsibility—that it be offered to, not imposed upon, the free choice of mankind. They must, under no circumstances, look upon themselves as an end, making their members an instrument of their activity.'

"A fresh evocation of the principle and practice of personal responsibility can revivify our society and help to stem the seemingly inexorable march toward the automation of human beings and the steady loss of that freedom which is man's distinctive attribute.

"It will cure the mental lethargy and inertia which permits organizations to usurp, mainly by default, the rights of their members. It will stimulate self reliance which will automatically restore the balance between freedom and security. It will reject unwarranted pressure from groups that seek unjustly to aggrandize their power and will restrict them to lawful ends.

"It will see in all business ventures of whatever size a means of serving others as well as self. It will have an immediate effect in every sphere of life—in the home, in the office, as well as in the workshop, the factory, in our schools and in our cultural groups.

"An effective response to a call for personal responsibility need not wait for a mass movement. The response belongs to the individual person. As our Holy Father indicated:

'Fully conscious of what is at stake, moved by his apostolic zeal, he then makes a personal engagement with these communities that surround him, the result of a free and justified choice of careful thought about himself, his destiny and the world.'

"Such a response by a representative number, given only in the silent sanctuary of the heart, will begin to have its leavening effect. Our appeal for action is made directly to our Catholic fellow citizens, but it reaches out also to all Americans who face the same problems as ourselves.

"Before it is too late, we must revive in our midst and present to the world, the ideals that have been the real source of national greatness.

"For America will fulfill its destiny when we have achieved that spiritual maturity, described by Pope Pius XII, as:

'Men established in their inviolable integrity as images of God. Men proud of their personal dignity and of their wholesome freedom. Men justly jealous of their equality with their fellow creatures in all that concerns the most intimate depths of human dignity. Men solidly attached to their land and their tradition.'"

XX—April, 1972 Rudolph M. Unger

FROM THE PASTOR'S DESK

ARCHBISHOP SHEEN IS ALIVE AND WELL

We all know Archbishop Fulton J. Sheen of TV and radio fame. Since his retirement from the Bishopric of Rochester, N.Y., he has still been devoting his time and talent to writing and speaking. Recently, he was one of the main speakers at the 15th Congress of the Laywomen's Retreat Movement held in Los Angeles. He gave an unusually strong message to the 2,000 women who were in attendance. He emphasized that retreatants must balance off certain extremes in our culture—and said that there is too much emphasis on activism.

"We should indeed go into the world as the whole world belongs to Christ," Archbishop Sheen stressed, "but we should not just bring Christ TO people; we should bring Christ OUT in people." He went on, "We should go into the world, but we have to PREPARE FOR IT BY OUR OWN SPIRITUAL LIVES." He added that "there are too many go-go's, but not enough come-come's," and said "Christ did admonish His Apostles to go into the world, but He also said, 'Come to Me.'"

Decisions are important in the Archbishop's eyes. "Our lives have to change and we have to change this modern world which is full of evil," he said. "There is too much 'going down' to make religion popular with our young people and everyone." He stated that our youth are looking for something to lift them up—religious values and virtues to challenge them.

This brought to his mind the time he went to speak at a college recently, where the students had just burned down two buildings. He thought to himself that he would have to speak on something that would really challenge these students and make them think. He spoke of "chastity." The president of the college remarked to Archbishop Sheen that it was the first time that the students stood to applaud the speaker and then went to the podium to speak to him afterward. Archbishop Sheen continued. "There is no need to meet man in his mediocrity. Lift him up!"

The ways to lift men up came when the Archbishop spoke directly to the retreatants about their duties. He stressed that we have not been giving Christ to the world, and said that Jesus People should have found Our

Lord through us, and instead they found Him on their own.

"Retreatants and others must center on Christ. They must restore the guilt sense in others, then get them to go to Christ and have it pardoned." He went on, saying, "We need the true sense of guilt to preserve us from the demonic."

"Demonic" is the state of the world in which we live, according to the Archbishop. He said the "demonic" is destroying everything—the individual, the family, the State. He defined this demonic as nudity, violence, and disintegration of personality.

"The demonic is loose in the world today," he said, adding, "Our Blessed Lord Himself is the only one to conquer the demonic." He asked the entire group to make a continuous hour of meditation each day, preferably before the Blessed Sacrament, or, if this is not possible, at their own leisure. (It is well known that the Archbishop himself makes a daily Holy Hour.) He quoted Christ in the Gospels as using the word "hour" whenever He was speaking of the demonic and satanic. In speaking of His Passion, He said, "My hour has not yet come." He asked the Apostles to "Watch one hour with Me." When Judas kissed Him on the cheek, Jesus said, "My hour has come."

Although the Archbishop said we will probably never have another schism or live in an age of heresy, because there are not enough thinking people in the world to be heretics, there was real sense of urgency in his voice when he said: "WE have to do SOMETHING TO SAVE THE CHURCH. Things will only be better if we have more and more people to intercede." He stressed, "We will never save our Church, our children, our people if WE DON'T DO SOMETHING HARD." He called the weakness of Western civilization "The picking up of the cross without Christ."

"Lord, make me an instrument of your peace. Where there is hatred, let me sow love. Where there is injury, pardon; where is doubt, faith; where there is despair, hope; where there is darkness, light, and where there is sadness, joy.

"O Divine Master, grant that I may not so much seek to be consoled as to console, to be understood as to understand, to be loved as to love. For it is in giving that we receive. It is in pardoning that we are pardoned. And it is in dying that we are born to eternal life."

St. Francis of Assisi

Chapter 21

In his Christmas message in 1953, the saintly Pope Pius XII remarked—"True democracy cannot exist and thrive except in an atmosphere of respect for God and observance of His commandments, as well as for the Christian solidarity of brotherhood."

In 1947, in writing on "Christian Rebirth", Pius had this to say about the great enemy of such rebirth—secularism. "To wish to draw an exact line of separation between religion and life, between the natural and supernatural, between the church and the world, as if they had nothing to do with each other, as if the rights of God were valueless in all the manifold realities of daily life, whether human or social, is entirely foreign to Catholic thought and is positively anti-Christian."

The desacralizing of life in America has been afoot for many years and is now coming apace with such acceleration and wide sweeping compass that it threatens to engulf and profane all of us in an Orwellian hell.

There are those who now, in search of a scapegoat, claim that this a natural outgrowth of our system and what else did we expect—that America and Christianity were always irreconcilable and never in accord.

That's a lie. The failing lies in us, Christians, who have been given every opportunity under our form of government to grow in the faith and to transmit it to others. The fault is not in the system. The fault is in us.

No where, in no nation, in any period of history, have both religion and liberty had the rich, fertile soil to grow in as in America.

In the appendix to his classic work on the American system, "The Key to Peace", Dean Clarence Manion presented an opinion of the United State Supreme Court, which clearly underscored the fact that from its very discovery this has been a religious nation.

Written in 1892, the opinion ruled that a law of congress regarding immigrants was never intended to prevent a church here from hiring a clergyman abroad to minister religion here. Because, of its very essence, as the court wrote, "This Is A Religious Nation." The opinion read as follows:

"No purpose of action against religion can be imputed to any legislation, state or federal, because this is a religious people. This is historically true. From the discovery of this continent to the present hour, there is a single voice making this affirmation.

"The Commission to Christopher Columbus is from—'Ferdinand and Isabella, By The Grace of God, King and Queen of Castile' and recites that 'it is hoped that by God's assistance some of the continents and islands in the ocean will be discovered.'

"The First Colonial Grant, that made to Sir Walter Raleigh in 1584, was from 'Elizabeth, By The Grace of God, of England, France and Ireland, Queen, Defender of the Faith'. And the grant authorized him to enact statutes of government provided that 'they be not against the true Christian faith now professed in the church of England.'

"The First Charter of Virginia, granted by King James I in 1606, commenced—'We, greatly commending, and graciously accepting of their desires for the furtherance of so noble a work, which may, by the Providence of God Almighty, hereafter tend to the glory of His divine majesty, in propagating of Christian religion to such people, as yet live in darkness and miserable ignorance of the true knowledge and worship of God.'

"The celebrated Compact made by the pilgrims in the Mayflower in 1620 recites—'Having undertaken for the glory of God and advancement of the Christian faith, and the honor of our king and country, a voyage to plant the first colony in the northern parts of Virginia, do by these present, solemnly and mutually, in the presence of God and one another, covenant and combine ourselves together into a civil body politic.'

"The Fundamental Orders of Connecticut instituted in 1638 commences—'For as much as it hath pleased the Almighty God by the wise disposition of His Divine Providence so to order and dispose of things that we are now dwelling upon the river of Connecticut...and well knowing where a people are gathered together, the word of God requires that to maintain the peace and vision of such a people, there should be an orderly and decent government established according to God.'

"In the Charter Granted by William Penn to Pennsylvania in 1701 it is stated—'Because no people can be truly happy, though under the greatest enjoyment of civil liberties, if abridged of the freedom of their consciences as to their religious profession and worship, and Almighty God being the only Lord of conscience, father of lights and spirits, and the author as well as the object of all divine knowledge, faith and worship, who only doth enlighten minds and persuade and convince the understanding of people, I do hereby grant…'

"Coming nearer to the present time, The Declaration of Independence recognizes the presence of the divine in human affairs in these words—'We hold these truths to be self evident, that all men are created equal, that they are endowed by their creator with certain unalienable rights, that among these are life, liberty and the pursuit of happiness. We, therefore, appealing to the supreme judge of the world for the rectitude of our intentions, do in the name and by the authority of the good people of these colonies, declare…And for the support of this declaration, with a firm reliance on the protection of Divine Providence, we mutually pledge to each other our lives, our fortunes and our sacred honor.'

"If we examine the constitutions of the various states we find in them a constant recognition of religious obligations. Each of them recognizes a profound reverence for religion and an assumption that its influence in all human affairs is essential to the well being of the community. For example:

"The Constitution of Illinois, 1870—'We, the people of the State of Illinois, grateful to Almighty God for the civil, political and religious liberty which he hath so long permitted us to enjoy, and looking to Him for a blessing upon our endeavors to secure and transmit the same unimpaired to succeeding generations…'

"In the declaration of rights in The Constitution of Maryland, 1867: 'As it is the duty of every man to worship God in such manner as he thinks most acceptable to him, all persons are equally entitled to protection in their religious liberty…no religious test ought ever to be required to hold any office of profit or trust other than a declaration in the existence of God.'

"In The Constitution of Massachusetts, 1780: 'It is the right as well as the duty of all men in society to publicly worship the supreme being, the great creator, and preserver of the universe…as the happiness of a people and the good order and preservation of civil government essentially depend upon piety, religion and morality.'

"In The Constitution of Mississippi, 1832: "No person who denies the being of God, or a future state of rewards and punishments, shall hold any office in the civil department of this state...Religion, morality and knowledge—being necessary to good government, the preservation of liberty, and the happiness of mankind—schools and the means of education shall forever be encouraged in this state.'

"The Constitution of the United States states: 'Congress shall make no law respecting an establishment of religion or prohibiting the free exercise thereof.'

"There is no dissonance in these declarations. There is a universal language pervading them all, having one meaning. They affirm and reaffirm that this is a religious nation. These are no individual saying, declarations of private persons. They are organic utterances. They speak the voice of the entire people.

"While because of a general recognition of this truth, the question has seldom been brought to the courts. We find in 'Updegraph vs. Com., it was decided—'Christianity, general Christianity, is, and always has been, a part of the common law of Pennsylvania. Not Christianity with an established church and tithes and spiritual courts, but

"If we pass to A General View of American Life we find: The oath with appeal to the Almighty; opening sessions of all deliberative bodies with prayer; the prefatory words of all wills—'In the name of God, Amen'; the laws respecting the Sabbath with the general cessation of all secular business and closing of government offices; the churches and church organizations which abound in every city, town and hamlet. This is a Christian nation."

XXI—May, 1972 Rudolph M. Unger

Chapter 22

Probably the most astute foreign observer ever to come to America to study this great experiment in self-government was Alexis de Tocqueville. The young Frenchman, of aristocratic background, a lawyer and judge, and later politician in France, came to the United States in 1830 to study and analyze this democratic republic.

Subsequently he set down his findings and views, pro and con, in his classic work—"Democracy in America." For balanced, objective, disciplined, dispassionate, cool, analytical appraisal, his work has no peer. Some of his unbelievably sage insights, pro and con, into the future of a people seeking to govern themselves, portraying the potential good and the potential pitfalls, are all the more remarkable when viewed with the benefit of 140 years hindsight.

In the following two issues of this newsletter, we shall read his observations and comments on the role of religion and its relationship to liberty in a nation whose people has striven to live equally under the law and unequally otherwise.

"In America, religion is the road to knowledge and the observance of the divine laws leads man to civil freedom," de Tocqueville wrote.

He then referred to the comments to the citizenry by Massachusetts Governor John Winthrop, distinguishing between liberty and license, in which Winthrop remarked:

"Nor would I have you mistake the point of your own liberty. There is a liberty of a corrupt nature which is effected by men to do what they will and this liberty is inconsistent with authority, impatient of all restraint.

"This liberty is the grand enemy of truth and peace and all the ordinances of God are bent against it.

"But there is a civil, a moral liberty which is the proper end and object of authority. It is a liberty for that only which is just and good. For this liberty you are to stand with the hazard of your very lives and whatever crosses it is not authority but a distemper thereof."

De Tocqueville than proceeded:

"The remarks I have made will suffice to display the character of Anglo-American civilization in its true light. It is the result (and this should be constantly presented to the mind) of two distinct elements, which in other places have been in frequent hostility, but which in America have been admirably incorporated and combined with one another. I allude to the spirit of religion and the spirit of liberty.

"Religion perceives that civil liberty affords a noble exercise to the faculties of man and that the political world is a field prepared by the creator for the efforts of intelligence. Content with the freedom and the power which it enjoys in its own sphere and with the place it occupies, the empire of religion is never more surely established than when it reigns in the hearts of men unsupported by aught besides its native strength.

"Religion is no less the companion of liberty in all its battles and its triumphs; the cradle of its infancy, the divine source of its claims. The safeguard of morality is religion. And morality is the best security of law and the surest pledge of freedom.

"No true power can be founded among men which does not depend upon the free union of their inclinations. And patriotism or religion are the only two motives in the world which can permanently direct the whole of a body politic to one end.

"After the idea of virtue, I know no higher principle than that of right. Or to speak more accurately, these two ideas are commingled in one. The idea of right is simply that of virtue introduced into the political world. It is the idea of right which enabled men to define anarchy and tyranny and which taught them to remain independent without arrogance as well as to obey with out servility.

"There are no great men without virtue and there are no great nations without the notions of rights. For what is the condition of a mass of rational and intelligent beings who are only united together by force?

"I have previously remarked that the manners of the people may be considered as one of the general causes to which the maintenance of a democratic republic in the United States is attributable. Under manners, I comprise the whole moral, intellectual condition of a people.

"Every religion is to be found in juxtaposition of a political opinion, which is connected to it by affinity.

"The greatest part of British America was peopled by men who, after having shaken off the authority of the Pope, acknowledged no other religious supremacy. They brought with them into the new world a form of Christianity, which I cannot better describe, then by styling it a democratic and republican religion.

"This sect contributed powerfully to the establishment of a democracy and a republic. From the earliest settlement of the emigrants, politics and religion contracted an alliance which has never been dissolved.

"About 50 years ago, Ireland began to pour a Catholic population into the United States. On the other hand, the Catholics of America made proselytes and at the present moment more than a million Catholics, professing the truths of the Church of Rome, are to be met within the union.

"These Catholics are faithful to the observance of their religion. They are fervent and zealous in the support and belief of their doctrines. Nevertheless, they constitute the most republican and most democratic class of citizens which exists in the United States. And although this fact may surprise the observer at first, the causes by which it is occasioned may easily be discovered upon reflection.

"I think the Catholic religion has erroneously been looked upon as the natural enemy of democracy. Among the various sects of Christians, Catholicism seems to me, on the contrary, to be one of those which are most favorable to the equality of conditions.

"On doctrinal points, the Catholic faith places all human capacities on the same level. Its subjects the wise and the ignorant, the man of genius and the vulgar crowd to the details of the same creed. It imposes the same observances upon the rich and needy.

"It inflicts the same austerities upon the strong and the weak. It listens to no compromise within mortal man, but reducing all the human race to the same standard, it confounds all the distinctions of society at the foot of the same altar, even as they are confounded in the sight of God.

"No sooner is the priesthood entirely separated from the government, as is the case in the United States, than it is found that no class of men are more naturally disposed than Catholics to transfuse the doctrine of the equality of conditions into the political world.

"Most of the Catholics are poor, and they have no chance of taking a part in the government unless it be open to all citizens. They constitute a minority and all rights must be respected in order to ensure them the free exercise of their own privileges.

"These two causes induce them, unconsciously, to adopt political doctrines which they would perhaps support with less zeal if they were rich and preponderant. The Catholic clergy of the United States has never attempted to oppose this political tendency, but it seeks rather to justify its results.

"The priests in America have divided the intellectual world into two parts. In the one, they place the doctrines of revealed religion, which command their assent. In the other, they leave those truths, which they believe to have been freely left open to the researches of political inquiry. Thus the Catholics of the United States are at the same time the most faithful believers and the most zealous citizens.

"It may be asserted that in the United States, no religious doctrine displays the slightest hostility to democratic and republican institutions. The clergy of all the different sects hold the same language. Their opinions are consonant to the laws and the human intellect flows onward in one sole current."

XXII—June, 1972 Rudolph M. Unger

Chapter 23

This is the continuation of the comments of Alexis de Tocqueville in his 'Democracy in America" on the relationship of religion and liberty in America's experiment in self government.

"I believe the indirect influence of religion upon politics in the United States is more considerable than the direct influences.

"Each sect differs in respect to the worship which is due from man to his creator, but they all agree in respect to the duties which are due from man to man. Each sect adores the deity in its own peculiar manner, but all the sects preach the same moral law in the name of God.

"Moreover, almost all the sects of the United States are comprised within the great unity of Christianity and Christian morality is everywhere the same.

"There is no country in the whole world in which the Christian religion retains a greater influence over the souls of men than in America. And there can be no greater proof of its utility and of its conformity to human nature than that its influence is most powerfully felt over the most enlightened and free nation on the earth.

"I have remarked that the members of the American clergy in general, without even excepting those who do not admit religious liberty, are all in favor of civil freedom. But they do not support any particular political system. They keep aloof from parties and from public affairs.

"In the United States, religion exercises but little influence upon the laws and upon the details of public opinion. But it directs the manners of the community and by regulating domestic life, it regulates the state.

"I do not question that the great austerity of manners which is observable in the United States, arises, in the first instance, from religious faith. Religion is often unable to constrain man from the numberless temptations of fortune. Nor can it check that passion for gain which every incident of his life contributes to arouse.

"But its influence over the mind of woman is supreme and women are the protector of morals. There is certainly no country in the world where the tie of marriage is so much respected as in America, or where conjugal happiness is more highly or worthily appreciated.

"In Europe, almost all of the disturbances of society arise from the irregularities of domestic life. To despise the natural bonds and legitimate pleasures of home, is to contract a taste for excesses, a restlessness of heart, and the evil of fluctuating desires. Agitated by the tumultuous passions which frequently disturb his dwelling, the European is galled by the obedience which the legislative powers of the State exact.

"But when the American retires from the turmoil of public life to the bosom of his family, he finds in it the image of order and peace. There his pleasures are simple and natural, his joys are innocent and calm. And as he finds that an orderly life is the surest path to happiness, he accustoms himself without difficulty to moderate his opinions as well as his tastes.

"While the European endeavors to forget his domestic troubles by agitating society, the American derives from his own home that love of order which he afterwards carries with him into public affairs.

"In the United States the influence of religion is not confined to manners but it extends to the intelligence of the people. Christianity therefore reigns with universal consent. The consequence is that every principle of the moral world is fixed and determinate, although the political world is abandoned to the debates and experiments of men.

"The human mind is never left to wander across a boundless field. It is checked from time to time by barriers which it cannot surmount. These habits of restraint recur in political society and are singularly favorable both to the tranquility of the people and to the durability of institutions.

"Nature and circumstance concurred to make the inhabitants of the United States bold men. But the revolutionists of American are obliged to profess an ostensible respect for Christian morality and equity which does not easily permit them to violate the laws that oppose their designs.

"Hitherto no one in the United States has dared to advance the maxim that everything is permissible with a view to the interests of society, an impious adage which seems to have been invented …to shelter all tyrants.

"Thus whilst the law permits Americans to do what they please, religion prevents them from conceiving and forbids them to commit what is rash or unjust.

"Religion in America takes no direct part in the government of society, but it must nevertheless be regarded as the foremost of the political institutions of that country.

"I do not know whether all the Americans have a sincere faith in their religion, for who can search the human heart? But, I am certain that they hold it to be indispensable to the maintenance of republican institutions. This opinion is not peculiar to a class of citizens or to a party but it belongs to the whole nation and to every rank of society.

"The Americans combine the notions of Christianity and of liberty so intimately in their minds that it is impossible to make them conceive the one without the other. Religious zeal is perpetually stimulated in the United States by the duties of patriotism.

"Missionaries traveling to the western reaches will tell you—'All the American republics are collectively involved with each other. If the republics to the west were to fall to anarchy or be mastered by a despot, the republican institutions which flourish on the Atlantic shore would be in great peril. It is therefore our interest that the new states should be religious, in order to maintain our liberties.'

"If any persons hold that the religious spirit is the very thing most amiss in America and that the only element wanting to the freedom and happiness of the human race is to believe in some blind cosmogony, I can only reply they have never been in America and they have never seen a religious or free nation.

"Despotism may govern without faith but liberty cannot.

"How is it possible that society should escape destruction if the moral tie be not strengthened in proportion as the political tie is relaxed?

"And what can be done with a people which is its own master, if it be not submissive to the divinity?

"The philosophers of the 18th century explained the gradual decay of religious faith in a very simple manner. Religious zeal, said they, must necessarily fail the more generally liberty is established and knowledge spread.

"Facts are by no means in accordance with their theory. There are certain populations in Europe whose unbelief is only equaled by their ignorance and debasement. While America, one of the freest and most enlightened nations in the world, fulfills all the outward duties of religion with fervor.

"In France, I had almost always seen the spirit of religion and the spirit of freedom pursuing courses diametrically opposed to each other. But in America, I found that they were intimately united and that they reigned in common over the same country.

"I questioned American clergymen of all different sects. I expressed my astonishment and explained my doubts. They mainly attributed the peaceful dominion of religion in their country to the separation of church and state. I do not hesitate to affirm that during my stay in America, I did not meet with a single individual, of the clergy or laity, who was not of the same opinion on this point.

"I learned with surprise that clergymen in America fill no public appointments, not one of them is to be met in the administration, and they are not even represented in the legislative assemblies.

"In Europe, Christianity has been intimately united to the powers of the earth. Those powers are now in decay and Christianity is, as it were, buried under their ruins.

"The living body of religion has been bound down to the dead corpse of super-annuated polity. Cut the bonds which restrain it and that which is alive will rise once more.

"Religion, in obtaining a power to which it has not claim, risks that authority which is rightfully its own."

XXIII—July, 1972 Rudolph M. Unger

Chapter 24

The spiritual God-Father of a strain of Secularism which has had startling success inside the post-Pius church has been uncovered, thanks to a masterful new book by a Jesuit priest, Father Vincent P. Miceli.

In his monumental work, entitled "The Gods of Atheism", Father Miceli has delineated—among many others—the brilliant, mad French thinker whose perverted concepts have strongly influenced the modernist pseudo-liberals who have had the run of the church in the past decade.

He is Auguste Comte, son of ardent Catholic parents, but a child of the French revolution, who coined the word "sociology" and inserted this discipline in place of theology and metaphysics, enroute to his replacement of the triune God as the object of worship with social humanity.

The next two issues of this newsletter will be devoted to excerpts from Father Miceli's most significant portrayal of this rebel, who has spawned such influential offspring in today's church.

"In the chaotic aftermath of the French revolution, in an atmosphere of flagrantly avowed and triumphally marching atheism, Auguste Comte, thrived," begins Father Miceli.

"He is a typically French thinker whose ideas do not rise directly from Kantian or Hegelian roots, though his ideals have much in common with his German contemporaries.

"Emile Saisset noted—'Monsieur Auguste Comte in Paris, like Herr Ludwig Feurbach in Berlin, offered Christian Europe a new God to worship—the human race.'

"Revolution had already crushed the ancient regime, dissolved the powers and coherency of the church, rendered existing institutions morally and economically ineffective, disoriented the thoughts and beliefs of men and sent society wandering off in all directions, its actions ungoverned and misdirected.

"Comte felt called to the mission to replace disorder with order, to bring about the total reconstruction of society.

"A new society had to be created over the ruins of what was once the church and state. A new faith had to replace the decadent belief of tired Christianity.

"The new society, the new humanity, would have to rest on man himself.

"God, metaphysics, transcendent destinies, traditional beliefs, religious rituals and feelings had all failed man. Man's destiny, henceforth, was in his own hands, not God's.

"His society was to be his own creation, not the church's. His religion was to be his worship of himself, thus would man finally achieve mental, social and theological coherence and cohesion.

"Though a prodigy, Comte was also a problem child. Product of the revolution, he was in revolt against all authority, against all conformity. He drew special delight from destructive activities. At 14 he claimed he was already an atheist. 'I don't believe in God' he would repeat incessantly.

"Comte rejected metaphysics and theology as sources of natural and superior knowledge. They were to him fictional viewpoints on the ladder of humanity's climb from its depths of superstition to its summit of positive wisdom.

"For Comte, scientific methods alone captured and reflected accurately the real world. Science alone gave real knowledge. Comte, by his positivism, had immersed himself totally in the prison of his senses, refusing to even admit the possibility of transcendent being.

"Comte, like Hegel, subtly used his system of thought as an instrument for the demolition of philosophies of life which preceded their own, especially for the destruction of the Christian metaphysical and theological view point. The technique is to claim that the time for the Christian ideal is past.

"For Comte, the new superior synthesis would be fully rational human society, perfected by positive philosophy.

"The basic affinity of Comte's atheistic adventure to those of Marx and Nietzsche, despite their obvious differences, is perceptively reported by Father Henri de Lubac as follows:

'To anyone observing the great spiritual currents of our age, positivism will seem less the antagonist than the ally of the Marxist and Nietzschean currents. By other methods, in another spirit and in competition with them, it strives for the same essential object.

'Like them, it is one of the ways in which modern man seeks to escape from any kind of transcendancy and to shake off the things it regards as an unbearable yoke—namely faith in God. To discover a man with no trace of God in him was Comte's self appointed task.'

Father Miceli then continued:

"Theology and physical science were utterly incompatible in Comte's mind. Physical nature, of course, replaced a personal God or an abstract first cause as the source of order in the whole universe, in Comte's view.

"All human knowledge is knowledge of the world as men experience it, he said, but since the world and man are in evolution, all human knowledge is limited, never final, never absolute, Comte said. Thus the major tendency of the positivistic mind is to substitute the relative for the absolute in all cases. There are no eternal truths or principles of human conduct.

"Comte was convinced he was the man of genius destined to bring about the maturation of evolving society by the discovery and application of what he called at first 'social physics' and later renamed 'sociology'. He claimed that this 'positive science' was the last stage of development in the physical domain of man's progress. Theology must wane and disappear as sociology waxes and advances, he concluded.

"Positive philosophy, Comte claimed, is unaware of the existence of a real personal God. This is a myth in the imagination of men. But having passed far beyond the infantile state of man, positive progress views the God idea as the key idea in a cultural system that has long ago been swept into oblivion by the winds of revolutionary history.

"Comte was not an ordinary atheist. He planned to go beyond mere negative atheism through a positive program. His historical, positivistic dialectic was aimed at delivering the coupe de grace to a dying theologism.

"So thorough is Comte's campaign to eliminate God as an illusion of man's arrested youth, so zealous and successful is that campaign, that Comte must be compared not to pale atheists, but to those famous anti-theistic God killers—Feurbach, Marx, Nietzsche and Heidegger.

"His plan was to bring about the dethronement of this decrepit God who ruled despotically over mankind through the instrumentality of organized religions, particularly Catholicism. All of which were presently rotten to the core.

"The battle cry of the regime of science would be – 'Nothing is absolute, everything is relative!'

"Later in his life, Comte would transform the philosophy of positivism into the religion of positivism, i.e., the religion of humanity. Comte, the cold, positive scientist would come forth as Comte, the compassionate lover and founder of the religion of humanity. The science of humanity was replaced by the religion of humanity.

"Though he expanded his philosophy into a religion, Comte did not bring back either the God of the Christians, or their theology. Humanity was man's new God. Comte created a religion without a belief in God, a religion of the infidel.

"The statue of humanity would have as its pedestal the altar of God.

"In Comte's vision, the fallen God himself was to be the footstool of the 'grand etre', the real and ideal humanity, comprising the past, present and future of the human race, conceived as a continuous, progressing whole and holy reality.

"And everywhere, 'the servants of humanity' would convert or drive out 'the slaves of God'. On this point, Comte was adamant. He excluded from leadership in his positivism kingdom—'Catholics, Protestants, Deists.'

"He said, 'We must discard God, once and for all.'"

XXIV—August, 1972 Rudolph M. Unger

Chapter 25

Herein is the continuation of Father Vincent P. Miceli's description of Auguste Comte's creation of a cult of man worship, which has so insidiously found its way into the thinking of some of the most influential leaders in the present day church.

"Comte concentrated his attacks against the spirit of Christianity for it begot, he argued, persons unnaturally preoccupied with death, indifferent to earthly ideals, dreamers of happiness in the solitude of heaven.

"It exaggerated, he said, the importance of the personal and individual to the detriment of the social. It sought personal sanctity and salvation without regard to the welfare of humanity at large.

"After all, St. Peter said, 'Let us look upon ourselves on earth as strangers or pilgrims' and St. Paul said, 'We have not here a lasting city but we look for one which is to come.'

"Among the documents of Christianity criticized by Comte, the gospels came in for special scorn. He rejected them for the 'mental and moral void' which prevailed in them.

"Moreover, reminiscent of Nietzsche's wrath against Christ, Comte too displayed a shockingly jealous hatred for the person of Jesus. He banned Christ from the calendar of positivist saints, considering him as 'essentially a Charlatan', a religious adventurer, the false prophet and founder of a false religion.

"Though socially superior to Christianity, in Comte's thinking, Catholicism was still infected with its egotistical, absolutist one God. Comte was determined to eliminate the God of Catholicism, immanentize its mission in temporal power and political wisdom, after having rejected Christ and the gospels.

"The religion of humanity was to make use of the organization, worship, cathedrals, even clergy if possible, of Catholicism.

"How did Comte plan to effect this marvelous transformation? Was a desecrated, desacralized, secularized Catholicism, now known as the religion of humanity, possible?

"For Auguste Comte it was a thrilling, realizable messianic mission.

"There already existed within this monotheistic monolith, doctrinal and liturgical currents which could breach the fortress of faith in one God and lead on to the eventual establishment of the religion of humanity.

"Comte proves to be a man of masterful imagination at discovering and linking up doctrines of Catholicism which are heralds of humanity's deification in positivism.

"In Comte's view, the incarnation unites mankind with the absolute God and thus already manifests 'our growing tendency towards a real homogeneity between worshippers and worshipped.' The Eucharist, in his eyes, indicated the God of Catholicism is slowly being assimilated into the God-humanity, the God of positivism.

"Then too, he said, the cult of the saints moved towards the displacement of the worship of the one God by the worship of the many great humans, the worship of humanity.

"Thus far we have briefly treated the Comtian version of the evolution of religion from Christianity to positivism. Now we must give some of the details of the Comtian cult of humanity.

"Comte wrote, 'The necessary basis of the human order is the entire subordination of man to humanity.' For man is and lives through humanity, he said, and therefore the human race should be the focus of all his speculations, affections and worship. The human race was the new supreme being, composed of 'its own worshippers, substituting herself (the race) for God.'

"In the Comtian ethics of altruistic atheism, the 'science' of sociology had demonstrated to man that humanity is the great being which is advancing society through the tragedies of history to communal maturity (ala Lenin). The social good of the human race becomes thus the ultimate standard of good and evil.

"In the church of humanity, individuals have no rights whatsoever,. They merely have duties and all their happiness will be attained in the fulfillment of their social duties.

"Comte wrote, 'The idea of right has to disappear. All human rights are as absurd as they are immoral. The final state of society admits only duties as a consequence of functions.'

"The faithful must live an open, totally socialized existence. Religious and social privacy are banned and the great being becomes the big brother.

"Here are Comte's orders to his Godless priesthood: (again, ala Lenin)

'Seize hold of the world of society, for it belongs to you. Not according to any law but because of a manifest duty, resting on your exclusive capacity to direct it properly. Let there be no dissembling the fact that today the servants of humanity are ousting the servants of God, root and branch from all control of public affairs.(!!!)

'As for those who claim to combine God and humanity (peaceful co-existence) their mental inferiority is at once evident, since they propose to reconcile two wholly incompatible regimes.'(John, Paul, Nixon, Brandt – the lambs) (Khruschev, Chou-Enlai, Brezhnev—the foxes).

"Such then is the atheism of the religion of humanity. In practice it creates the tyranny of a totally socialized society. The individual is wholly bound over to the great social idol.

Can it be said that the menace of the Comtian idol is still with us? Father Henri de Lubac thinks so. He wrote:

'To my mind it is one of the most dangerous menaces that besets us. Many of the present campaigns against individualism already derive their inspiration from Comte and his disciples, too often at the cost of the human person.

'The accommodation and alliances favored by Comte have already borne fruit. They were followed by a period of spontaneous assimilation and the faith, which used to be a living adherence to the mystery of Christ, then came to be no more than attachment to a social program, itself twisted and diverted from its purpose. Without any apparent crisis, under a surface which sometimes seemed the reverse of apostasy, that faith has slowly being drained of its substance.'

"In our age of positivism, scientism and relativism, which Comte did much to nourish, we have the divorce of the human from divine love. Producing not human reformation but human deformation.

"In Comtian thought, truth reflects what is wanted from reality, not what is there and offered by reality. Ethics, even among Christians, identify with what is being done by the majority, not with what ought to be done. The situation creates the ethics.

"The goals of modern Christians have become quite Comtian. Increasing interest and messianic zeal is focused on creating a better world in which the individual tends to be absorbed by the collectivity.

"Christians, indeed often the clergy, who flock to the banners of expanded rights, are more zealous for the creation of a humane society than for the coming of the kingdom of Jesus Christ in the hearts of all men.

"The social apostles themselves disassociate themselves from the gospel, preferring to be inspired by the spirit of the times.

"This blinded age suffers from a dual illusion. The first, that a man's adherence to the triune, transcendental, absolute God is a superstitious enslavement of man. The second, that the liberation and ennoblement of man lies in his discovery through the physical sciences that God and the world are one.

"Only the reality of God and the leap of faith to Him can dispel this double illusion and restore vision to this blinded age.

"Those who refuse to rise above the adventures of the time are condemned to suffer serfdom under idols of their fashioning.

"No greater calamity can afflict a people than its rejection of a worship that transcends, in wonder and reverence, to the all Holy God. For a rejected faith cannot long remain without a replacement, some idol.

"And every idol is a total tyrant, demanding of its victims, self-immolation to the extremity of annihilation.

"The idol of humanity is no exception. For there are no idols friendly to man."

XXV—September, 1972 Rudolph M. Unger

Chapter 26

In the classic film, "The Sound of Music", in the midst of a tender love scene, Oscar Hammerstein II, the greatest lyricist of all and a superb student of human nature, presented a profound philosophical truth.

Capt. Von Trapp had just asked Maria to become his wife and the mother of his seven children. Maria, being the generous person she was, accepted his proposal. As she reflected on why she should be blessed with this greatest of all human gifts—love—she sang, "Somewhere, in my youth or childhood, I must have done something good. For nothing can come from nothing, nothing ever could."

And there, for all the world to see and hear, was the presentation of a truth that shattered the false Gods and false philosophies that have tormented modern man and threatened his dignity, his liberty, his sanity, his very existence.

Those false prophets telling him—that everything is relative and hence ultimately meaningless; that he is at once everything and nothing; that he came out of nothing and will return to nothing; that there is no God to love and guide him; that he is really a helpless victim of a cosmic process beyond his control; that good and evil are superstitions; that life is a madman's joke; that he should eat, drink and be merry for tomorrow he dies, never to rise.

It is no accident that mankind instinctively poured out to see this beautiful, masterful film, portraying a true love story about real people, a film panned by the "sophisticated" critics of our media as "soapy sentimentalism". A film seen by more persons than any other movie in history.

Like "A Man for All Seasons", "The Sound of Music" was an example—all the doubting Thomases among us not withstanding—that God's Providence is still with us, still watches over us, and still seeks to save us, if only we have the simple sense to want to be.

Hammerstein in his superb simplicity restated what a man back in the 13th century lucidly spelled out for mankind. St. Thomas Aquinas called it the law of cause and effect. Nothing comes from nothing. Every effect proceeds from a cause. Good comes from God and men inspired by God. Evil comes from the devil and men influenced by him. That God, being good, was Almighty. That evil, being a vacuum, an absence, a negation, was a weak and self-destructive force.

And Thomas was simply restating what another man, the God-man, said 13 centuries before him. "As you sow, so shall you reap." "A good tree does not bear bad fruit. A bad tree does not bear good fruit. By their fruits you will know them." "Without me, you can do nothing." So spoke He whom Thomas called the prime mover.

What has all this to do with the price of life in the shank of the 20th century?

Any honest, thoughtful person who looks at the world around him today knows that it is not the best of all possible worlds. That, in all candor, it is a world that in many ways is sick unto death. This is not a statement of frenzied, emotional prophesying of gloom and doom. It is simply a statement accurately portraying reality on our earth in our times.

In the east, there dwells a militant atheism that denies God, tells man he is God. And proceeds in its insatiable devouring of men, making them the slaves of Satan.

In the west, there is a more "altruistic" "humanistic" atheism that has corroded and corrupted the Christian world and has even infiltrated the one, true church. It has so dimmed the mind and weakened the will of Christian man that he is being led, inexorably, along the primrose path of "peace" to sheep-like lay his head upon the chopping block.

So we find ourselves poised on the possibility of cataclysmic events. Let us not wonder that we have arrived there. For we have been walking the path a long time, a path well paved by "humanistic" "benign" "benevolent" "lovers" of mankind.

In these next issues of Counter-Reformation, we will continue to draw upon the wisdom of Father Vincent Miceli in his prodigious "The Gods of Atheism", as he retraces the route that mankind has come these past 450 years.

From the Reformation through the Enlightenment, the French Revolution, the Napoleonic era, the French and German schools of rationalism and their flowering—in the east, in the power vehicle called communism,—in the west, in the disintegration of Christianity and its morality.

Who is Father Miceli?

Well, according to Cardinal John Wright, prefect of the Sacred Congregation For The Clergy and the highest ranking American in the Vatican:

"Father Miceli is the most recent of a valiant company within the Society Of Jesus who clearly perceives that God is the heart of the matter...who sees this as the central issue in our culture and our crises. Man cannot exist without God. And if he rejects the true God, he will invariably, instinctively, even perversely, create his own false God.

"Father Miceli's passion to share the truth, unto the salvation of others, identifies him as the servant of the God of love. It is a privilege to commend "The Gods of Atheism" to all those who have found God, with whatever fragile hold, and to those who seek Him, with whatever reluctant fear, lest having Him, they must have naught besides."

Father Miceli, in his introduction, remarks –"That atheists, like saints, are made, not born. It is not easy to be a saint. Left to himself, man cannot manage the climb. His sin-weakened nature is in absolute need of divine grace. God alone can develop sanctity in man. But man, endowed with intelligence and freedom, must cooperate in his own sanctification.

"Paradoxically, it is not easy to be an atheist either. It is terrifying to attempt to escape from the divine lover. The road leads down to violent serfdom. No one becomes an atheist unknowingly or unwillingly.

"Man is intrinsically burdened with an incurable hunger for transcendence. And history demonstrates that man is inconsolable without the true God. Why then are there so many atheists alive and flourishing?

"Because, as Kirilov in Dostoyevsky's 'The Possessed' explains, they have accepted the role of being their own God.

"The great sin of contemporary atheism is that it consists, through a sustained act of self-will, in a total pre-occupation with the human. This atheism induces man to fall down before himself in narcissistic adoration and love.

"These atheists reject the one true God and the God-man whom He sent to divinize man in a valid way. 'Not thy will but my or our human will be done' is their sole creed.

"Atheism's feebleness is demonstrated by its utter inability to cure the contradictory crisis it creates between man, whom it would advance in freedom, and its own new God, whom it cannot restrain from devouring man.

"In 'The Possessed' Kirilov says, 'For three years I have been searching for the attribute of my divinity, and I found it. The attribute of my divinity is—self will! That's all I can do to prove my defiance and my new terrible freedom, for it is very terrible. I am killing myself to show my defiance and my new terrible freedom.'

"It is hoped that this study may lead readers to reject the paths that run to the temples of the strange Gnostic Gods of humanistic atheism. For in these temples the masses are trapped in the millennium of temporality."

XXVI—October, 1972 Rudolph M. Unger

Chapter 27

At the outset of his portrayal of man's suicidal wanderings in the briar patch of atheism, Father Vincent Miceli remarks, "Atheism has from the dawn of creation been the great temptation for intelligent creatures.

"Atheism arises from a mentality and attitude which involves a flight from the invisible to visible, from the transcendent toward the immanent, from the spiritual toward the material.

"It represents a choice the creature makes of himself and his universe in preference to his creator.

"In the contemporary world, atheism has attracted millions of souls throughout the world. In the east, it is organized, politicized. Its leaders hold the reins of political and economic power. It is dynamic, apostolic, dramatic and demands heroic sacrifices of its adherents. It is scientific, messianic, militant. It has organized and dominated over a billion people in its crusade to eradicate God from the hearts and minds of men.

"The west is also seriously ill with the disease of bland atheism that is rapidly becoming virulent. Many of its loves are repulsively materialistic, its morals decadent, its crime rate soaring. Quantity has replaced quality as one of its ideals. Its new God is science and technology. Its new allies and alliances are expedient agreements made with tyrannical regimes at the expense of honesty and fidelity to the true God and its true friends. Its goal seems to be peace and prosperity at any price, even the price of changing its true God for an idol.

"Pope Paul has said, 'In the world of thought everything is doubted today and consequently religion too. It seems as if the mind of modern man finds no peace except in total negation, in abandoning any kind of certainty and any kind of faith. He is like a person with infected eyes who finds no rest except in obscurity, in darkness.'

"On Nov. 7,1967, Moscow celebrated the 50th anniversary of the rise of red atheism to tyrannical power over unhappy, Holy Russia. There was nothing golden about this anniversary for the people of Russia, of Christian Eastern Europe, of Cuba, for the hundreds of millions of Chinese.

"Yet how did the west for the most part respond, but with tributes and congratulations pouring into Moscow, that headquarters of hell on earth. For having successfully created a concentration camp of many countries, for one billion souls.

"Why where there no statesmen of the free world who dared to recall to their subjects the tremendous cost in millions of bodies, minds, souls who were and are presently still being tortured, degraded and murdered that the revolution may continue to advance.

"Was it the magnitude and frequency of crimes that developed callosities on the Christian consciousness? Why has the Christian consciousness lost its Christ-like compassion and sensibility at the afflictions unjustly imposed upon millions? Moral indifference—the disease of diluted Christians.

"Can it be that the Christians of the west have become cold to their suffering brethren behind the iron and bamboo curtains because they have become cold to Christ? Dull in themselves, have they become dead to others?

"In 1949, Charles Malik, Chairman of the Lebanon delegation, told the U.N.—'Rights that are natural and inalienable, rights that inhere in the very nature and dignity of man as a person, are rejected by communism and trampled upon communist states. The communist state necessarily suffocates spontaneity, inner dynamism, freedom and diversity. The spirit of man, which can be itself and its best self only in freedom and love and genuine communion, is choked, annihilated by this evil.

'Communism in general and the Soviet Union in particular do not really wish peace. Every peace offensive on the part of the Soviet Union is but a strategic or tactical device, a phase, of communism's overall war plan.'

"On Nov. 7, 1967, very few voices in the press and communication media of the free world had the courage to remind the atheistic tyrants, even timidly, of the crimes they have perpetrated upon the peoples of the whole world.

"Where heaven is obliterated the earth becomes a jungle. But what is surprising is that so few in the Christian world, known as the haven of religious liberty, spoke up to break the silence shielding the red tyranny.

"The slow assassination of millions through these 50 years,

unspeakably ghastly, has been the prolonged crucifixion of holy Russia. The steady strangulation of liberty, literature, art and prayer has been a sacrilege of a heinous sort. But perhaps the most satanic project of the revolution is its program to extinguish Christian hope, the hope of transcendent life hereafter, in the hearts of all men. This is an especially demonic program because hope alone can sustain and inspire men to make something worthwhile of this life.

"When we realize how silent religious leaders of the west have been in the face of this project for despair, we cannot fail to ask—why has this attack on Christian hope raised such little counter-attack in the west? Why have even the Catholic press been paralyzed before this anti-theistic assault?

"One had hardly grown reluctantly accustomed to this apathetic scandal of silence when a new and far more detestable scandal was enacted in the west. One is rendered speechless with astonishment at this new perversion.

"Attaining the same end as the communist project to extinguish Christian hope, the horror of this new crime arises from the fact that the project to destroy hope is now undertaken and carried through, not by professional atheists, but by men who through special training, positions and duties, are supposed to be dedicated Christian leaders.

"Priests and bishops, whose vocation is to sustain and foster faith and hope in themselves and among the faithful, have become advocates for the prostitution of religion to the purposes of atheism.

"When ordained ministers and consecrated bishops tell the faithful that 'God is dead', when these teachers of the gospels declare their inability to accept any longer the virgin birth, the divinity of Christ, the resurrection, the ascension, the real presence, the immortality of the soul; hell, heaven, sin, grace, redemption.

"When, under the guise of re-interpreting the Holy Scripture, these teachers repudiate Christianity, then has the spirit of anti-Christ become incarnate in men and the most demonic form of atheism is attacking the church.

"For then Christendom's anointed ones have become atheists, and, still vested as angels of light, they disown the Lord in His own house, cause truth to be maligned, introduce destructive sects into the church, exploit the faithful with specious arguments and lead men to follow their ungodly ways. Is it any wonder Malik said:

'There are many phases of western life which are repulsively materialistic. The spirit of business and gain, the maddening variety of things that excite concupiscence, the utter selfishness. There is a general weakening of moral fiber. To the superficial observer, who is unable to penetrate to the core of love and truth which is still at the heart of the west, there is little to choose between the soulless materialism of the west and the militant materialism of the east. I must say in all humility that the leadership of the west in general does not seem to be adequate to the unprecedented challenges of the age.'

"Our learned atheists, the avant-garde of humanity-come-of-age, have erased the horizon of heaven. They have accepted the responsibility of creating heaven here on earth. It would be a mistake to take them as mere dreamers. They know what they want. They have drawn up plans about how they are going to get it. Their books are everywhere to be read. Their actions are everywhere to be witnessed.

"They are at total war with the religious consciousness of men. They rightly see as their most deadly enemy the religious consciousness of Christians. Thus their messianic drive to bring all men within their Godless utopia.

"Modern atheism has developed a rigid philosophy of human nature and the cosmos. In the East, it is organized into a political monolith, in the West, it is organized into an establishment through a kinship of humanism and progressivism. This atheism has an arbitrary code of ethics, flexible, conspiratorial tactics, and a messianic imperialism which excludes no man from insertion into its great uniform ant-hill hegemony. It is the most efficiently ruthless system ever devised for inflicting man's inhumanity upon man."

XXVII—November, 1972 Rudolph M. Unger

Chapter 28

"Within the last two decades the crust of man's theological landscape has trembled and split wide open as a result of the volcanic forces that have exploded beneath it.

"For the Christian savant who has carefully followed the formation and development of various layers of modern thought, this shaking of religious foundations was not unexpected. Indeed it was long overdue. Underground pressures had been building against the city of theology for at least three centuries."

So wrote the Rev. Vincent Miceli, S.J., in his "Gods of Atheism" as he prepared to describe the current vintage of the "There ain't no God—I dare him to strike me dead" prophets.

"In a sterile and self contradictory venture the Godless theologians have substituted the suicidal science of a theology without God for the authentic discipline of theology about God,' Father Miceli wrote.

"Moreover, the secular city is now rising over the ruins of the Christian city. This new city promises its citizens an earthly paradise and a civilization that is founded on a new creed—'There is no God! In man—come of age—we trust!'

"Needless to say, this Godless city is doomed to even greater destruction than that which struck faithless cities before it. For it is built on the sands of a double fault—that of philosophical atheism and theological nihilism.

"When the underground, volcanic fires of disbelief, desperation and despair build to the point of violent friction that can no longer be suppressed, then the shining city of Godless, secular culture will explode and be consumed by fire like Sodom and Gomorrah and, like them, will disappear into the bowels of the earth as a city of eternal night.

"But perhaps if Christians understood the past and present causes that are hastening Godless society toward self-annihilation, they might once again so bestir themselves as to change the face of the earth through a renewal of faith and zeal that God would be moved to spare and bless His cities.

"For social upheavals do not occur in a fatalistic manner. Man chooses these freely with open eyes. Often in defiance of God's offers to save man from himself. Man need only return to God in faith and repentance to be rescued from social suicide.

"The plant of modern atheism took root in the seed bed of a period, a flood of wild thoughts and violent passions, which in history books is called 'The Age of Enlightenment.'

"Earlier, at the time of the Protestant Reformation, Luther had radically altered the concept of the nature of the Christian God. In his eyes, God was the supreme being of absolute sovereignty who decided the fate of men in a purely arbitrary manner, saving those He liked, damning those He disliked. Calvin hardened this cruel predestination into a ruthless dogma of faith.

"Naturally, men shrank from this God who devoured their intellectual, volitional and personal existences. In the name of human freedom and dignity the men of The Enlightenment turned against this despot God, who as the exemplar of human rulers, was invoked to justify the unbridled political omnipotence of tyrannical princes and kings.

"The Frenchman, Rousseau, created the euphoric atmosphere that fostered man's complete confidence in his own natural goodness and faith in the power of his reason. Robespierre, his devoted disciple, promulgated his master's doctrine and in 1794, from the tribunal of the French Revolution convention, decreed that the religion of civil humanity, delineated in Rosseau's 'Emile', was henceforth the state religion.

"According to Engels this establishment of a civil religion was the herald of a new awakening, a new spring. D'Holbach insisted that 'the God who was on trial was the God of the Christians'. He thundered against God as a tyrant who had to be done away with. Much ahead of Marx he labeled faith a drug.

"Voltaire himself had no use for God, heaping ridicule upon Him and the Catholic church. Marx shrewdly remarked that, 'Voltaire taught atheism in his text and faith in his footnotes and people believed the text, not the footnotes.'

"Though in the end he returned and died in the Catholic faith, Voltaire left behind him a nation of agnostics whose faith he had sapped by the ridicule and mockery that filled his brilliant books.

"Voltaire altered the tyrant-God of Luther and Calvin into the deistic God of The Enlightenment. This was a God who abandoned the world to the devil, caring not at all for the miserable plight of humanity. Men rose against a God who had betrayed the world, demanding His annihilation.

"When the political revolution, the reign of blood, and the Napoleonic wars added their vast carnage to this flood of free-thinking, the faith of France, eldest daughter of the church, was almost obliterated.

"Soon, many German scholars, ardent admirers of such French men of letters as D'Holbach and Voltaire, joined the chorus of enlightened mockers. Hegel, Fichte, Feuerbach, Marx slashed at the Christian God and church.

"Feuerbach declared that God was the image of man, not man the image of God. Theology was anthropology, not vice versa. It was time man dismissed God and lived up to his own image. Marx, the atheist of action, set to work to reduce the Christian world to a desert swept clean of Christian institutions. His classless utopia could be built only on the ruins of the city of God.

"Kant, originally a rationalist and man of the Enlightenment, was stung by the criticisms of David Hume, the English empiricist. Kant analyzed and found wanting—metaphysically—the existence of God, the immortality of the soul, the liberty of man. God's existence was incapable of metaphysical proof. At this point, positivism replaced rationalism.

"Following the footsteps of Kant came Hegel. Hegel, tortured by Christianity with a sense of sin, rejected all faith in a personal God. Later, Nietzsche, feeling God keeps man forever frightened and sick and hence dependent upon Him, rejected God as the eternal enemy of man.

"Hegel downgraded God to a mere dialectical 'process', clashing, twisting, unwinding and obliterating in history through the principle of contradiction. Hegel told man his glory consisted in allowing himself to be kneaded into this collective, historical, necessary 'process.'

"In Hegel we find allusions that God must die if man is to be cured. That man's longing for a transcendent happiness with God beyond time was a despicable flight from the challenge of time, a cowardly fear of the good earth. Neitzsche later warns man in a warning which still echoes and re-echoes in our day, 'Brothers, remain true to the earth! Beware of the siren God of Christianity who would seduce you from your earthly greatness!' The entire death-of-God movement takes its rise in this philosophic assault of man on heaven to recover for man the treasures he squandered on God.

"As George Siegmund wrote, 'Hegel's intellectual revolution began with the fundamental religious decision he made against a personal God. His principle of dialectics became one wherein a world spirit came into its own in the world process. God is identical with the world, never complete, forever in the process of becoming. Only in man does God attain full self-consciousness, for God and man are one and the same.' (ala Teilhard de Chardin.)

"In our time, some have asked, 'In our scientific age does the idea of God make any difference in the betterment of man?' There are others who believe the idea of God is positively harmful, a roadblock to progress. They say the idea of God is used to conserve the unjust established order, justifying this order's existence, institutions, and policies.

"In a desperate effort, therefore, to throw off the yoke of God and the corrupt status quo, these men have taken to streets and campuses in violence.

"All these accusations against God have been systematically developed and given the fashionable ring of genuineness over the past several centuries through such rationalists as we have mentioned, and later, through such existentialists as Camus, Sarte and Heidegger, mentioned elsewhere in this work, they molded our age of atheism.

"In 1926, Oswald Spengler wrote of western civilization—'You are dying. I see you in all the characteristic stigma of decay—your revolutions, your atheism, your pessimism, your cynicism, your immorality, your broken marriages, your birth control. These were the characteristics of the dying ages of Egypt, Greece, Rome.'"

XXVIII—December, 1972 Rudolph M. Unger

Chapter 29

Historians looking back on the 20th century will record that the year 1917 was the most significant year in the century.

Conscious of St. Paul's counsel that—"We wrestle not against flesh and blood, but against principalities, against powers, against the rulers of the darkness of this world, against spiritual wickedness in high places"...

... They will note that it was in 1917 that the antagonist, the adversary of man—the anti-Christ—surfaced in Russia in the form of communism under the leadership of Lenin. And, that it was also in 1917 that the protagonist, the protector of man—Christ – descended and made himself present to modern day man in Portugal through his beloved mother, the Blessed Virgin.

Lenin returned to Russia at Petrograd on April 16, 1917 to make his God forsaken quest for power. Mary first appeared to the three shepherd children at Cova da Iria near Fatima in Portugal on May 13, 1917.

Lenin succeeded in his diabolical endeavor on Nov. 7, 1917. Our Lady made her last of six appearances to the children at the Cova on Oct. 13, 1917.

That struggle of principalities and powers for the soul of man has been going on ever since with the powers of darkness, 56 years later, holding a decided advantage and stranglehold on the windpipe of mankind.

And holding it for one reason and one reason only—modern man just doesn't believe he is the stake in this eternal poker game, and, instead of reaching out to clasp that heavenly hand proffered so lovingly, he continues to wallow stupor-like in the pig sty, arrogantly insisting on casting his pearls before devilish swine.

The last three pontiffs of Christ have lend their presence to the urgency of this, His heavenly admonition and request made at Fatima through His mother. Pius through radio and John, as Cardinal Roncalli, and Paul as Pope, in person. And yet precious little is heard of this message in the present day, enlightened church. One would hardly think that the only thing at stake was everything.

In these next issues of Counter-Reformation we will present the occurrences surrounding Fatima and their portent for the terrestrial well being and celestial joy of man.

We will draw upon the observation and investigation of William T. Walsh, an American historian, who went to Fatima in 1946, and after studying the history of the events, speaking to Lucia, the only survivor of the three shepherd children, and drawing upon her four unpublished memoirs, came away to write the book—"Our Lady of Fatima". Because, as he said—"The future of our civilization, our liberties, our very existence may depend upon the acceptance of this heavenly lady's commands."

And to make it explicitly, unmistakably clear, to anyone with any modicum of intelligence, what Walsh meant, we quote from the 1954 forward to the book by Msgr. William C. Mcgrath:

"Where Russia tomorrow to feel assured of final victory in an all-out atomic struggle, we should all too soon be shocked into a realization of the pathetic futility of our contemporary gestures of appeasement and compromise, of our refusal to take a strong and uncompromising stand in the face of an enemy that respects and understands nothing else."

On Oct.13, 1917, our Lord, for the benefit of those of little faith or none at all, such as the freethinker masons who then controlled Portugal, performed the miracle of the sun before 70,000 persons to verify that indeed His mother was present at Fatima and that the three little children were not psychological psychopaths or pathological liars.

Among those present that day was a correspondent for one of the major news services in the United States. He cabled a long and impressive story from Lisbon, but it was never published. The long dispatch was relegated to one sentence on a back page, buried amidst the details of the truly momentous event then engaging the American people—the world series between two teams whom no one today could from memory recall.

Chicagoans packed a ball park for a Bears-Cardinal Game in December, 1941 when America was drawn into one of the events forecast by Our Lady at Fatima as the bombs came tumbling down at Pearl Harbor.

Pray tell, at what other truly important affair shall we American people be in attendance, when the perhaps key scene in this battle of principalities and powers comes bursting down, hurling us into eternity?

Providence, proceeding in its usual prudential pattern, prepared the three little children—Lucia, 10, and her two cousins, Francisco, 9, and Jacinta, 7—for the momentous appearances of Our Lady in 1917.

The first prefatory events occurred in the summer of 1915. One day, Lucia and three other girls were keeping watch over their sheep, saying their rosary together after lunch, when, as Walsh writes:

"They saw a strange white something that was moving majestically from East to West, far over the deep valley. As it approached them it came to a pause over the pine grove and remained suspended in the air for some time.

"As Lucia remembers, it was, 'A figure-like statue made of snow which the rays of the sun had turned somewhat transparent.' It seemed to have the form of a human being. As they finished the rosary it disappeared. The same thing occurred twice again that summer."

During the next summer, that of 1916, Lucia, Francisco and Jacinta were minding their sheep and had just finished saying their rosary when, as Walsh relates, "Without warning, a strong wind began to blow across the top of the pines, which swayed and moaned as never before.

"Startled, they then saw a light far over the top of the trees. It was moving over the valley from East to West and coming in their direction. Lucia recognized in this the strange whiteness of that figure she had witnessed the previous summer with the three other girls.

"It seemed indeed to be wholly made up of radiance more white than snow and this time it drew near and became distinguishable as the form of 'a transparent man' about 15 years of age, as Lucia recalled. And now they could see that he had features like those of a human being and was indescribably beautiful.

"Stupefied, speechless, they stood regarding him.

'Do not be afraid', he said. 'I am the angel of peace. Pray with me.'

"And kneeling on the ground, he prostrated himself until his forehead touched it, saying—'My God, I believe, I adore, I hope and I love you! I beg pardon of you for those who do not believe, do not adore, do not hope, and do not love you!'

"Three times he spoke the same words, while the children, as in a daze, repeated them after him. Then arising, he said, 'Pray thus. The hearts of Jesus and Mary are attentive to the voice of your supplications.' With that he disappeared as if he had been dissolved in sunlight.

"A few weeks later, the angel appeared again to the three. This time at the well in the shade of the fig tree behind Lucia's home. 'What are you doing?' he demanded. 'Pray! Pray a great deal! The hearts of Jesus and Mary have merciful designs for you. Offer prayers and sacrifices constantly to the most high!'

'How must we sacrifice?', Lucia asked.

"'With all your power offer a sacrifice as an act of reparation for the sinners by whom He is offended, and of supplication for the conversion of sinners. Thus draw peace upon your country. I am its guardian angel, the angel of Portugal. Above all, accept and endure with submission the suffering which the Lord will send you!'

"The angel's third and last appearance came one day as they were tending the sheep. After they had said the rosary and were reciting the prayer the angel had taught them.

"This time he held a chalice in one hand and a host in the other. He left them suspended in the air and prostrated himself on the ground and said:

'Most Holy Trinity, Father, Son and Holy Spirit, I adore you profoundly and offer you the most precious body, blood, soul and divinity of Jesus Christ, present in all the tabernacles in the world, in reparation for the outrages, sacrileges and indifferences with which He is offended.

'Through the infinite merits of His Sacred Heart and of the Immaculate Heart of Mary, I beg of you the conversion of poor sinners.'

"Giving the children communion, the angel asked them to 'console your God!' and left."

XXIX—January, 1973 Rudolph M. Unger

Chapter 30

On May 5, 1917, Pope Benedict XV, in a memorable letter, lamented, "The cruel war, the suicide of Europe", narrates William T. Walsh, the American historian, in his book, "Our Lady of Fatima."

"After begging God to turn the hearts of rulers toward peace and urging all to purge themselves of sin and pray for peace," Walsh noted, "The pope continued that since all graces were dispensed 'by the hands of the most Holy Virgin, we wish the petitions of her most afflicted children to be directed with lively confidence, more than ever in this awful hour, to the great Mother of God'. And he directed that the invocation 'Queen of Peace, pray for us' be added to the litany of Loreto.

'To Mary then', implored Benedict, 'She who is the mother of mercy and omnipotent by grace, let loving and devout appeal go up from every corner of the earth—from noble temples and tiniest chapels, from royal palaces and mansions of the rich as from the poorest hut—from blood drenched plains and seas.

'Let it bear to Her the anguished cry of mothers and wives, the wailing of innocent little ones, the sighs of every generous heart, that Her most tender and benign solicitude may be moved and the peace we ask for be obtained for our agitated world.'

Walsh then continued:

"On May 13, 1917, an uncommonly fine Sunday morning, Lucia Abobora, 10, and her two cousins, Francisco Marto, 9, and Jacinta Marto, 7, took their sheep to the Cova Da Iria near Fatima in Portugal.

"Suddenly they were startled by a flash so brilliant that they took it to be lighting. Without stopping to ask how it could have come from that cloudless sky, they ran down the slope toward a certain Holm-oak. They had just found shelter beneath it when there was a second flash of light. Again frightened, they left the tree and ran again.

"Then they stopped in amazement, for just before them, on top of a small evergreen, they saw a ball of light. And in the center of it stood a lady. As Lucia described Her, She was 'A lady all of white, more brilliant than the sun. Her face was indescribably beautiful, not sad, not happy, but serious.'

"Her hands together as in prayer at her breast, pointing upward, with rosary beads hanging down between the fingers of the right hand. It was almost impossible to look steadily at the face. It dazzled and hurt the eyes and made one blink and look away.

"'Don't be afraid', she said, in a low musical voice, never to be forgotten. 'I won't hurt you!'

"The children felt no fear now, in fact, but only a great joy and peace. Lucia asked, 'Where does your excellency come from?' The lady replied, 'I am from heaven.' Lucia asked, 'And what is it you want of me?'

"The lady answered, 'I come to ask you to come here for six months in succession, on the 13th day at this same hour. Then I will tell you who I am and what I want.'

"Lucia then asked, 'And shall I go to heaven too? 'The lady said, 'Yes, you will.' 'And Jacinta?' 'Also.' 'And Francisco?' 'Also, but he will have to say many rosaries.'

"The lady then asked—'Do you wish to offer yourselves to God, to endure all the suffering that He may please to send you, as an act of reparation for the sins by which He is offended, and to ask for the conversion of sinners?' 'Yes, we do.'

"'Then you will have much to suffer. But the grace of God will be your comfort.'

"As the lady spoke, she opened her lovely hands and from her palms there radiated intense streams of light that enveloped the children and, as Lucia described it, 'Making us see ourselves in God, more clearly than in the best of mirrors.'

"An irresistible impulse forced them to their knees and made them say, 'O Holy Trinity, I adore you! My God, my God, I love you in the most Blessed Sacrament!'

"The lady then said, 'Say the rosary every day to obtain peace for the world and the end of the war.' She then rose serenely, glided toward the East and disappeared.

"Lucia later learned that Francisco had seen the lady but had not heard what she said, just as when he had seen the angel. When she and Jacinta told him what the lady said, he was intensely happy, especially over the promise that he was going to heaven. Folding his hands over his head, he cried, 'O my, Our Lady, I will say all the rosaries you want!'

"On June 13, the feast of St. Anthony, the Portuguese saint who went to Italy, the children, accompanied by persons who had learned of the May apparition, returned to the Cova and recited the rosary. Upon completing it, Lucia rose from the ground, crying, 'Jacinta, there comes Our Lady. There is the light!'

"The three children ran to the tiny evergreen where the lady again stood. Lucia asked her, 'What does your excellency want of me?' The lady replied, 'I want you come here on the 13th day of the coming month, recite five decades of the rosary every day and learn to read. I will tell you later what I want.'

"Lucia then said, 'I should like to ask you to take us to heaven.' The lady answered, 'Yes, Jacinta and Francisco I will take soon. But you remain here for some time more. Jesus wishes to make use of you to have Me acknowledged and loved. He wishes to establish in the world the devotion to My Immaculate Heart.'

"Lucia, in dismay, said, "I stay here? Alone?'

"'No daughter', the lady said. 'And do you suffer a great deal? Don't be discouraged. I will never forsake you. My Immaculate Heart will be your refuge and the road that will conduct you to God.'

"The lady then again opened her hands from which streamed the heavenly radiance enveloping the children.

'In it we saw ourselves as if submerged in God.' Lucia said. 'Jacinta and Francisco seemed to be in the part that went upward to heaven and I in that part which spread itself over the ground.

'Before the palm of the right hand of Our Lady was a heart encircled by thorns which seemed to have pierced it like nails. We understood that it was the Immaculate Heart of Mary, outraged by the sins of humanity, for which there must be reparation.'

"Now the children saw both Jesus and Mary in that vision of the most Blessed Trinity that enfolded them. Our Lady seemed neither sad nor joyful, but always 'serious.' But the impression left by the Word of God, on the mind of Francisco, at any rate, was one of infinite sadness. As this tremendous revelation faded from their view, The Lady arose, glided swiftly to the East until She could no longer be seen.

"On July 13, accompanied by a somewhat larger crowd, the three children returned to the Cova, where following the recitation of the rosary, the lady appeared in the same manner as before, saying, 'I want you to come here on the 13th day of the coming month, continue to say five decades of the rosary every day in honor of Our Lady of the Rosary to obtain peace of the world and the end of the war, for She alone will be able to help.

'In October, I will tell you who I am and what I wish and will perform a miracle that everyone will have to believe.

'Sacrifice yourself for sinners, saying, 'O Jesus, it is for your love, for the conversion of sinners, and in reparation for the sins committed against the Immaculate Heart of Mary.'

"The lady then again opened her hands from which streamed the radiant light, but this time it seemed to pass into the earth, disclosing beneath, as Lucia said, 'A sea of fire and plunged into this fire the demons and the souls…among shrieks and groans of sorrow and despair…'

"The lady said, 'You see hell, where the souls of poor sinners go. To save them, God wishes to establish in the world the devotion to My Immaculate Heart. If they do what I will tell you, many souls will be saved, and there will be peace. The war is going to end. But if they do not stop offending God, another worse one will begin in the reign of Pius XI.

'When you shall see a night illuminated by an unknown light, know that it is the great sign that God gives you that He is going to punish the world for its crimes by means of war, of hunger, and of persecution of the Church and of the Holy Father. To prevent this, I come to ask the consecration of Russia to My Immaculate Heart and the communion of reparation on first Saturdays.'"

XXX—February, 1973 Rudolph M. Unger

Chapter 31

When Our Lady on July 13, 1917 told the three shepherd children at Fatima that she was asking for the consecration of Russia to Her Immaculate Heart and the communion of reparation on first Saturdays, She said:

"If people listen to my requests, Russia will be converted and there will be peace. If not, she will scatter her errors throughout the world, provoking wars and persecution of the Church. The good will be martyrized, the Holy Father will have much to suffer, various nations will be annihilated.

"In the end My Immaculate Heart will triumph. The Holy Father will consecrate Russia to Me and it will be converted and a certain period of peace will be granted to the world. In Portugal the faith will always be kept.

"When you say the rosary, say after each mystery—'O my Jesus, pardon us and deliver us from the fire of hell. Draw all souls to heaven, especially those in most need.'"

Our Lady did not make Her scheduled appearance at the Cova on August 13 because the three children were forcibly kept from going there by the freethinker mason who was the administrator of the district in which they lived.

Instead, she appeared to them on August 19 in an area not too far from the Cova. She told them, "I want you to continue to go to Cova da Iria on the 13th day and to continue to recite the rosary every day. In the last month I will perform the miracle so that all shall believe. Pray, pray a great deal and make sacrifices for sinners. For so many souls go to hell because they have no one to sacrifice and pray for them."

On September 13, accompanied by a yet larger crowd, the three children kept their rendezvous at the Cova with their lady. She told them:

"Continue to say the rosary to bring about the end of the war. In October our Lord will come also and Our Lady of the Sorrows of Carmel, and St. Joseph with the child Jesus, to bless the world. God is content with your sacrifices. In October I will perform the miracle so that all will believe."

"On the eve of Oct. 13, 1917, a cold driving rain storm pelted across Portugal," wrote William T. Walsh in his "Our Lady of Fatima." "Yet there were thousands of human beings on the roads of the little republic that night.

For faith is stronger than doubt and love is hardier than hate

"Devout Catholics in every village of the land had heard by this time that Our Lady had promised to return to the Cova to perform a miracle on Oct. 13. Rain or shine, that was all they needed to know.

"Fathers and mothers carried sick or lame children in their arms for incredible distances. Fishermen from Nazare, sailors from Porto and the Algarve, factory workers from Lisbon, were plodding through the mud under the pouring rain that night. Like a great scattered army converging on Fatima, hoping to find there some favor of health or conversion, forgiveness of sin, consolation for sorrow, the beginning of a better life, the blessing of God's mother.

"Fragments of old hymns would echo back from the wet cliffs, 'Ave, Ave, Ave Maria!' The rosary was recited by the pilgrims as they marched through the wet, dark night. Not for nothing had the ancestors of these people sung the 'Salve Regina' on the decks of galleons in the Indian Ocean or whalers in the China Sea.

"Also enroute to Fatima was Avelino de Almeida, managing editor of 'O, Seculo', the largest newspaper in Lisbon. He was a freemason who made no secret of his dislike for priests, sacraments, creeds and dogmas. He was covering the story because it had been too much talked about to be ignored and he was one of the best newspaper men in Portugal.

"When the three shepherd children set out for the Cova that morning it was a long and slow journey. The high road was crowded all the way from Fatima to Cova da Iria. Men and women were kneeling in the thick slime on both sides of the road.

"When they arrived at last, there were fully 70,000 men, women and children, people of all ages and conditions, standing patiently in the rain waiting for them—a dark mass under innumerable umbrellas, dripping sombreros and soaked blankets.

"Nearly all the people were reciting the rosary in various rhythmical cadences when Lucia cried 'Put down your umbrellas!' Why she never knew. Moments later, looking East, she cried, 'Jacinta, kneel down, for now I see Our Lady there. I can see the flash!'

"With the rain falling on her face, Lucia asked, 'What do you want of me?' The lady replied, 'I want to tell you to have them build a chapel here in my honor. I am the Lady of the Rosary. Let them continue to say the rosary every day. The war is going to end and the soldiers will soon return home.'

"Our Lady opened her hands and it seemed to Lucia that the light emerging from them ascended to where the sun ought to be, directly overhead, and it was brighter than any sunlight.

"Perhaps it was at this moment that the crowd saw the clouds separate like two vast curtains rolled apart and the sun appeared between them in the clear blue, like a disk of white fire. Certainly many heard Lucia cry, 'Look at the sun!' But she said this in ecstasy and has no recollection of it. For she was wholly absorbed in something she saw where the sun must have been.

"As our lady disappeared in the very radiance that came from her out stretched hands, there stood out in the zenith above three tableaus which symbolized, one after another—the joyous, the sorrowful and the glorious mysteries of the rosary.

"The first was a distinct representation of the Holy Family. Our Lady Herself in Her traditional dress of white with a blue mantle and Saint Joseph beside Her, holding the child Jesus on His arm—St. Joseph in white, the infant in bright red. Lucia was heard to say, 'St. Joseph is going to bless us!' All three children saw this first vision and saw the saint make the sign of the cross three times over the crowd. The Holy Child did likewise.

"The next vision, seen by Lucia alone, was one of Our Lady of Sorrows in the somber garb assigned to Her by tradition, the Mater Dolorosa of Good Friday, but without the sword in Her breast. Beside Her stood Her Divine Son grieving as when He met Her on the way to Calvary. He looked pityingly on the crowd for whom He had died and raised His hand to make the sign of the cross over them.

"Our Lady then appeared in a third vision of glory as Our Lady of Mount Carmel, crowned as Queen of Heaven and the World, Her infant son on Her knee.

"The crowd saw nothing of this. What they all did see, however, was something stupendous, unheard of, almost apocalyptic. The sun stood forth in the clear zenith like a great silver disk which, though bright as any sun they had ever seen, they could look straight at without blinking, and with a unique and delightful satisfaction. This lasted but a moment.

"While they gazed, the huge ball began to 'dance'—That was the word all of the beholders applied to it. Now it was whirling rapidly like a gigantic firewheel. After doing this for sometime, it stopped. Then it rotated again, with dizzy, sickening speed.

"Finally there appeared on the rim a border of crimson, which flung across the sky, as from a hellish vortex, blood red streamers of flame, reflecting to the earth, to the trees and shrubs, to the upturned faces and the clothes, all sorts of brilliant colors in succession—green, red, orange, blue, violet, the whole spectrum in fact.

"Madly gyrating in this manner three times, the fiery orb seemed to tremble, to shudder and then to plunge precipitately, in a mighty zigzag, toward the crowd.

"A fearful cry broke from the lips of thousands of terrified persons as they fell on their knees, thinking the end of the world had come. Some said that the air became warmer at that instant. They would not have been surprised if everything about them had burst into flames, enveloping and consuming them.

"This had lasted about 10 minutes, perhaps. Then all saw the sun begin to climb, in the same zigzag manner, to where it had appeared before. It became tranquil, then dazzling. No one could look at it any longer. It was the sun of every day.

"The people stared at one another in joy and amazement. 'Miracle, miracle, the children were right! Our Lady made the miracle! Blessed be God. Blessed be our Lady!'

"Some were laughing, others weeping with joy. Many were making the discovery that their drenched clothes had become perfectly dry."

XXXI—March, 1973 Rudolph M. Unger

Chapter 32

In Our Lady's first appearance to the three little shepherd children near Fatima in 1917, She asked them—"Do you wish to offer yourselves to God, to endure all the suffering that He may please to send you as an act of reparation for the sins by which He is offended, and to ask for the conversion of sinners?"

Lucia, speaking for the three, replied, "Yes, we do." And Our Lady responded, "Then you will have much to suffer. But the grace of God will be your comfort."

How did this generous acceptance of the cross of suffering affect the lives of these little ones? We look particularly into the remaining short lives of Francisco, 9, and Jacinta, 7, to see how they mortified themselves to rise to great heights of holiness, thereby providing us with superb exemplars to follow, if we but dare.

As William Walsh wrote in his "Our Lady of Fatima": "One day the three children were wondering, 'The sacrifices? How are we going to make them?' Francisco had an idea. 'We can give our lunches to the sheep and make the sacrifice of not eating any lunch.'

"Jacinta thought of a better way of disposing of their lunches. One day they saw some poor children from Motta, a half mile away, coming to beg. 'Let's give them our lunches for the conversion of sinners', she said. And they did.

"Every day from then on Jacinta made a lunch of bitter acorns or of sour unripe olives. Lucia said one day, 'Jacinta, don't eat those. They are very bitter.' Jacinta replied, 'It is for the bitterness that I eat, to convert sinners.'

"It was not long before the children of poor families began to wait for them along the roadsides to ask for their lunches. The three always gave them cheerfully and then ate whatever they happened to find as they roamed about the Serra. 'We use to eat pine cones', Lucia remembers. 'Roots of bindweed, a little yellowish flower; mulberries, mushrooms and roots of fine trees.'

"The most resolute in carrying out The Lady's wishes regarding sacrifice was Jacinta, if we are to take literally the modest recital of Lucia. One sweaty day, after giving away their lunches, and a long hot walk, they were tired, hungry and parched.

"Finally Lucia obtained from a shepherd woman a small piece of bread and a jug of water. She offered it first to Francisco. 'I don't want to drink,' he said. 'Why?' she asked. 'I want to suffer for the conversion of sinners.' 'You drink', Lucia told Jacinta. 'I want to sacrifice for sinners too,' she said.

"Then, Lucia recalled, 'I poured the water into a hollow of the rock for the sheep to drink.' Later Jacinta remarked, 'Tell the crickets and the frogs to keep quiet. It gives me a headache.' Francisco said, 'Don't you want to suffer this for sinners?' Jacinta, pressing her head between her little hands, said, 'Yes, I do. Let them sing!'

"And Francisco, what a comfort he was. He seemed not only to accept suffering but to love it, as the saints do who follow in the footsteps of the crucified. 'Our Lady told us we would have much to suffer,' he would say, 'that, doesn't matter to me. I will suffer everything as much as she wants!'

"Another characteristic of the saints that Francisco began to manifest after the apparition of Our Lady was the love of solitude. One day he laid alone atop a high rock, refusing to eat. Finally the girls struggled up to where he was, demanding, 'What have you been doing all this time?'

'I have been thinking of God, who is so sad because of so many sins', he answered seriously. 'If only I could give Him joy!'

"The two girls could think of nothing else but the horrors divine wisdom had disclosed to them—hell, war—but Francisco for some reason was much less shaken by the experience.

"He would fix his thoughts on God, upon his goodness and His glory. 'How wonderful God is!' He would cry ecstatically. 'There is no way to say it. All you can say is, that nobody can say it! But isn't it too bad that He is so sad. If I could only console Him!'

Once Jacinta grasped the idea that God's justice is the counterpart of His mercy, and that there must be a hell if there is to be a heaven, nothing seemed important to her except to save as many souls as possible from the horrors she glimpsed under the radiant hands of the Queen Of Heaven.

"Lucia would say, 'Eat, Jacinta.' 'No, I will offer this sacrifice for poor sinners who eat too much,' she would answer. 'Drink, Jacinta,' Lucia would say. 'No, this is for those who drink too much,' she replied.

"She would say suddenly to Lucia, 'I am sorry for you. Francisco and I are going to heaven but you stay here alone. When you see war, don't be afraid - in heaven I will be praying for you.'

"One day Lucia asked her, 'Jacinta, what are you thinking about?' She answered, 'Of that war that is going to come and of so many people who are going to die and go to hell. What a pity there must be a war and they must go to hell because they won't stop sinning!'

"Time and again this thought recurred with sickening impact. She would say, with a look of terror, 'Hell, hell! How sorry I am for the souls that are going to hell!' Then she would fall on her knees, clasp her hands and repeat over and over the prayer Our Lady had taught them to add to each decade of the rosary—'O my Jesus, pardon us, save us from the fire of hell. Draw all souls to heaven, especially those in most need!'

"One day Jacinta demanded of Lucia, 'Why doesn't Our Lady show hell to sinners? If they saw it, they would never sin again, so they wouldn't go there. You must tell Our Lady to show hell to all those people. You will see how they will be converted!'

"' Don't be afraid,' Lucia tried to reassure her one day. 'You are going to heaven.' 'Yes, yes I'm going. But I want all those people to go there too!' She replied.

"One day she said to Lucia, 'Don't you see such a long street, so many roads and fields full of people weeping with hunger, and they have nothing to eat? And the Holy Father in a church before the Immaculate Heart of Mary, praying? And so many people praying with him?'

"Another time, Jacinta said, 'Don't you see the Holy Father? I don't know how it is, I see the Holy Father in a very large house on his knees before a table, with his hands over his face, crying. In front of the house there are many people, and some are throwing stones at him, others are cursing him and saying very foul words to him. Poor little Holy Father! We must pray a lot for him!

"One day the three children found a rope. Lucia picked it up and it scratched her. 'Look, this hurts! We can make a girdle of it and offer this sacrifice to God.' Dividing the rope, each one wore a piece of it wrapped around the body, next to the skin. What was health compared to saving souls from hell? And what was comfort to the joys of an eternal heaven?

"There were many objective signs that these penances were pleasing to God and that Jacinta in particular was advancing on the road to sainthood. She had become more patient, more long-suffering, more affectionate. She had many visions of things that later came to pass. And in Lucia's opinion, Jacinta must have received by this time, the gift of infused wisdom. One day she said three 'aves' for a wretched woman with a terrible disease and all the symptoms vanished.

"One day the two girls found Francisco lying motionless along a wall and asked, 'Why don't you come and pray with us?' He said, 'I'd rather pray alone, to think, and to console Our Lord, He is so sad.' They said, 'Francisco which do you like better, to console Our Lord or to convert sinners so that their souls won't go to hell?' He replied, 'I'd rather console our Lord. I want to console Our Lord first and then convert sinners so they won't offend.'

"Another day the girls could not find him and shouted for him. They at last found him, prostrate behind a pile of rocks. Still no answer. He hardly even stirred when they shook him. When he finally got up, he seemed hardly to know where he was. He said he had said the prayer of the angel and then had remained there thinking. He had not heard the girls' shouts. The boy obtained notable cures and conversions."

XXXII—April, 1973 Rudolph M. Unger

Chapter 33

"It was October, 1918 and the war was about to end as Our Lady had promised, but the great epidemic of influenza, one of the concomitant scourges of the almost universal punishment of man's apostasy, was laying low millions of persons throughout the world."

So wrote William T. Walsh in his "Our Lady of Fatima", noting that epidemic made its first appearance at Fatima toward the end of October, strickening all in the Abobora family but Lucia and in the Marto home sparing only the father, Ti.

"Francisco, the first to be put to bed, had a severe case, ending with bronchial pneumonia." wrote Walsh. "It was heartbreaking for his parents to see him welcome the illness as the beginning of the journey that The Lady had promised him.

"He became so weak that he could hardly move, yet he never complained. He took the bitter medicines without making a face. 'This gave us hope that he would get well, 'recalled Olimpia, his mother. 'But he was always telling us that it was no use, that Our Lady was coming to take him to heaven'.

"Jacinta became ill a few days after Francisco. One day Lucia found her strangely elated. 'Our Lady came to see us,' she told Lucia. 'She said that she is coming very soon to take Francisco to heaven. And she asked me if I still wanted to convert more sinners and I said yes.

'Our Lady wants me to go to two hospitals, but not to be cured. It is to suffer more for the love of God, for the conversion of sinners and in reparation for the offenses committed against the Immaculate Heart of Mary.'

"Lucia asked Francisco, flushed with eyes much too large and bright, 'Do you suffer much?' 'Yes' he answered, 'but it doesn't matter. I suffer to console Our Lord and in a little while I shall be with Him.'

"Shortly thereafter the boy made his first confession and communion. He was radiant with joy. He looked so ethereal that Lucia doubted she would see him again. He pressed her hand hard for a long moment and looked deeply into her eyes and both were blinded by tears. 'Goodbye

Francisco, till heaven,' she said, weeping as she left. She could stand no more.

"In the morning he asked his mother's blessing and pardon for any trouble he had caused her in his life. At 10 a.m., April 4, 1919, his life passed almost imperceptibly. There was still a faint smile on his lips when Jacinta and Lucia came to look at him.

"In the days that followed, though Jacinta knew where Francisco was and who had taken him, she missed him terribly.

"She had purulent pleurisy as a result of bronchial pneumonia. She was taken to a hospital in Ourem. A month later her mother hardly knew her. She was so thin, pale, transparent and emaciated. There was a great open wound in her chest. Two months later, a priest friend who visited her, described her as a living skeleton, her arms nothing but bones. Her face, eyes and cheeks wasted by fever.

"It was only to Lucia that she would reveal the terrible pain she had in her chest, but it was to honor the Immaculate Heart of Mary. 'Tell all the people that God gives them graces through her,' Jacinta told Lucia. 'I don't know how it is, I feel Our Lord inside of me. I understand what He says and I don't see or hear Him! But it is good to be with Him.

' Look, do you know what? Our Lord is sad because Our Lady told us not to offend Him any more because He is so much offended, and nobody pays any attention. They keep right on doing the same sins.'

"Three times during the year 1919, Jacinta saw her "Little Mother Of Heaven" standing by her bed, encouraging her. The last of these visions came in December. 'Our Lady came to see me last night,' she said joyfully. 'She told me I am going to Lisbon to another hospital. She said that after I suffer a great deal I will die. But She told me not to be afraid, for She will come and find me and take me to heaven.

'I will never see you again, Lucia! Pray for me a lot for I die alone. We shall never meet again. Pray for me a lot until I go to heaven and afterwards, I'll pray a lot for you. Love Jesus and the Immaculate Heart of Mary a great deal and make many sacrifices for sinners. Goodbye Lucia.' 'Goodbye, Jacinta.'

"Before going to that hospital in Lisbon, Jacinta was put in an orphanage there operated by a lay nun.

"Mother Dona Godinho, a Franciscan, had a great devotion for Our Lady and felt Jacinta was a saint. She and Jacinta had many conversations which later were written down by the nun.

"Jacinta told Mother Godinho, 'Wars are nothing but punishment for the sins of the world. Our Lady can no longer hold back the arm of Her Beloved Son from the world. It is necessary to do penance. If people reform, Our Lord will save the world. But if they do not reform, He will punish it.

'Pray much for sinners. Pray much for priests. Pray much for religious. Priests should occupy themselves with the affairs of the church. Priests should be pure, very pure. The disobedience of priests and religious to their superiors and to the Holy Father offends Our Lord very greatly.

'Pray for those who govern. Alas, for those who persecute the religion of Our Lord! If the government leaves the church in peace and gives liberty to the holy Faith, it will be blessed by God.

'Do not walk in the midst of luxury. Flee from riches. Be very friendly to holy poverty and silence. Have great charity even for the wicked. Speak ill of no one and flee from those who do. Be very patient, for patience carries us to heaven. Mortification and sacrifices please Our Lord a great deal.

'Confession is a sacrament of mercy. For this reason it is necessary to approach the confessional with confidence and joy. Without confession there is no salvation. The Mother of God wants more virgin souls, which bind themselves to Her by the vow of chastity. To be a religious it is necessary to be very pure in soul and body. Those who do not keep the promises they make to Our Lady will never be happy in their affairs.'

"Mother Godinho asked Jacinta, 'Who taught you all these things?' She replied, 'It was Our Lady. But some I think of myself. I like very much to think.

"At last she entered 'the hospital in a dark building' Our Lady had foretold her, the hospital of Dona Stefania, where, on Feb. 10, 1920, two of her ribs were removed, leaving an opening large enough for a fist.

"The doctors felt the operation was a success. Jacinta knew better.

"The pain was excruciating. 'Oh My Lady' moaned the child. Then she would murmur 'Patience.' It is for Your love, my Jesus. Now You can convert many sinners, for I suffer much.'

"She had many conversations in the hospital with Mother Godinho, who visited her every day. On the night of Feb. 16, she told the nun she had seen Our Lady. 'She told me She was coming for me very soon and would take away my pains.'

"From then on she had no more pain. On the evening of Feb. 20, she called her nurse, 'My little Aurora' and told her she was about to die and wanted the last sacraments. At 8 p.m. she made her confession and the priest promised to bring her communion the next morning.

"Jacinta was not there the next morning. At 10:30 p.m. that evening the nurse had left her for a few moments and returned just in time to see her breathe her last, a rosy flush on her cheeks, a half smile on her lips.

"It was night in the dingy hospital, but it was forever dawn in the soul of Jacinta, as the Mother of God bent over bed 60 and gathered her into the arms that had enfolded the Christ in infancy and in death.

"In 1935, when Jacinta's remains were removed from a cemetery in Ourem to be reunited with her brother's in the cemetery in Fatima, her coffin was opened and her face was intact and incorrupt and the good odor of paradise hung about her. In 1946, Dom Jose Silva, the Bishop of Leiria, ordered evidence taken in the cause for the beatification of Jacinta and Francisco.

"In 1930, he had officially recognized and accepted the devotion to Our Lady Of The Rosary at Fatima, declaring the visions of the three children worthy of faith. In 1942, Pope Pius XII consecrated the entire world to the Immaculate Heart of Mary."

In 1967, the 50th anniversary of The Lady's appearances, Pope Paul went to Fatima to lead three million persons in homage to The Mother Of God.

'Hail Mary, full of grace, The Lord is with Thee. Pray For us sinners now and at the hour of our death, Amen.'

XXXIII—May, 1973 Rudolph M. Unger

Chapter 34

The message conveyed by Our Lady at Fatima—of the need for prayer and sacrifice for the reparation of sins and for the conversion of sinners—is central to the one true faith and has been preached by the church since her inception.

It lies at the heart of Our Lord's passion, the reason for His taking on our nature. Suffering is the price of salvation and He offered us the model to follow. The church has taught this message down through the ages. And sometimes Our Lord decides to use extraordinary means to re-emphasize the importance of this message, to reaffirm in the minds and hearts of men the church's teachings.

Fatima was one such example, one in which He chose to operate through His Mother. In another, exactly 300 years ago, He chose to convey the urgency of His message Himself.

Three months after little Jacinta Martro breathed her last for her Lord, Feb. 20, 1920, the church, on May 20, 1920, canonized the saint to whom Our Lord revealed His Sacred Heart, in all it's flaming love for man and in all its thornful hurt at man's rejection of this infinite love – St. Margaret Mary Alacoque.

It was two days after Christmas in 1673 that Our Lord first disclosed His Sacred Heart to the Visitation nun in Paray-le-Monial, France and asked her to spread the devotion of love and reparation to His Heart.

In her autobiography, Margaret Mary recalled that revelation:

"As I was before the Blessed Sacrament, God's presence enveloped me completely. For a long time He kept me leaning on His breast, while He revealed the wonders of His love and the mysterious secrets of His Sacred Heart.

"Until then He had always kept them hidden. But now, for the first time, He opened His Heart to me, saying – 'My Divine Heart is so passionately fond of the human race, and of you in particular, that it cannot keep back the pent-up flames of its burning charity any longer.

'They must burst out through you and reveal My Heart to the world, so as to enrich mankind with my precious treasures. I am letting you see them now and they include all the graces of sanctification and salvation needed to snatch men from the very brink of hell.'

"On the first Friday of each month there was a repetition of the favour. I would see His Sacred Heart like a dazzling sun, its burning rays shining right into my heart—setting it ablaze so fiercely, I'd keep thinking I was going to be reduced to ashes.

"Once as I was before the exposed Blessed Sacrament, Christ appeared to me—a blaze of glory—His five wounds shining like five suns, flames issuing from His form, especially His Breast, which was like a furnace and which He opened to disclose His utterly affectionate and lovable heart, the living source of all those flames.

"It was at this moment that He revealed to me the indescribable wonders of His pure love for mankind and the extravagance to which He had been led for those who had nothing for Him but ingratitude and indifference.

'This hurts me more than everything I suffered in my passion, 'He told me. 'Even a little love from them in return…but no. All my eager efforts for their welfare meet with nothing but coldness and dislike.

'Do me the kindness, then—you at least—of making up for all their ingratitude, as far as you can.'

"When I pointed out my incapacity, he replied, 'Here you are! This will make good your deficiencies, every one of them! His divine heart opening as He spoke. Such a scorching flame shot forth as I was sure would devour me. It went right through me and when I could bear it no longer, I begged Him to take pity on my weakness.

'I shall be your support,' He told me. 'Don't be afraid. You are to receive me in the Holy Eucharist as often as obedience allows. Accept any mortification or humiliation that may result, as a token of my love.

'You also are to receive communion on the first Friday of each month. Then every Thursday night I shall give you a share in that fatal sadness which I allowed myself to feel in the Garden Of Olives.

'Death couldn't be so hard as the agonized state to which this sadness will reduce you. You are to get up between 11 p.m. and midnight to keep Me company in humble prayer to My Father, exactly as I spent that night of my agony…to soothe in some way the heartache I felt when my apostles deserted Me, when I had to reproach them for being unable to watch even one hour with Me.'

"In June, 1675, as I was kneeling one day before the Blessed Sacrament, I was deluged with God's loving favours. He disclosed His Divine Heart as He spoke:

'There it is, that Heart so deeply in love with men. It spared no means of proof—wearing Itself out until it was utterly spent. This meets with scant appreciation from most of them. All I get back is ingratitude—witness their irreverence, their sacrileges, their coldness and contempt for Me in this sacrament of love.

'What hurts most is that hearts dedicated to My service behave in this way. That is why I am asking you to have the Friday after the octave of Corpus Christi set apart as a special feast in honour of My Heart—a day on which to receive Me in Holy Communion and make a solemn act of reparation for the indignities I have received in the Blessed Sacrament while exposed on the altars of the world.

'I promise you, too, that I shall open My Heart to all who honour Me in this way and who get others to do the same. They will feel in all its fullness the power of my love.'"

Years later, in letters written to her religious superiors, Margaret Mary wrote:

"Our Lord has brought home to me afresh the delight He takes in being honoured by His creatures, and His promises include—no one who has a deep devotion to the Sacred Heart will ever lose his soul. Blessings will be lavished on those places where an image of the Sacred Heart is displayed to win Him love and honour. In this way, He will mend broken homes, help and safeguard families in time of need.

"Communities, where this image is honoured, will be permeated with the soothing influence of His love and He will dispel the threat of God's just anger by restoring them to His favor, if sin caused them to fall from His grace. For the first person who will do Him the kindness of having this image made, He has a special promise—to make them holy and save his soul.

"Our Lord has again corroborated my impression of the untold pleasure He takes in being known, loved and honoured by His creatures. He has promised that all those who have a true devotion to Him and consecrate themselves to His Sacred Heart will never lose their souls.

"Families divided by discord, who will honour His Divine Heart as He asks, He will bring together again. He will also be the shelter and help of any family faced with trouble and which calls on Him with confidence.

"He has given me to understand that His Sacred Heart is the holy of holies, the sanctuary of love. He wants the world to recognize Him now as the mediator between God and man, unlimited in power, He can give the world peace—averting the punishment which our sins bring on us, and winning mercy.

"One Friday, during holy communion, Our Lord told me:

'I promise you out of the prodigal pity of My Heart, that My all powerful love will grant to those who receive holy communion on nine consecutive first Fridays of the month, the grace of final perseverance, so that they shall not die in disfavour without the sacrament. My Divine Heart will be their sure refuge.'

"The Sacred Heart is a treasure house of graces and blessings past all counting. I know of no other devotion in the whole range of spiritual life which affords the same guarantee of lifting souls in a very short time to the peak of perfection, allowing them to relish the sweetness of serving Jesus.

"My Divine Master has told me that those who labor for the salvation of souls will acquire the art of touching the hardest of hearts, if they have a tender devotion to the Sacred Heart and use their influence to establish it.

"People will find in the Sacred Heart a home and shelter all their life long—but, above all, at the hour of death."

XXXIV—June, 1973 Rudolph M. Unger

Chapter 35

Life is a mystery. Always was. Always will be. The mystery of God's love. And central to that mystery is the Passion of Our Lord. The great paradox that the route to joy and peace lies through suffering and sorrow. And as Chesterton explained, the paradox is the orthodox in this mystery of life.

The ever haunting, beckoning, frightening, never fully understandable mystery that lies at the heart and end of being. It's the story of the cross and the crown that is perpetually renewed in the holy sacrifice of the mass.

It is Christmas, Holy Thursday, Good Friday and Easter all wrapped up in one inseparable, integral mystery.

It says that the greatest gift the gentle God can bestow on those who walk in His wake is the full bittersweet cup of suffering. Those who have come closest in life to fathoming the depths of this mystery are the saints. And certainly one such was the magnificent St. Margaret Mary Alacoque.

She, whose confessors said, had never committed a mortal sin, felt so keenly the stain, injustice and ingratitude of sin, that she took on the burden of mortification and suffering to such a degree that it all but shatters our comprehension.

But then, really, is it all that incomprehensible? After all, what in life hurts, but that which involves failures in justice and love. The closer we are to someone, the greater the vulnerability of wound if we or they are hurt, or worst of all, if we hurt one another.

The writing of her autobiography at the command of her confessor was bitter penance for the saint.

"I take up my pen out of obedience," she wrote at the outset. "It is only because I love you, my God. For pity sake, good Jesus, never let anyone else see these pages. I don't want this manuscript to become an obstacle to my permanent burial from human memory and esteem."

She wrote: "Our Lord explained that His aim was the undisputed mastery of my heart and that my earthly life would be one of suffering like His. I came to learn, O Lord, what it cost Your Sacred Heart to bring me to birth on Calvary. That the only source of nourishment for this life of the spirit is the cross and that suffering was to be my favorite food.

"Our Lord told me, 'I am the eternal truth, with whom there is no deception. I am faithful to My promises and the graces I have given you can stand any kind of test and trial.'

"I was being drawn to mental prayer. The urge was so strong, it hurt. He taught me to humble myself in His Presence, ask pardon for my sins, and after an act of adoration offer Him my prayer, although I had no clear idea of where to go from there.

"He let me see Him, after that, under whatever aspect He wanted me to think of Him. My mind would be riveted to Him, all the powers of my soul absorbed in Him. All I felt was an overwhelming desire to love Him and this gave me a longing for Holy Communion and suffering, which I could never satisfy.

"He gave me a deeper appreciation of the beauty of virtue. My usual reading was a book of the saints' lives. I used to ask Him to make me a saint. To love and to obey—that was all I wanted, but I had no idea how to achieve it.

"His answer was to make me very fond of the poor. I would teach them their catechism and their prayers. I tested myself by being submissive to those I liked least, obeying them. I simply couldn't bear the sight of wounds. To cure myself of this, I started to kiss the wounds of the poor and then to dress them. Even the most alarming wounds healed in a surprisingly short time. God's Providence my only ointment.

"Frequent communion! That was the height of happiness for me. If only they'd have let me spent whole nights alone with the Blessed Sacrament. The sublimity of it plunged me into silent awe.

"I was dreadfully afraid of failing to please Our Lord. 'Aren't you satisfied with me?' came His reply. 'What are you afraid of? Your Father In Heaven is all powerful. No child in His arms can ever be lost—especially one I love as much as you.

"From babyhood upwards I have been patiently fashioning you, quietly waiting for you to come round. Just remember, you owe it all to me. I am the one to thank. If you forget, all your good will dry up.'

"As my royal master was doing the praying for me, the only thing I could do was obey.

Presently I'd be singing, 'Let sorrow come. Tis not to part, but bend me closer to His heart.' Then he would warn me, 'Remember, separated from me, you have no power to do anything. I will never leave you helpless as long as you always keep your nothingness and weakness buried in My strength.

'Always keep yourself ready, waiting for Me. I am going to make My home in your heart. Where we can talk and enjoy each other's company.' I began to see Him, feel Him near me, hear His voice, spiritual impressions which were much more vivid than physical ones.

"I had no hand in these. The effect of it all was self-abasement, of being flung into the depths of nothingness, annihilated, and so it has always remained. God's infinite goodness demands such respect and reverence that I've always felt I must kneel. Our Lord left me no peace in any less respectful posture.

"He began to favor me with visits under various disguises, sometimes a dear friend, sometimes the fondest of bridegrooms, sometimes a father wrapped up in his only child. He showed me His twofold holiness—the holiness of love and the holiness of justice.

"I was then given the chance to relieve the sufferings of those Holy Souls in purgatory whom God would allow to turn to me for help. I was made to suffer for them by feeling the severity of God's justice.

"He gave me an insight into the mystery of His passion and death. It is too deep to write about. I'll only say it gave me such a love for the cross, I couldn't live for a moment without suffering. But I had to suffer in silence, without consolation, comfort or pity.

"My life became one long round of physical suffering. I was also suffering spiritually. I could see God being offended. I was persecuted, thwarted and humiliated by those around me. I was tempted by the devil, who never left me alone. And there was myself, the worst adversary I've ever had and the most difficult to get the better of.

"My royal master told me He wanted my life to be one long sacrifice. The only sweetness I would know in this world would be found in the bitterness of Calvary. All the things that normally would make for joy in this world, for me, would turn out to be—ordeals akin to martyrdom.

"He warned me that whenever He felt like washing His hands of any souls He wanted me to suffer for, He'd treat me like a damned soul, letting me experience the loneliness that comes over it at the hour of death. I've never met with anything so terrible. There are no words to describe it. I volunteered to suffer whatever God's justice demanded as long as He wouldn't forsake the soul.

'Strike my God, cut, burn, spare neither body, life, flesh, nor blood of mine, but save that soul!' I would cry.

"One day after communion, Our Lord appeared to me carrying His cross. He was a mass of wounds and bruises, His precious blood flowing freely. 'Will no one take pity on me?' He asked, His voice saddened with pain. 'Will no one have the sympathy to share my sufferings in the pitiful state to which sinners have reduced me?'

"Tearfully, sorrowfully, I threw myself at His sacred feet as a volunteer, my shoulders bent to the heavy load of that nail studded cross. The sensation of its crushing weight made me aware of the gravity and malice of sin. Horrible sin, what a loathsome way to treat so good a God!

"Whenever He intended to bestow a new cross on me, He used to prepare me for it by untold endearments and such tremendous spiritual delights, I couldn't have endured them permanently.

"Once I saw the Heart of Jesus, so lovable, so worthy of adoration, outshining the sun. It appeared to be the center of flames of love. And all around were seraphim singing in wondrous harmony—'Love's triumphant, love delights, love His Sacred Heart excites.'

"They invited me to join them, these blessed spirits. In their praises of that Divine Heart, to join them in paying an unending homage of love, adoration and praise."

XXXV—July, 1973 Rudolph M. Unger

Chapter 36

Now we all know that this is the age of liberation.

Men, of course, have long been liberated. Giving what they want from the paycheck to the spouse to run the house, feed and clothe the kids, whether it be sufficient or not.

Out drinking with the boys when he wants and carousing with some babe when he is of the mind to. And if the old lady doesn't like the way he does things, why maybe an occasional lick to the chops to remind her who the master of the house is.

The liberation of youth in our times is, of course, already legendary. No parents, teachers, or clergymen, no one that isn't a peer, is going to tell them they can't have pre-martial sex, or that marital is important at all. No one is going to tell them they can't smoke pot, pop some downers or some uppers, or shoot some of the hard stuff.

Grooming, manners, cleanliness, respect, industry at school, in the home and at a job…those are all outmoded hang-ups of an uneducated, hypocritical older generation. So long as the old man or old lady or some other working sucker coughs up enough bread to sustain youth's emancipated life style, that's all that counts.

And, of course, how could anyone be unaware of the liberation of woman—cigarettes, pants, careers, bleached hair, artificial faces, ersatz bodies, bar stool drinking, vulgarity, immodesty, incontinency, sloth.

Couples, married or single, "adult" men and women, "free, white and 21", this is the swinging generation: fornication, adultery, perversion, dishonesty, cheating, theft, misrepresentation; say man, this is the "now" generation—contraception, sterilization, abortion, artificial insemination, euthanasia.

Masculinized women, feminized men, adulterated youth, emasculated elders. This is the day of the existentialist—"Don't tell me there are rules or regulations, right or wrong, good or evil. Nothing exists, nothing is for me until I try it and decide for myself – I'm liberated modern man…doing my own thing. And that's all that counts—me, mine, I! You dig?"

And what, who are we really running from? Ourselves, our loved ones, our needy brothers. Yes. But these are all only partial expressions of this central flight of ourselves—from God.

He's the one who created our nature, wrote the principles, rules, commands of our lives and the world we live in. He's the one we are really running from, no matter how we try to confuse others and deceive ourselves in our rush from reality into our illusionary, never-never land of self deception, self enslavement, and self destruction.

This is what the attack on the individual's dignity in the name of dignity, the person's freedom in the name of freedom, society's security in the name of security, man's harmony in the name of harmony, is all about.

Man, woman, child, family, society, school, state, church, and always finally and logically, God, are the targets of those who would destroy man in the name of man, society in the name of society, and the God-man in the name of man making himself God.

In coming months in Counter-Reformation we will seek to apply some Christian antidote to this disease which is poisoning the human soul, the society of man, the harmony of man and nature, the relation of creature and creator. The disease of slavish pride which denies the liberty of love in God, murders it in others, and then immolates it in self.

We will draw upon the wisdom of one of the finest discussions of love, marriage, family, and society—for time and eternity—ever written – "Three To Get Married" by Fulton J. Sheen.

"Love is trinity. It takes three to make love – the lover, the beloved, and love," writes Sheen in presenting the central idea of his book.

This he says is so, on every level of love. Be it the general love that exists between any two persons, whatever the nature of the relationship be. Be it in the most intimate relationship on a human level, between a man and a woman in the married state. Be it on the level of the divine itself, in the Holy Trinity.

"The basic error of mankind has been to assume that only two are needed for love – you and me, or society and me, or humanity and me," writes Sheen.

"Really it takes three—self, other selves, and God; you and me and God. Love is triune or it dies.

"Love for other hearts is intended to lead to the love of the Divine Heart. For all love is—an inclination to seek good, the impetus to perfection, a flight towards immortality.

"There are two basic loves which everyone has without exception – love of self and love of others. The first is the basis of self preservation. The second is the root of friendship and community.

"Love is useless when alone, incomplete, sterile. It craves involvement with others because love is essentially a relation. Love is really possessed only by giving it to others, love of self becomes the love of others.

"But human beings are only lovable. They are not love. Only God is love. Love of self and love of neighbor both require love of God. True love passes from an affection for outer appearances to those inner depths of personality which embody the divine spirit.

"Eros (carnal love) is intended to be a stepping stone, the gateway to agape (love of person) which itself is the embryo of the love of the divine.

"In marriages that are truly Christian the love of God increases through the years. Not in the sense that husband and wife love one another less, but that they love God more.

"This transformation from Eros primacy to agape primacy takes place in sacrifice. No love ever mounts to a higher level without a touch of the cross.

"What happens when the divine order is not worked out and the erotic love doesn't develop into an embryo for the divine? This question puts the finger on the failure of most modern marriages.

"When marriages are devoid of religion, which alone can suggest that the love of the flesh is the preface to the love of the spirit, then the other partner is often made the object of worship in place of God.

"The partners then try to live a moment in which Satan's promise would be realized – 'You will be like Gods.' Each partner eventually begins to feel the torturous contradiction between the infinite longing for divine love he spurned and its poor finite realization in the human form.

"The furies are unleashed—the sense of betrayal, deception, disappointment—when the other partner is discovered not to be a God.

"Only God can give what the heart wants. In Christian love, the husband and wife see God coming through their love. Eliminate the divine third from human love and there is left only the substitution of the cruel ersatz for infinity. The need of God never disappears. Those who deny the existence of water are still thirsty. Those who deny God still want him in their craving for goodness, truth, beauty, love, and peace, which He alone is.

"Love that is only a search, a quest, is incomplete. All incompleteness ends in frustration. The search was for the garden but ended in eating the apple. The quest was for the melody but the discovery was only a note.

"At this point Christianity suggests—'Do not think that life is a snare or an illusion. It would be only if there were no infinite to satisfy your yearnings.'

It says husband and wife should determine—'We both want a love that will never die and that love lies beyond both of us. Let us therefore use our marital love for one another to bring us to that perfect love which is God.'

"God never intended that the 'I' and 'thou' should be separated. God is no obstacle to the full enjoyment of self, nor is he a competitor to the love of the other. But when love becomes triune, God is installed in the center of the 'I' and 'thou', saving 'I' from egotism and 'thou' from slavery.

"Such love is God in pilgrimage. Such marriage is then a spark from the great flame of eternity. Such love becomes a river running to the sea.

"For since God is boundless, eternal love, it will take an ecstatic eternal chase to sound its depths. There will be one same eternal moment containing a limitless receptivity and boundless gift –a possession of the greatest revelation ever given to the world – God is Love!"

XXXVI—August, 1973 Rudolph M. Unger

Chapter 37

"Freudianism interprets man in terms of sex. Christianity interprets sex in terms of man," wrote Fulton J. Sheen in his "Three To Get Married."

"There is a world of difference between sex loving sex and a person loving a person. In sex the male adores the female. In love the man and woman together adore God.

"There are two extremes to be avoided in discussing married love. One error—Victorian—is the refusal to recognize sexual love. The other—Freudian—is giving primacy to sexual attraction.

"To the Christian, sex is inseparable from the person. Certain Victorians practically denied sex as a function of personality. Certain sexophiles of modern times deny personality and make a God of sex.

"The male animal is attracted to the female animal. But a human personality is attracted to another human personality. The attraction of beast to beast is physiological. The attraction of human to human is physiological, psychological, and spiritual.

"The human spirit has a thirst for the infinite. If sex does not mount to heaven, it descends into hell. There is no such thing as giving the body without giving the soul. The two are inseparable.

"Sex in isolation from personality does not exist. Man has no organic functions isolated from his soul. There is involvement of the whole personality.

"Nothing is more psychosomatic than the union of two in one flesh. Nothing so much alters a mind, a will, for better or worse. Those who seek to separate sex and spirit are rehearsing for death. For the separation of soul and body is death.

"Sex is one of the means God has instituted for the enrichment of personality. The enjoyment of the other's personality through one's own personality is what love is.

"Love is primarily in the will, not in the emotions or glands. Love is soul contact. Person needs person. And a person is a person only when seen in an image of God.

"In sex can be seen mirrored that wider world of love. But when sex is divorced from love there is a feeling that one has been stopped at the vestibule of the castle, that the heart has been denied the city after crossing the bridge.

"Happiness consists in interiority of the spirit, the development of personality to a higher destiny. Frustration of such destiny results in sadness and melancholy. There is a closer correlation between the animal view of sex and mental instability than many suspect.

"There is no doubt whatever that sex is an important energy in human life. But, is it the basic energy as so many psychologists contend? Or is it, better, only one of the branches on the tree of life? Instead of being the reservoir of vita, of life, is it not but one of the channels thru which that vita, that life, flows, is communicated?

"Most psychologists are narrow in that they choose one of the channels of life in exclusion to the others. Freud takes sex and forgets the others. Adler takes pride and ignores the others. Jung takes security, to the ignorance of the others.

"Psychology will never give a total understanding of man until it incorporates all three of these channels and relates them to something more basic in man—the vita, that fundamental soul-body unity in man.

"These three distillations of the vita are in themselves good because given by divine goodness. And all three emanations go together. One relates to the person himself (pride), another to other persons (sex), and the third to material things (security).

"Through original sin, vita, the fundamental soul-body unity in man, lost its balance. It did not become intrinsically corrupt. But a derangement occurred affecting the three channels or outlets of vita.

"There sprang up in the vita what is called libido, or concupiscence, a tending toward certain things in defiance of rational restraint. Abnormality was introduced in the three channels.

"Legimate pride or self love now could become egotism, selfishness; sex could become lust, and the quest for security could become avarice, greed.

"Sacred scripture tells us that before the fall, Adam and Eve were 'naked but not ashamed.' they were naked and not ashamed because the

passions were completely subject to reason and there was not yet in the human body a tendency on the part of the passions to rebel against reason.

"It was only after our first parents rebelled against God that they disturbed the equilibrium of their human nature. The disruption of the union of God and man had an echo in the disturbance of the union of soul and body.

"The two words most often abused today are 'freedom' and 'sex.' Freedom is often used to mean absence of law. Sex is used to justify absence from restraint. Sometimes the two words are fused into the one—license.

"There is no quarreling with those who say, 'be yourself.' the point is, which is your true self? To be a beast? Or to be a child of God? A person may be self-expressive either by obeying the laws of his nature, or, by rebelling against them, which rebellion ends in frustration and slavery.

"It is true that God gave us a nature equipped with certain impulses. It is also true that he expects us to obey nature. But our nature is not primarily animal, but rational. Since it is rational, our impulses ought to be used rationally. That is, for the highest purposes, not for the lowest.

"The Lord Of The Universe, in the first of the beatitudes, said, 'Blessed are the clean of heart for they shall see God.' The pure of heart shall see God because they do His will. Purity does not begin in the body, but in the will. From there it flows outward, cleansing thought, imagination, and finally body. Bodily purity is an echo of the will's purity. Life is impure only when the will is impure.

"Purity is a vision, the seeing of the soul in the body, a holy purpose in the flesh. Purity is the reverence paid to the sanctity of personality. Purity is the guardian of love.

"Sex is a function of the whole personality. It is the self, the human personality, that has sexual desires, and not the body's organs.

"Precisely because it is essentially bound up with the body-soul unity of a human, sex affects him mentally, morally, and socially.

"Our Divine Lord warned that personality must keep itself integrated by refusing to allow carnal explosions to disturb its right reason.

"If there had been no disharmony in man because of the original rebellion against God, there would be no need of taming the body. It now revolts against the spirit because the spirit revolted against God.

"The Christian idea of the body is based on the sanctity of the soul which vivifies it. The body is holy because the soul is holy. The more the soul is united with God, the more sacred the body becomes. The church knows not the body alone nor the soul alone, but the person.

"There is a law running through human nature, that he who does not spiritualize the flesh, will carnalize the spirit. Sex and spirituality do not walk hand in hand. Rather one leads the other. As one must learn to see eternity in time, one must learn to see the spirit in the body.

"The alternative presented to every bride and groom is whether to eroticize marriage or eternalize it; whether to base it on sex or on spirit. This does not mean choosing between one or the other, but rather choosing which shall receive the primacy, which shall lead the other.

"Marriage by its very nature tends toward unity. God intends the physical impregnation to be closely associated with the spiritual impregnation.

"He intends the unity in flesh to be enduring, symbolizing and intensifying the union of the souls. Unity in body, in spirit, in ideals, in love.

"God intends there should be a growing together. What started as a passion of love becomes an act of love and then a habit of love. The body of each moves the soul of each. Then the soul of each moves the body of each.

"And at the height of their mutual togetherness, God moves the body and soul of each to Himself."

XXXVII—September, 1973 Rudolph M. Unger

Chapter 38

"Our entire outlook on life, conception, and birth, changes once these are seen not as an evolution from slime, but as a gift from the divine."

So wrote Fulton J. Sheen in his "Three To Get Married."

"Human generation," he noted, "is not a push upwards from the beast but rather a gift downwards from The Trinity. The begetting of children is not an imitation of the beasts of the field, but a feeble reflection of the eternal generation of the second person in the bosom of the father.

"God made the universe fecund. The understanding of this mystery will throw a new light on the family. It is the very nature of life to be enthusiastic, for all life tends to diffuse and communicate itself and even to overflow its perfections in order that others may share its joy of living.

"The fountainhead of all generation, the source of all artistic creation, the prototype of the birth of children, the archetype of every mind that generates a thought, if carried back to its ultimate source, is the goodness of God, who diffuses Himself internally by the eternal generation of the son, and externally in creation.

"Behind the urge to procreate is the hidden desire of every human to participate in the eternal. Human generation is related in a special way to eternity. Sex love is not meant for death. Love is for life.

"The creative act of God is necessary to the human act of generation. Nothing is more religious in nature than procreation. It is the sign of both unity and continuity.

"The disjointed, separated, and egotistical have no use for the child. Only those who have immortality in their hearts really yearn to prolong that immortality through the child.

"An impoverished heart has nothing to contribute to another but its emptiness and, therefore, nothing to transmit to posterity. The will not to prolong life is a confession that one lacks life. When the spirit has become sterile, then even human life seems worthless. And if one cannot bear the ennui and boredom of his own life, there is no urge to give to others.

"The denial of the offspring is a sign of the deadening of the spirit.

"But the begetting of new life is a sign that the heart is so full of happiness and love that it will die unless it overflows. For body and soul, generation is the condition of wholeness, sanity, and order.

"As humans lose the consciousness of the Divine Image within them and as the body becomes the sole existent, the instinct for renewal is lost. The consciousness of the soul and the desire for procreation go hand in hand, as do materialism and sterility.

"The more a marriage union is based on the divine, the more the husband and wife are in harmony with God, the more they find in each other that eternal fascination and satisfaction which transcends earthly frailties and disappointments.

"Lovers always speak of the immortality of their love, and cynics scoff at them, but the lovers are right. Their love can become immortal. It is sufficient to steep it in God and it becomes impervious to time and space. God is unending life and eternal love and the lovers united to Him are caught up in His ceaseless joyous current.

"The initiative which is given earthly fathers to beget new fountains of life is a participation in divine fatherhood. And the good father will so educate his children that they will go back again to God from whom they came.

"There are no great physiological changes in the father at birth as in the mother, but he undergoes profound psychological changes. The consciousness of fatherhood does something to one's mental vision of the world.

"Love does not mean merely the joy to possess. It means also the will to see a new life born out of that love. The realization that he has passed on the torch of life and can see it flowering before his eyes in 'his own image and likeness' is the basic reason why a man when he has become a father is no longer just a man.

"It is time's best moment when a man feels within himself the shimmering refraction of the eternal joy of an eternal father begetting an eternal son, saying, "Thou are my son. I have begotten Thee this day.'

"Not only is it a bond with a child, but it is also a bond with the mother. The newborn child not only unveiled fatherhood in the husband, but also motherhood in the wife. From that moment on, she appears before him in a relationship which never before existed. He will never again be the same in the face of that double mystery of fatherhood and motherhood.

"Planned un-parenthood is the deliberate and willful decision on the part of a husband and wife to exclude from God the opportunity to create another to His image and likeness. It is human will freely frustrating divine will.

"The non-serviam of Lucifer has had its catastrophic effect throughout creation and particularly in those who say, 'I refuse to accept from God that which is His Holy Will, the increase and multiplication of life.' The refusal to be a cooperator with God is to spoil and maim oneself.

"Medical opinion today is that the increasing psychoses and neuroses in women are due to a flight from motherhood. Five out of every six cases of divorce stem from marriages having no children.

"As the bearer of seed, a woman throws herself completely on God, saying with Mary, 'Behold The Handmaid Of The Lord.' The submission is sacrificial.

"A woman is capable of more sustained sacrifice than man. Man is more apt to be the hero in one great, passionate outburst of courage. But a woman is heroic through the years, months, and even seconds of daily life. Not only her days but her nights, not only her mind, but her body, must share in the Calvary of mothering.

"She, therefore, has a greater understanding of redemption than man, for she comes closer to death in bringing forth life. If mothers but realize it, they are prolonging the passion of Christ through the centuries, and, at each birth in the flesh, telling mankind that only through labor and self-effacement does one become a child of grace.

"The father and mother leave a memorial of their love in their children. As witnesses through history, they will testify to the parents who once walked the Earth. As the poet wrote, 'You are the bows from which your children as living arrows are sent forth.'

"Children have a messianic character in the family. They represent the conquest of love over the insatiable ego. They symbolize defeat of selfishness and the victory of charity. Each child begets disinterestedness, inspires a sacrifice. Love's greatest luxury is to spend itself on others.

"A wise father once said to his son about to be married: 'Try to make it last for only ten years. After those ten years, your heart will be full of memories and your house full of children and you will never want it to end.'

"Children beget humility. Before an infant, the big feel little and the proud so insignificant. There is something about a baby that disarms, attracts, and makes even the evil want to appear as good.

"Before an infant, the wise men discovered wisdom and the shepherds discovered their shepherd. Every child in taking us back to the source of life, takes us back to God who is the fount of life.

"The intelligentsia, who are educated beyond their intelligence, stay away from children for the same reason that they stay away from God. They cannot bear the vision of the source of life.

'But the humble like to get as close to it as possible and from this flows the family. There is something awesome about a child, for it is the unveiling of love. In each child, God whispers a new secret to the world, adds a new dimension of immortality to creation.

"In that new life, that as yet wordless word, the parents see not the increase of their image but the very image and likeness of God.

"Only two classes of people found in The Word Made Flesh that littleness who is greatness, the shepherds and the wise-men. Those who knew they did not know anything and those who knew they did not know everything.

"For those who conspire against life, there will one day come the haunting conscience described by John Davidson:

'Some night, when darkness, silence and the sleeping world give vision scope, you will lie awake and see the pale sad faces of the little ones who should have been your children, as they press their cheeks against your windows, looking in with piteous wonder...Homeless, famished babes.'"

XXXVIII—October, 1973 Rudolph M. Unger

Chapter 39

"If love be what the heart wants above all else, why does it not grow in love?"

This agonizing question is asked by Fulton J. Sheen in his "Three To Get Married." His reply:

"It is because most hearts want the impossible. They want a love that, like cupid, does not grow, rather than a love which dies in order to ascend. They refuse to surrender the horizontal for the vertical, because it demands sacrifice. And thus they condemn their hearts to mediocrity and staleness.

"Love is no bargain. The cross is a far better picture of what love really is than cupid.

"The cross is something one sees on the roadway of life a long time ahead and the invitation to carry it to a resurrection of love is frightening indeed. That is why the Sacred Heart has so few lovers. They want the cross streamlined, without Him, who said:

'If any man will come after Me, let him deny himself and take up his cross daily and follow Me.'

"The ascension of love in marriage proceeds through three stages, each of which has its transfiguration—sex love, personal love, and Christian love.

"Nowhere else but in Christian love is the tortuous contradiction between infinite desire and finite being resolved, for here all human limitations become the channels to the spiritual and eternal.

"This elevation of love from one stage to another is inseparable from the crushing of selfishness, which is the enemy of love.

"As the burdens of married life appear the marriage may fail, unless there is an ascension through deeper faith. If the other partner, despite all his failings, is seen as a trust and a responsibility before God, then God is brought more into the marriage to heal its wounds.

"What God has begun to work in the partners He will perfect in the end. It is He who is the bond of their unity. It is He who sanctifies them in their love for one another. It is His love which sustains them. This vision becomes clearer as life goes on.

"The greatest joys of life are purchased at the cost of some sacrifice. One cannot enjoy love without a certain amount of self-denial. Whenever love is imperfect, there must be suffering, for such is the cost of love's purification.

"All love craves a cross by the very fact that love is forgetful of self for others. But even in the midst of sacrifice, it can say – 'Suffering is in me, but I am not in it.' The joy which is seen forthcoming as the result of the trial makes one in some way independent of it.

"No one ever climbs to the heavens without passing through the clouds. As the violin needs tuning, as the block of marble needs cutting before it can make a statute, so the love of husband and wife needs purification before it can rise to new heights.

"The trials which come into married life are merely so many contacts with reality which God sends into every life. If these moments are thorns, they are as the thorns given to the flesh of Paul the apostle; they are the means to grow in love, for it is the purification of love which saves love.

"Dryness in marriage is like that dryness in the spiritual life known as the dark night of the soul. They are really actual graces. God's finger is stirring the waters, creating discontent, so that new efforts may be put forth toward purification, toward perfection. Aridity in love is not the defeat of love, but rather its challenge.

"Love has its price. No one ever became a saint or made a marriage a joy without a renewed struggle against one's ego.

"Nothing is reborn to a higher life without a death in the lower. No one loves who cannot love through disenchantment, disillusion, and deception. The heart has its cycles but, impelled by love, its movement is an upward spiral and not in a thread-wheel circle.

"The husband who began by loving the other for his own sake, and then for her sake, now begins to love for God's sake. He who has touched the body, now discovers the soul of the other person. The partner ceases to be opaque and begins to be transparent, the glass through which God and His purposes are revealed. Good Friday passes through the resurrection of love into Easter.

"The crisis of nothingness which in marriage follows the dream come true needs its purification, its cross. The cross is not a roadblock on the way to happiness. It is a ladder up which one climbs to a heaven of love.

"Another name for the purification of love is transfiguration, which means the use of a loss, or a pain, or a mediocrity, of a disillusionment, as a stepping stone to a new anointing of joy.

"Transfiguration in marriage comes through an intensive retraining of the ego. The more one gives up the self, the more one possesses self. Transfiguration is based on the idea that love resides in the will, not in the emotions.

"Those who identify love and the will and admit the third, He who is love, find that age never affects love. The will really can grow stronger as the body becomes weaker. Therefore, one always has it within his power to lift himself to new heights through a willed and deliberate sacrifice of the ego.

"There can be no happiness in the home without the sacrifice which transfigures love. The world is full of people who give up instead of going forward in marriage. Instead of being loyal and faithful, they break their trust.

"No wound caused by quarrels can fester when the ego is willing to humble itself and give the delicate attention to the partner which sacrificial love engenders. It is sacrifice alone which can make possible this necessary spiritual adjustment which leads to happiness.

"In selfish love, the burdens of others are regarded as impeding one's own happiness. In Christian love, burdens become opportunities to serve.

"Suppose 'for better or for worse' turns out for the worse? Selfish love then seeks to get rid of the other person because he or she is a burden. Christian love takes on the burden.

"If it be objected that God never intended that anyone should live under such difficulties, the answer very flatly is that he does. 'If any man will come after Me, let him deny himself and take up his cross daily and follow Me.'

"No human being has a choice of whether he will go through life with or without suffering, because this to a great extent is beyond his control. But each one has this choice—will the suffering open on a cross and therefore see the joy beyond, or, will it be closed to the cross and therefore be the beginning of hell on earth?

"The great difference between a Christian and a pagan in suffering is that for the Christian the suffering is a trial permitted by God which affords a means for self-purification and sanctification. The pagan lacks this Christian perspective. He cannot see the place of suffering in the universe for it negates his egotism, it cancels his love of pleasure. Therefore, for him, the cross becomes unbearable.

"The Christian, seeing that the innocent God-man voluntarily bore a cross, sees that then somehow or other the cross must fit into his own life which is far from innocent.

"If, then, husband and wife reflect the love of Christ by continuing to love, even in disaster, sickness, or trial, it will be as redemptive as His love.

"The pagan, seeing the gold mixed with the dross, throws away the treasure because he has no knowledge of how to refine it. The Christian, however, can extract the divine gold from the dross of suffering. To the pagan it is but suffering. For the Christian it becomes joy. Life for him then becomes a conquest, a triumph.

"Our Lord never promised that His followers would be without a cross. Rather did He promise they would have one. He did guarantee, however, that by His grace we would never be overcome by it. 'My grace is sufficient for you.'

"This mystery of the cross before the crown, the egotist cannot understand. And for that reason did St. Paul call it 'the folly of the cross.' But those who have sounded its depths know that God gives the strength to carry it! 'You are distressed now. But one day I will see you again and then your hearts will be glad and your gladness no one will take from you.'"

XXXIX—November, 1973 Rudolph M Unger

Chapter 40

"There are only two words in the vocabulary of love—'you' and 'always,'" wrote Fulton J. Sheen in "Three To Get Married."

"'You', because love is unique. 'Always', because love is enduring.

"All love songs have the ring of eternity about them.

"Social culture demands a permanent bond between man and woman, for no civilization can endure without responsibility and loyalty to one's trust.

"When fifty percent of married couples feel that they can throw overboard pledged loyalty in order to suit their own pleasure or convenience, then the hour has struck when citizens will no longer feel a need to keep their pledges to America as citizens.

"Once a citizenry does not feel bound to the most natural and democratic of all self-governing commonwealths, the home, it will not be long until it ceases to feel bound to a nation.

"When Mrs. White is ready to call herself Mrs. Brown, then it will only be a short time before Americans will be calling themselves soviets. The traitors to the home today are the traitors to the nation tomorrow. A people who are not loyal to a home will not be loyal to a flag.

"The permanence of the bond is necessary also for sacrifice. So long as a nation of families learns to renounce the 'mine' in 'ours' there is strength. The family then becomes a training school in self-discipline. It crushes egotism for the sake of unity as all members learn the supreme lesson of living with others for the sake of others.

"If every emotion, whim, appetite, and fancy has a right to be satisfied even at the cost of another person, then what shall happen to the sacrifice so necessary for a nation in time of crisis and conflict?

"The fewer sacrifices a man is required to make, the more loath he will be to make those few. His luxuries soon become necessities, children a burden, and the ego a God.

"Whence will come our heroes in a crisis, if we no longer have heroes in the home? If a man will not put up with the trials of a household, will he put up with the trials of a national emergency?

"Once the need of sacrifice for maintenance of the home is uprooted, the need for sacrifice for the maintenance of a nation is likewise uprooted.

"Only a nation that recognizes sweat, toil, hardship, and sacrifice as normal aspects of life can save itself and these virtues are first learned in the home.

"The decline in the permanence of family life is, therefore, intrinsically bound up with the decline in democracy. Here democracy is understood as a system of government which recognizes the sovereign worth of a man.

"Nowhere is the dogma of the worth of a man better preserved and practiced than in the family. In the family a person is valued because he 'is'. Existence is 'worth' in the home.

"The family is the training school and novitiate for democracy. As persons lose a sense of loyalty and obligation to all in the family, particularly to the crippled, the sick, those of no economic value to the family, the state picks it up.

"State socialism, understood as state control not only of the means of production but also of life itself, is the political expression of psychological laziness and irresponsibility first manifested in the family.

"The most stable youths, from a moral point of youth, come from those families where the creative instinct is inseparable from an unbroken and perpetuating love; where sex relationships are inseparably bound up with the moral and spiritual side of life; where instead of momentary self-indulgence, there is integration into a lifelong bond.

"It is highly significant that Jesus began His miracles at a marriage feast. The sanction for the perpetual bond of husband and wife to love one another until death do part them comes from God's own order.

'What God, then, has joined, let not man put asunder.' 'No more male and female, you are all one person in Christ.'

"The charity that one spouse has for the other will aid their complete spiritual development until Christ be formed in them. The avidity to possess the other in love is superseded by the interest in seeing the other grow in love of God.

"The partner cannot give the infinity which love demands, but he or she can point the way to it. Then the creature gives what it has not, as it points to love of Christ, who is now in their midst to unite the couple more than ever in soul as well as in body.

'You have only to live on in Me and I will live on in you. The branch that does not live on in the vine can yield no fruit of itself. No more can you, if you do not live on in Me. I am the vine, you are its branches. If you live on in Me and I in you, then you will yield abundant fruit. Separated from Me, you have no power to do anything.'

"Because divinely strengthened, marriage takes on a deeper significance. When husband and wife live their married life as a reflection of the divine prototype, their relation with one another becomes a source of merit. They save their soul through union with one another. Sacramental grace is communicated in the marriage act.

"As the church prays in the nuptial mass:

'May the God of Abraham, Isaac, and Jacob be with you, may He fulfill His blessing in you, and may you have life everlasting by His grace.'

"The great advantage of the vow, which binds until death, is that it guards the couple against allowing the moods of time to override reason. It may be hard to keep, but it is worth keeping because of what it does to exalt the characters of those who make it.

"It is too terrible to contemplate what would happen to the world if our pledged words were no longer bonds. International order vanishes as domestic society perishes through the breaking of vows.

"As Pope Pius XI wrote:

'The love of which we speak is not that based on the passing lust of the moment but in the deep attachment of hearts whereby a man and wife help each other, day by day, in forming and perfecting themselves in the interior life, so that through their partnership in life they may advance ever more in virtue and, above all, grow in true love toward God and their neighbors.'

"The passing of time wears out bodies, but nothing can make a soul vanish or can diminish its eternal value. Nothing on earth is stronger than the fidelity of a heart fortified by the sacrament.

"Fidelity is strength. It is unity in plurality. Such fidelity is not discovered. It is made. It is not automatic. It requires renewed efforts at mutual understanding in order that finally there may result an alliance of mind, soul, and destiny.

"Everyone believes in the eternity of love, and eternal love is found only in God. Earthly love remains abiding only to the extent that its sparks spring from the great hearth, the great heart of God. They who possess this 'fides' every now and then, are cast into the ecstasy of love wherein in the sweet anticipation of heaven, they whisper, "If the spark is so great, oh, what must be the flame!'

"History is filled with many noble examples of how faithful love, ground in God, can overcome seemingly insurmountable obstacles. Princess Maria Volkonskaya had married a distinguished officer and nobleman who was convicted of a political crime and condemned to work in the mines of Siberia.

"She went to see him on the eve of his departure for that dreaded land and he entreated her to forget him. After many difficulties she obtained from Czar Nicholas II permission to go to Siberia.

"Selling all her jewels to pay for the expenses, she set off on the hard journey over the objection of her father to such 'folly'. She told him, 'I cannot stay. If I remain here, I shall always hear the quiet reproachful voice of my husband, and in the faces of my friends I will read the truth concerning my behavior. In their whispers, I shall get a sentence, in their smiles my reproach.

'My place is not at a ball but in a distant and savage land where a woeful prisoner, a prey to gloomy thoughts, suffers alone without help. I must share his disgrace and banishment.' At long last, after a terrible journey, she arrived at the mines of Nertchinsk, went down into the depths of the earth, and in the gloom flung herself before the dazed, unbelieving man, and kissed his chains."

XXXX—December, 1973 Rudolph M. Unger

Chapter 41

In the months to come, in this newsletter and its sister epistle, we will consider the key issue of our times—faith and freedom or slavery, Christian liberty or communist tyranny.

It is not a pleasant subject. It is one that western man and his spiritual and secular leaders do not like to have to consider. They shy away from consideration, discussion, and action regarding this bitter, hard reality.

Rather they indulge themselves in talk about peace and coexistence, negotiation and cooperation, and hope that this meaningless repetition of illusionary catch-phrases, along with their silence about the hard bitter reality, will make that bitter reality go away.

It will not!

In the next issues of this newsletter we will consider a spiritual figure whose name has become a symbol, synonymous with the fight of Christian liberty against diabolical tyranny.

The lead of this hardheaded man of common sense—who knows that this is an Armageddonian struggle from which one of the mortal foes will not walk away alive; who knows that it is 'the truth that shall make you free' and not illusions—is not being followed.

He is Cardinal Joseph Mindszenty of Hungary, who like Cardinal Wyszynski of Poland, Cardinal Slipyj of Ukraine, and Cardinal Stepinac of Yugoslavia, has known first hand the reality of communism, who like they laid his life on the line against this evil.

As Bishop James McNulty of Buffalo has written:

"Cardinal Mindszenty had complete contempt for communist threats. He rejected communist doctrine. He refused even the least compromise with this evil.

"When friends pleaded with the cardinal to go to Rome for safety's sake, he replied, 'A pastor of souls must stay with his flock and cannot flee like a hired servant.

'I stand firmly for God, church, and country in my historic responsibility to the nation which has repeatedly stood alone against the enemies of western civilization.'"

From the evidence available, and it is rather meager for silence seems to be the rule, it is not Mindszenty's counsel which prevails today.

Rather the counsel that seems to prevail is that stated by Cardinal Koenig of Austria who was reported by the press as stating in a conference in Toronto in 1967 that:

"It would be better for the churches to seek ways to enable them to exist under communist governments rather than waste their time looking for occasions to combat them. Many Marxists, communists, and atheists are not indifferent to religious values."

In 1965, in Vienna, Koenig said, "The first aim must be for us and the atheists to recognize that we have to live together in one world. If they fight us, we cannot live together. We must find a basis of accommodation. The atheist must be told, '1 won't convert you, but you must be reasonable. You must recognize spiritual problems cannot be settled by force, only by talk.'"

The Vatican II council in all its vast pronouncements on the role of the church in the world today does not even so much as mention the word communism.

The silence of Christian spiritual leaders on the subject is deafening. The Jews have stood up and cried out in their usual bold, gallant manner for their brethren.

But the Catholic church, the universal church, listen, what do you hear? Do you hear anything? Aside from Pope Paul's meetings with communist leaders?

At the masses on Sunday, prayers are said for everyone and everything. But never is one raised to God for the victims of communism. Nor are any raised for the communists themselves.

The prayers once said in every Catholic church after every low mass for the conversion of Russia have been eliminated in the name of renewal.

Those prayers which pleaded to God "For the conversion of sinners and for the liberty and exaltation of Holy Mother Church." Those prayers which ask "St. Michael the Archangel, defend us in battle, be our protection against the malice and snares of the devil...Do thou, O Prince of the Heavenly Host, by the divine power, thrust into hell Satan and the other evil spirits who roam thru the world seeking the ruin of souls."

The Lutheran minister Richard Wurmbrand wrote:

"When I was released the communists told me I could preach about Christ but not against communism. In the free world many clergymen gave me the same advice. I am very sad. The church can never have peaceful coexistence with atheism. How can a man preach God is good and not preach communism is evil?"

Whitaker Chambers when he broke from the communist party told his wife: "You know, we are leaving the winning world for the losing world."

He added, "At the heart is this critical conflict of the two irreconcilable faiths of our time—communism and freedom. The history of our times can end only in the destruction of one or both of these two forces.

"A witness is a man whose life and faith are so completely one that when the challenge comes to step out and testify for his faith, he does so, disregarding all risks, accepting all consequences.

"Economics is not the central problem of this century, faith is the central problem of this age. The western world possesses the answer to this problem. But only provided that its faith in God, and the freedom he enjoins, is as great as communism's faith in man."

Edmund Burke wrote, "All evil needs to do to succeed is for good men to do nothing." William Yeats said, "The best lack all conviction while the worst are full of passionate intensity."

Patrick Henry declared, "Is life so dear, or peace so sweet as to be purchased at the price of chains and slavery? Forbid it, Almighty God! I know not what course others may take, but, as for me, give me liberty or give me death."

Christ said—"Be not overcome by evil, but overcome evil with good... You are either for Me or against Me. You either gather with me or scatter from me... Thou art neither cold nor hot. I would thou wert cold or hot. But because thou art lukewarm and neither cold nor hot, I will begin to vomit thee out of My mouth... He that shall deny Me before men, I will also deny him before My Father Who is in heaven...

"Do not think that I came to send peace upon the earth. I came not to send peace, but the sword... He that taketh not up his cross and follow Me is not worthy of Me...he that shall lose his life for Me shall find it...

"I am the Good Shepherd. The Good Shepherd giveth His life for His sheep. But the hireling and he that is not the shepherd, whose own the sheep are not, sees the wolf coming and leaves the sheep and flees, because he is a hireling and he hath no care for the sheep… I am the Good Shepherd. I know mine…And I lay down My life for My sheep."

Phyllis Schlafly, the prominent American author who with Father Joseph Vecsey, Cardinal Mindszenty's secretary, wrote the book we will be drawing upon—"Mindszenty The Man"—said in her introduction:

"The crying need of our times is for noble leaders who have the courage to stand fast, who persevere in their principles, who cannot be seduced or scared, who listen to the voice of conscience instead of the roar of the crowd, who are willing to pay the price that leadership demands.

"The last several decades have been singularly lacking in enough nobly dedicated leaders to defend the ramparts of civilization against the enemies of freedom and religion.

"By any standard, Cardinal Mindszenty is a leader. He has accepted the responsibilities of leadership, he has paid the price many times over. He has retained the loyalty of freedom lovers all over the world. The principles he stands for are universal and eternal. He is truly a man for all seasons."

XXXXI—January, 1974 Rudolph M. Unger

Chapter 42

Father Joseph Vecsey, secretary to Cardinal Joseph Mindszenty, who collaborated with American author Phyllis Schlafly to write the book, "Mindszenty The Man" explains at the outset his purpose.

"It is my hope that this book will give readers a realistic insight into the everyday life of the people who live under communist tyranny. The record of inhuman treatment and cruelty behind the iron curtain is often difficult for those in the free world to believe.

"The content of this book is the drama of real history. I have simply and plainly recorded the facts as I saw them, without embellishment or theatrics. My only aim is to be a faithful historian and, in a spirit of humility and fidelity, to be a witness to the truth.

"Cardinal Mindszenty's valiant struggle to save the Catholic Church in Hungary is important to everyone in the free world, no matter what his faith. In order to understand fully the reality of communism's war on religion, it is necessary to study this case history of how diabolical and deceitful tactics were used to transform man's natural religious inclinations into an instrument of the communist state.

"The cardinal is a Hungarian of enormous significance for mankind. He has come to symbolize the defense of universal and eternal values. His 23 years of captivity in Budapest are a constant reminder to the free world of the evil and danger of communism—always ready to crush that freedom of spirit which is the basis of human dignity and, indeed, of all human culture.

"His very name expresses his defense of individual liberty against tyranny. When the Nazis instituted a campaign to induce Hungarians of German descent to discard their Hungarian names and take German names instead, the man who was born Joseph Pehm expressed his defiance of the Nazis by dropping the name which revealed his German ancestry and adopting instead the Hungarian name of Joseph Mindszenty.

"Taken from his native village of Mindszent, this name more accurately reflects the fact that his people have been Hungarian natives for 400 years.

"The career of Cardinal Mindszenty is strongly linked with the life of a country woman of deep spirituality and sound common sense—his mother. The son inherited the basic traits of her character. By her sacrifices and prayers, she prepared him for his great place in history.

"As the cardinal wrote in the foreword of his book, "The Mother", 'Whatever I have become is due to the merits and prayers of my mother.'"

Father Vecsey and Mrs. Schlafly then launch into the description of the cardinal's early years and the first two skirmishes with tyranny which prepared him to cope with his great battle with communism—the reds' first futile endeavor to conquer Hungary in 1919 in the aftermath of World War I, the Nazis' occupation of the nation during World War II.

"In February, 1919, Father Mindszenty was arrested by two communist plain-clothes policemen in Szombathely and interrogated by a Mr. Obal who tried to terrify him by threatening him and asking him why he was writing and speaking against the revolution.

"He meant the October revolution of 1918. Under the flag of this red revolution, irresponsible elements within three months destroyed much of Hungary's wealth and productivity.

"The cardinal's reply—'Because it is my duty to spread the truth.'

"The revolutionaries were very angry at him because they found it impossible to organize any successful revolutionary units. They were unable to win over the youth or the workers. They believed father's pastoral work was partly responsible for this.

"That was true. He gave lectures, sermons, and most important, he edited a weekly newspaper. It was widely read and supported and was an outspoken critic of destructive and extremist elements.

"There was another reason why the communists were against him. One day he was walking through the town square of Zalaegerszeg and saw an enormous crowd of people. The workers had been ordered by their bosses to attend a meeting to hear a speech by a party leader from a Budapest. Coming closer, father heard the communist thundering the 'Reactionary Clergy.'

"The next moment, the church bell started ringing the angelus. The communist speaker seemed unnerved by this. Father seized this moment of hesitation and in his strongest voice started to pray the angelus. The whole crowd joined him and, by the first Ave Maria, everyone was praying loudly.

"At the end of the angelus, father made the sign of the cross and went home. The entire crowd did the same.

"On the 10th day of his imprisonment, a revolutionary chief offered to free Father Mindszenty if he would change his attitude toward the revolution and never return to his church post in Zalaegerszeg. He refused. He was threatened with a 15 year prison sentence. He would not give in.

"He was held in police custody until March 20, 1919, when the civil leader of the revolution turned over power to the communists, a tragedy which brought 133 days of bloody terror. That was the so called dictatorship of the proletariat in which the first step was to intimidate the people. He was one of the hostages taken and held in prison along with many Catholic laymen and civic leaders from all parts of the nation.

"On May 19, he was freed from prison under orders to work for good relationships between church and state. He was told that since he was a son of the common people, he must work for the dictatorship of the proletariat.

"His answer upon release was to openly meet with the men his captors ordered him to stay away from because the communists considered them to be 'reactionary.' He was ordered home to Mindszent where he had to report to the police twice a day, but continued to give public talks.

"One of his comments to the people was—'Remember, if power remains in the hands of the communists, even your scythe and spade will be stamped, 'government property!'". 'The Communist government collapsed on August 2.

"During World War II, the now Monsignor Mindszenty's newspaper was one of the few which carried articles critical of both communism and nazism, exposing their dangerous ideas and social programs.

"In March, 1944 he was appointed Bishop of Veszprem in Western Hungary. His mother in a letter reminded him of his 1919 imprisonment and warned him he probably would have to face even greater suffering in the future.

"His installation as Bishop came a week after Hitler's army occupied Hungary. A short while earlier, he had informed me (Vecsey) that he and

I were on the Nazi blacklist. He told me that I could flee the country, but as a pastor, he was obliged to remain.

"A summer of horrors began when on Hitler's orders there began the deportation of the Jews. The entire Hungarian Catholic episcopate protested with Bishops Apor and Mindszenty the most vigorous and vocal protesters.

"Bishop Mindszenty turned every religious house under his jurisdiction into a sanctuary for Jews hiding from the Gestapo. He said, 'If today we do not keep sacred and inviolable the Jew's personal freedom, his common and civil rights, tomorrow we may find that we have lost our own.'

"On November 27, 1944, the Bishop, whose residence had been turned into a home for refugees of the war, was arrested by the Nazis. The next day all 26 priests and seminarians who had followed him to the prison were arrested.

"On December 7, in the basement of the Veszprem prison, the Bishop ordained ten new priests, who together had only one candle, one cassock, and one surplice—but each had a separate armed guard standing over him with a loaded gun!

"Later, at Sopronkohida Prison, the 26 captive priests had been placed into one big hall but a small private room had been set aside for the Bishop.

"He objected to being singled out and was then permitted to stay with his priests and sleep on straw on the ground like them. He waited in line for his food as they did. He shared his spoon and cup with them. He shared their prison conditions completely.

"On the last day of March, 1945, after 4-1/2 months of captivity, he was freed. The release occurred at the very time the Soviet army reached the Hungarian border, thus fulfilling his dire warnings about the inevitable fate awaiting Hungary.

"Cities, villages, churches, schools, rectories, factories, and homes by the hundreds of thousands were in ruins, people were starving. Added to this was the drunken soldiers of the Red army engaged in an orgy of terror, intimidating a horrified population."

No. 42—February, 1974 Rudolph M. Unger

Chapter 43

In recounting the release of the then Bishop Mindszenty from prison by the Nazis in March, 1945, Father Joseph Vecsey and Phyllis Schlafly in their book "Mindszenty The Man" tell how the Bishop approached a town official to seek his aid in obtaining transportation back to his home.

"Mayor Sulyok", they wrote, "knowing what atrocities were being committed on all the roads by the Red army, felt strongly that the Bishop of Veszprem should not travel alone and suggested that he ask for a car and military escort from the soviet commanding officer in the town of Papa.

"Bishop Mindszenty replied to that suggestion by saying:

'A Hungarian Bishop cannot ask a favor from the soviet army.'

"He simply could not in conscience ask a favor from the agent of the atheist forces whose main goal was to destroy the church.

"Bishop Mindszenty had studied history well and he knew that whenever church leaders compromised with the church's persecutors, the persecutors were strengthened and their power prolonged.

"He had written in 1942—'New persecutors of the church are replacing the old ones. Swollen with pride at their whirlwind victories, they are temporarily on top. But the church always outlives them.'

"At the end of World War II, the Nazis persecutors of the church were replaced by the atheistic Bolsheviks. Following in the footsteps of the conquering Red army, Hungarian communists spread all over the country.

"The same man who had escaped to the Soviet Union after the collapse of their brief despotic rule in 1919, now returned to Hungary with the Red army to build a 'people's republic' in the Soviet pattern.

"The communists' main goal was to eliminate every courageous statesman and talented politician who would not cooperate with them. Simultaneously, they used agents and informers to cause discord and dissension among noncommunist political and social groups. They were successful in this objective even among Catholics because they cleverly made use of a few so called 'Progressive Catholics.'

"At first such persons were only pressed to make innocent statements about 'The necessity of cooperation between Marxists and Christians in a time of unprecedented national disaster.'

"Later, they were used to weaken the unity of the church and to diminish its resistance to the accelerated communist anti-religious activities.

"In the midst of this turmoil, Pope Pius XII appointed Joseph Mindszenty Archbishop of Esztergom and primate of the Catholic church in Hungary, the communists having already expelled the papal nuncio in March, 1945.

"The first words of the new primate were—'The Catholic Church does not hide when a storm is gathering, but is everywhere with and for the Hungarian People. It does not seek temporal, but only Divine Protection.'

"In his formal inaugural address, Archbishop Mindszenty added:

'Bleeding Hungary is drowning in the maelstrom of the worst moral, legal and economic collapse in our history. Our psalm is the De Profundis. Our prayer is the Miserere. Our prophet is Jeremiah. Our world is the Apocalypse.

'We sit at the waters of Babylon and captors try to teach us alien songs. I want to be a good shepherd who, if necessary, will give his life for his sheep, for the church, and our homeland.'

"The new primate knew only too well both the theory and the reality of communism, and its cunning and deceitful tactics. Beginning in 1919, he had continuously and thoroughly studied every phase of the persecution of the church in Russia.

"He knew that compromise had failed to secure any freedom for the church there. He knew the tragic case of the Russian Orthodox Patriarch Tikhon and his successor, the more 'diplomatic' Metropolitan Sergei.

"Archbishop Mindszenty understood that in Russia a diabolical atheistic power had confronted the leaders of the Orthodox Church. He had written years before—'Hell has never before mobilized such power. An officially atheistic dictatorship, with 5½ million atheist communist agents, fight unitedly and relentlessly with red-hot hatred against God, religion, and the church. They're in schools, radio, newspapers, literature, the theater, art, advertising,'

"In his inaugural speech, he exhorted:

'Let the nation storm heaven with prayers now! If we begin to really pray again, we will gain renewed strength and confidence. My trust is in a campaign of prayers by millions of the faithful; and in my mother's rosary, now held even more tightly in her hands.'

"He visited the packed concentration camps in and around Budapest where the victims of the new communist tyranny were eking out a pitiful existence. It was for these unfortunate people that he appealed in his first pastoral letter as primate:

'There are many who have been deprived of the basic right of personal liberty and who have been held in concentration camps for months without even being told why, without any court trial or sentence, sometimes even without being questioned.'

"He urged everyone to live a deeply pious life and he inaugurated a spiritual revival among clergy and people—a movement of prayer and atonement. He consistently set a good example himself.

"In monastic simplicity, he devoted himself exclusively to prayer and work. He slept very little and worked most of the night. He ate the simplest food. His priests often secretly mixed vitamins in his soup to prevent damage to his health from so much fasting.

"In another pastoral letter to the Hungarian people, the archbishop said, 'Human strength alone is not enough for man to live and progress. Man's struggle is in vain if not joined by God's blessing. We put all our hope in the hearts of Jesus and Mary. From them we ask for and hope to gain salvation.'

"In February, 1946, Pope Pius XII elevated archbishop Mindszenty to the cardinalate. Upon his return to Hungary, Lenten retreats and missions were held in every parish. A Catholic paper reported at Easter, 'Three-fourths of the faithful present in the churches were men, this year some 38 percent more men were present at sermons than last year and 51 percent more men were present at processions than last year.' In May, 100,000 men took part in a ten mile procession led by the cardinal. In August, 500,000 men took part in a procession the cardinal organized.

"In 1947, Cardinal Mindszenty announced a Marian year in honor of the Virgin Mary. He opened it on August 15, in a ceremony attended by 60,000 persons.

"There followed, in every section of Hungary, special Mary days and in a three week period some three million pilgrims participated at Szombathely; after that, on September 8, there were 100,000 pilgrims at Szombathely; on September 14, the primate led 100,000 men on a penitential pilgrimage to Mariaremente; on September 20, 120,000 persons attended his mass; in October, 150,000 boys and girls attended a Marian congress in Budapest, the meeting for workers at the congress drew 80,000, while 200,000 attended the session for parents, and 250,000 attended the Sunday high mass.

"At the Bishops' conference in September, Bishop Rogacs, in welcoming Cardinal Mindszenty, told him in the presence of the gathering:

'Your charismatic wisdom leads hesitant minds along the right way, gives strength to weary souls, and fortitude to those who have abandoned hope. Possessing the steadfastness of a St. Ambrose, you are the rock to which the Hungarian people, both Catholic and non-catholic, cling in order not to be swept away by the waves.'

"In a subsequent speech, Cardinal Mindszenty stated—'In the past great fortresses stood watch over our people. We cannot live without fortresses even today. Thank God. We have fortresses for our defense—the church of our native land, our catholic schools, the fundamental unit of the family.

'Amidst the storms and tempests which sweep our world today, stand guard, hold fast at their thresholds!

'Either the school will instruct in the spirit of the church to help produce saintly souls or it will become a workshop of evil, corrupted and corrupting. History teaches us that, as the school moves farther away from the church, it goes closer to the world of sin and damnation. The school must be the home of virtue and science. If virtue is not taught in it, God save us from its science.'

"It was during the bitter struggle over the Catholic schools that the decision was made in Moscow and Budapest to silence Cardinal Mindszenty."

No. 43—March, 1974 Rudolph M. Unger

Chapter 44

In "Mindszenty The Man" Father Joseph Vecsey and Phyllis Schlafly describe the classic communist pattern which was employed to take control of Christian Hungary.

"While publicly asserting their good will toward the church, the communists struck three major blows against it.

"They stripped religious organizations, institutions and schools of their financial support. They closed down all church newspapers, periodicals and magazines by refusing permits and limiting newsprint. They cleverly prevented any political parties of Christian orientation and ideology from running candidates in parliamentary elections.

"Cardinal Mindszenty, of course, treated these pre-planned measures against the church as grave violations of the right to freedom of religion. He often raised his voice to protest the way the church was restricted in the expression of its religious and social doctrine by being deprived of its own daily newspaper.

"Speakers at Catholic rallies would point out that Catholics made up more than two-thirds of the Hungarian population, but did not have any representation in the parliament because of the communists' dictatorial manipulation of the party system.

"In the national election of Nov. 4, 1945, the electorate could vote only for candidates of political parties permitted by the allied control committee. This committee was controlled by the commander of Russian troops in Hungary, General Voroshilov.

"Permission was granted only to those parties already represented in the provisional parliament, which were the several Marxist parties and the one non-Marxist party, the Smallholders party.

"When this party won the election with a 57.7 majority, its weak leaders were successfully pressured by the Russians to divide the ministerial portfolios 50-50 with the communists. Of course the communists made sure they got the minister of the interior, which had charge of the secret police.

"The communists took advantage of this coalition government to put through a policy designed to weaken the church even further.

"They proceeded to ban Catholic youth organizations, prohibit religious education and secularize the Catholic schools.

"In spite of the deteriorated political situation, Cardinal Mindszenty struggled successfully for nearly four years to defend Catholic organizations, religious education programs and Catholic schools against the accelerating communist policy of false propaganda and terroristic harassment.

"In the fall of 1947, the communists increased their power in the coalition government by means of fraudulent and falsified elections and by brutal persecution of opposition parties. This new communist 'coalition' government ordered the expropriation of all Catholic schools on June 16, 1948.

"Cardinal Mindszenty organized a nationwide protest. The expropriation and the introduction of required courses in Marxism alarmed the entire population.

"Everyone could see that the enforcement of this law passed by the communist pseudo-parliament was a clear violation of public promises made by the communists that any new 'reforms' would be passed by 'legal' means alone and 'according to the consent of the people.'

"Cardinal Mindszenty regularly submitted documentation of the religious persecution in Hungary to various western news agencies, especially the Catholic press, so that newspapers and radio stations throughout the world could expose the communist lies.

"The communists knew it was to their interest to mask their anti-religious tactics in Eastern Europe to avoid a public confrontation between church and state. The Hungarian Bolsheviks caught on quickly that as long as Cardinal Mindszenty headed the Catholic Church in Hungary, the forcible stamping out of religion would mean a life and death struggle between church and state.

"Despite many attempts to get him to 'cooperate' the communists simply could not divert him from his vigorous defense of religious freedom. They were just as unsuccessful with their tactics of intimidation.

"The top Hungarian communists reached a consensus in the summer of 1948 that the only way to avoid a violent struggle between church and state was to eliminate Cardinal Mindszenty from his leadership position. Henceforth, all anti-religious attacks were aimed specifically at the primate personally.

"The communist officials and their controlled press and radio hammered away at the 'anti-democratic' attitude of the cardinal, labeling him an 'enemy of the people.'

"They repeated ad nauseam that the cardinal refused to 'recognize' the republic, that he was organizing a 'revolution' to overthrow it,' that he 'obstinately' opposed peaceful relations between church and state by demanding the return of church properties; that he was 'causing irreparable harm' not only to the Hungarian republic, but to the whole Catholic church.

"Here is how Cardinal Mindszenty replied to these accusations:

'The trouble does not lie in my peaceful or un-peaceful disposition. Not everything is peaceful which is called peace. Who actually wears the mantle of justice and peace?

'The means of peace are not belligerent. Peace does not bring the fruits of war, which are—injustice, cruelty, vengeance, unjust deportations, hatred and violence.

'Every new Bishop is admonished at his consecration—'Don't turn light into darkness, or darkness into light. Don't call error truth. Don't call evil good or good evil.'

'To this, I would add, don't call it peace if it is not peace!'"

"The communists increased the number of secret police who followed the cardinal everywhere in order to put his trusted friends and co-workers under surveillance. A whole army of secret agents spread over the nation to investigate every place where the cardinal had been in three decades. Their object—to find something in his past with which they could compromise him.

"Cardinal Mindszenty was well aware of the danger to which he was exposed. This is why his sermons included the recurring theme that a pastor must serve his flock even at the cost of his life.

"When he consecrated Bishop Rogacs in the Szombathely cathedral on June 29, 1948, his sermon included words about the role of the church.

'Throughout the world, the battle rages between spiritual and worldly weapons, between conscience and the sword. The secular power is ill at ease in the presence of God, and even in the presence of the church which represents almighty God and the spiritual freedom He has given us.

'It is an everlasting blessing that there is someone who indicates even to the most powerful, what is right and what is wrong. What becomes of nations when truth is silenced?'

"During the week following I (Father Vecsey) went with the cardinal to the home of his mother in Mindszent. He failed to calm her fears that the communists were preparing for a final showdown to get rid of him. She earnestly declared her support of the way her son was 'defending the church so heroically and conscientiously.'

"On the other hand, she realized the danger that threatened him and asked him if he couldn't do something to save his life by easing tensions between church and state. He and I were both somewhat shaken by her anxious plea. Later, I again brought up to him the question she raise. He replied:

'This problem does not concern only the Catholic Church and Hungary, but the whole Christian world and western civilization.

'Several times in history, we Hungarians have been in a strategic spot where it was our mission to defend the universal church. Once, when our nation was great and strong, we fulfilled our duty with the sword.

'Today, we are no longer independent, but we still must courageously stand our ground in this struggle between Christianity and atheistic bolshevism.

'Our historic mission is to alert and warn the rest of the world of the communist threat. Fulfilling this task is far more important than winning a brief respite from our suffering at the price of humiliating compromise.'"

No. 44—April, 1974 Rudolph M. Unger

Chapter 45

"The communists continued their daily slanders against Cardinal Mindszenty in the summer of 1948. They accelerated and 'orchestrated' their attacks on the radio and through mass demonstrations.

"By autumn, posters and signs appeared with the slogan, 'We must liquidate Mindszentyism!' Communist commentators reiterated emotional warnings that 'peaceful co-existence between church and state' depended on eliminating 'Mindszentyism.'

So wrote Father Joseph Vecsey and Phyllis Schlafly in their book 'Mindszenty The Man.'

"The communists required the 'progressive' Catholics to join in mass demonstrations against the cardinal. School children and industrial workers were forced to listen to anti-Mindszenty harangues. The young people and workers were taught to repeat slogans and propaganda phases demanding that the 'obstinate' and 'short-sighted' cardinal be removed from his leadership of the church so that 'civil peace' could be restored.

"The national committee of communes, which was entirely controlled by the communists, was ordered to present petitions to the parliament demanding the arrest and trial of the cardinal.

"In an address to the nation on Nov. 18, 1948, the cardinal stated:

'In spite of repeated promises made since World War II, no elections have been held anywhere except in the capital. Thus, there is no legal basis for any governmental actions in the cities, counties or districts. Men are forced to make declarations contrary to general public opinion by being threatened with the loss of their bread or freedom.

'The majority has been silenced and excluded from the exercise of their constitutional rights. 'Freedom of speech' in this new 'democracy' does not permit criticism. If any is voiced, the critic is fired from his job. This has happened time and time again. All my sympathy goes out to those who oppose this regime. Their sterling examples of character, loyalty and courage are inspiring.'

"On that same day, the cardinal issued this message to reassure those worried about his life:

'I calmly watch the storm artificially blown about my person. In my position, storms are not uncommon. History provides many examples. Two of my predecessors died in battles. Two had all their possessions confiscated. John Vitez was thrown in prison. Martinuzzi was assassinated by hired killers. Pasmany, one of the greatest, was exiled.

'None of my 48 predecessors, however, was the victim of so many trumped-up lies. Obstinately repeated even though they have been refuted a hundred times.

'I stand firmly for God, church and country in my historic responsibility to the nation which has repeatedly stood alone against the enemies of western civilization. Compared to the suffering of my people, my own fate is not important.'

"The next day, Nov. 9, 1948, Father Andrew Zakar, the cardinal's personal secretary, was arrested. He simply was kidnapped on the street. Three days later, the secret police searched his apartment as well as some other rooms in the Archbishop's residence.

"Cardinal Mindszenty released a public statement in which he exonerated from guilt any Catholic man or woman who was forced to sign a declaration against him 'since he or she does not act deliberately.'

"On Dec.23, 1948, the Archbishop's residence was searched again. The secret police brought with them Father Zakar whom they had 'treated' and brainwashed for a month. He was in a pathetic dazed condition. He walked with strange dancing steps and babbled incessantly that he had been among kind people who had even given him 'bits of meat.'

"The secret police than took him into the cellar of the residence and emerged triumphantly with a large tin tube, which they said contained documents revealing a conspiracy against the government. They were immediately shown to the press which trumpeted the news about the 'cardinal's conspiracy.'

"That night, the cardinal drafted a statement, reading: 'I have never participated in any kind of conspiracy. I will not resign my office as Archbishop. I have nothing to confess and I won't sign anything.

'If you should ever read that I have confessed or resigned, and even seen it authenticated by my signature, remember that it will have been only the result of human frailty. In advance, I declare all such actions null and void.'

"He put the statement in an envelope, sealed it and wrote on it instructions that after his arrest, it should be given to the Archbishop Joseph Grosz, the vice chairman of the Bishops' conference.

"The cardinal's mother, who had come to spend the Christmas season with him, urged him to leave immediately for Rome in order to save his life. She said she had received numerous letters from friends who were worried about his life and they all pinned their hope for his safety on a flight to Rome.

"She told me (Vecsey) that her pleading obviously distressed the cardinal who replied that he would not desert either his country or his people in such troubled times.

'A pastor of souls must stay with his flock and cannot flee like a hired servant,' he told her.

'I know very well what my arrest and perhaps execution by the communists would mean to you at your age of 74. I know this would break your heart. I have known for a long time, mother, that a great grief would be your lot. But please take comfort from the Blessed Mother, whose heart was also pierced under the cross by the arrows of pain. For a long time I have prayed to the Sorrowful Mother to give you the grace to accept God's will about my suffering and death.

'With God's help, I was able to make you happy for a while. Now, you must take up your cross,' he said in parting.

"He knew that the torture and murder of other priests simply had made no significant impact on the western world. He felt that it was his responsibility to stay and confront the communists in order that the free world would learn how even the strongest man can be broken and debased by the diabolical tortures of the Bolshevik bosses.

"On Dec. 26, 1948, an armed squad of secret police broke into the Archbishop's residence and arrested him. His mother watched and bade him a tearful goodbye.

"Western newscasts in announcing his arrest, also read portions of the cardinal's Dec. 21 Pastoral letter to his priests:

'Everywhere and always, only that happens which God permits. What he has told us is valid for all times—'Do not worry about your life, or what you shall eat, or what you shall wear. Your Heavenly Father will care for you.'

'We cannot behave like men without faith or hope. Let us pray for those among us whose nerves are frayed by present events, and who alarm and panic others around them. Let us pray that the bell of peace will toll in their tormented hearts, and that their way will be lighted by the Lord's admonition, 'Why are you fearful, O Ye of little faith?'

'Let us recall the words of St. John Chrysostom, 'The waves roar and the storm rages, but we are not afraid because the rock of the church cannot be crushed…I despise that with which the world tries to frighten me. I laugh at the way the world tries to seduce me.'

'Therefore, my friends, don't worry about tomorrow. Let us find our consolation in the gospels. Our Christian and Hungarian ancestors have never enjoyed soft lives. Priests, religious and nuns are expected to give an example of standing firm at their posts. Our profession of faith must be a beacon to the faithful. Let us be a light shining in the darkness.

'Everything we have done has been to preserve the liberty of the church, safeguard our youth, help our suffering people, for peace, for higher spiritual values.

'Ours is the world of the sermon on the mount –'Blessed are those who suffer persecution for justice's sake. Theirs is the kingdom of heaven.'"

No. 45—May, 1974 Rudolph M. Unger

Chapter 46

The futile efforts of the mother of Cardinal Mindszenty to see her son and to provide a defense attorney for him after his arrest by the communists on December 26, 1948, was related in the chapter "The Mock Trial" by Father Joseph Vecsey, the cardinal's secretary, and Phyllis Schlafly in their book, "Mindszenty The Man."

Finally, the communists told his mother that they had provided a lawyer for her son, One Coloman Kiczko.

"When we told this to our two legal advisers," related Vecsey, "they were shocked because they knew Kiczko was an old-time communist who had played an important role in the 1919 communist dictatorship.

"This opened our eyes to the fact that the government was preparing a trial which would be a travesty of justice. This convinced our advisers that nothing could be done to help the primate.

"On January 19, 1949, the communists issued the so called yellow book which contained among other things a phony confession by the cardinal. I told his mother I thought the purpose of the book and 'confession' was to blackmail the Vatican and the Bishops conference in Hungary into negotiations.

"When I saw the cardinal years later in Budapest, on November 1, 1956, after his liberation by the Hungarian freedom fighters, he personally told me about his pre-trial detention and how he had been subjected to day and night interrogation, hour after hour without any sleep, by brutal interrogators working in shifts.

"He was forced to stand with arms raised high for days at a time under blinding lights during endless repetition of rapid-fire questions.

"The cardinal signed a 'confession' on January 11, when he felt on the verge of a complete breakdown and hoped to get rid of his interrogators for a few hours. Under his signature, he placed the letters, 'c.f.', for 'coactus feci', that is, 'I signed under force.'

"The secret police soon deciphered the meaning of the Latin letters and the relentless interrogation was immediately resumed.

"When he was physically broken by three weeks of grueling day and night interrogation, tormented with pain, and unable to say 'no' any longer, the 'treatment' with drugs began.

"The fraudulent yellow book 'confession' was prepared by interrogators and the cardinal never wrote or signed any confession at all.

"When his public trial finally opened on February 3, 1949, the effects of the drugs and brainwashing were obvious to everyone, he looked like a man broken physically and mentally.

"We had known him as a man of vigor and independence. At the trial, he appeared awkward, submissive, slavishly obedient to every directive of the court.

"He 'confessed' against himself in a long stream of self-accusations. If he forgot memorized lines and momentarily stumbled in reciting them, the court was always quick to help him continue the pre-written dialogue.

"At the end of this mock trial, Cardinal Mindszenty was convicted of treason, trying to overthrow the government, and foreign currency speculation, and he was condemned to life imprisonment.

"Even though drugs, sleeplessness, and forty days of psychological and physical pounding had manipulated the cardinal into playing a self-accusatory role at the trial, and even though the government carefully controlled the news accounts of the trial, the free world, nevertheless, saw through the mockery of justice.

"Shortly after the trial, Pope Pius XII told a crowd of some 100,000 persons in St. Peter's Square:

'The physical condition of Cardinal Mindszenty can only be explained by secret and unknown influences. This man, by nature so extremely vigorous, was suddenly changed into a frail and broken character—so much so that his behavior is an accusation, not against the accused, but against the accusers.'

"My original suspicion that the yellow book was designed to pressure and intimidate the Bishops was confirmed. The communists hoped to force them into negotiations during the cardinal's captivity.

"During the last week of January, Archbishop Grosz, who had succeeded as chairman of the Bishops conference after the Cardinal's arrest, received a 'letter from Cardinal Mindszenty' asking the Bishops to begin negotiations with the government.

"The majority of the Bishops rejected the letter as a fraud and Archbishop Grosz forbade any Bishop to appear at a meeting with the communists. Four of the sixteen Bishops attended anyway.

"Nevertheless, due to the strong resistance of Pope Pius XII, Archbishop Grosz, and the majority of the Hungarian Bishops, the government failed in its attempt to force the Hungarian church into 'negotiations' on communist terms.

"Even before the cardinal's arrest, the so-called 'Progressive Catholics' had been negotiating with the communists for a solution of the 'Mindszenty Problem.' As a result of this 'dialogue' the "Progressive Catholics' had been won over to the view that the Catholic church in Hungary could live in 'peaceful co-existence' under the present government, only if Cardinal Mindszenty were removed from his key position as primate.

"By December, 1948, when it became evident that the communists wanted to get rid of him at any price, the 'Progressive Catholics' considered the time right for asking the Vatican to arrange such a 'solution.' They were convinced that the six-month campaign of slander had adequately prepared world opinion, including the Vatican, for the cardinal's arrest.

"They hoped to persuade Vatican officials that the problems between the church and the Hungarian government were caused by the cardinal's 'obstinate' behavior. The 'progressives' offered their services to the government to try to solve the 'Mindszenty problem' by making an overture to the Holy See. As their messenger, they sent a Hungarian Jesuit who arrived in Rome at Christmas, 1948.

"When he arrived he heard of the cardinal's arrest and, left out on a limb, the 'Progressive Jesuit' was heard to remark, 'How could they commit such a stupidity at the very moment of my arrival in Rome?!'

"The Vatican replied to the Hungarian government:

'It is incomprehensible how the alleged desire for an agreement with the Vatican can be reconciled with the mistreatment given the cardinal—mistreatment that is very offensive to the Holy See.

'The Vatican position remains that the rights of the church and the right to freedom of conscience must be respected. This means not only freedom of worship, but freedom to give religious instruction, freedom to preach the gospel and propagate the faith, and especially freedom to give children a Christian education.'

"To other slanders that Cardinal Mindszenty's arrest was precipitated by his espousing religious and political views contrary to those of the Pope, Pope Pius himself replied:

'The uncalled for arrest of our beloved son, Cardinal Joseph Mindszenty, and his removal from his Episcopal seat, has grieved us most deeply. Such a lack of reverence and respect toward this highly esteemed prince of the church, is a deep offense to religion and human dignity.

'Therefore, conscience and duty compel us to openly express our sorrow and grief for these violations of the rights of the church. We voice an indignation and concern felt not only by Hungarian Catholics, but by Catholics everywhere. We solemnly protest this injustice inflicted on the whole Catholic Church.

'The great merits of this prince of the church as well as his unshakable faith are well known to us. We know also his apostolic courage and firmness in protecting Christian doctrine and the sacred rights of the church. As Archbishop, he fulfilled his unflinching duty to watch over the church with a courageous and steadfast heart.

'He rightly insisted that freedom of religion could not be limited to church services alone, but must include the schools, the press, pilgrimages to sacred shrines, and the activities of Catholic organizations.'

"Having failed in their efforts to trick the Vatican into negotiations on their terms, the communists proceeded with their mock trial of Mindszenty."

No. 46—June, 1974 Rudolph M Unger

Chapter 47

With their major enemy, Cardinal Joseph Mindszenty out of the way, safely behind prison walls following a mock trial charging him with treason, the communists—those champions of co-existence and negotiation—moved ahead with their plans to wipe out the church in Hungary.

As the cardinal's secretary, Father Joseph Vecsey, recalls:

"With Cardinal Mindszenty out of the way after his mock trial in February, 1949, the communist government no longer feared an open confrontation with the bishops. The bishops felt that any forthright defense of religious freedom could easily precipitate large scale persecution.

"Archbishop Grosz had succeeded to the chairmanship of the bishops conference. Instead of open confrontation he chose passive resistance. Following Archbishop Grosz' imprisonment in May, 1951, he was subjected for thirty-eight days to the same brainwashing techniques which had been used on Cardinal Mindszenty.

"His 'trial' was a carbon copy of the cardinal's. In a half conscious state he publicly confessed that he was 'a warmonger', had 'committed high treason', was 'a spy', and had 'dealt illegally in foreign currencies.' He received a fifteen year sentence.

"The communists needed to discredit archbishop Grosz in order to break resistance of the clergy against the 'priests' peace movement.'

"Archbishop Czapik succeeded Grosz as chairman of the bishops conference. His health was very poor, which undoubtedly influenced him to steer clear of any collision course with the government's persecution of the church. He dreaded prison, knowing that his failing strength could not stand the torture and suffering.

"All this was well known to the communists and they exploited the situation for their own anti-religious objectives. Archbishop Czapik's compromising attitude split the unity of the hierarchy.

"He adopted the policy that compromises had to be made to salvage whatever was possible. This attitude enabled the communists to put the entire Catholic Church under their yoke in a short time.

"After Archbishop Grosz was arrested the communists introduced a bill in the Parliament – the sponsor being a 'Progressive Catholic' – to establish a National Bureau for Church Affairs.

"His trial was still going on when personnel of the newly established bureau appeared with police escorts in three Episcopal sees where the police put the bishops under house arrest. They were invited to appoint priests from the 'peace movement' to the key diocesan posts of vicar general and chancellor.

"When they did not comply they were kept under house arrests to prevent them from attending the bishops conference meeting of July 3, 1951.

"Archbishop Czapik took the position that church officials should themselves dissolve all Catholic institutions which the communists would not tolerate, including the seminaries. He dutifully issued any statements the government demanded of him in order to publicly show his collaboration with the state, and then he persuaded the bishops to accept these decisions.

"At the July 3 meeting he persuaded them to sign a document in which they condemned 'those church officials whose subversive activities have just come to light'.

"Earlier, in June, 1950, in Cardinal Mindszenty's own Archdiocese of Esztergom, the communists forced the election of Monsignor Beresztoczy as Vicar General. One and one-half years before, he had been arrested by secret police and tortured. He was kept in prison several months and released on the condition that he would do whatever the communists wanted him to.

"The terror-stricken Monsignor under instructions from the communists had campaigned for his own election. The canons of the diocese, however, chose Dr. Bela Witz. Frail and timid, Dr. Witz did not dare to accept the position because he knew the communists were determined to have Beresztoczy in the job.

"On the second ballot the canons chose Bishop Zoltan Meszlenyi. He governed only two weeks before the communists arrested him and sent him to a concentration camp in Kistarcsa, where he died four years later.

"At the time Meszlenyi was elected, the secret police searched the homes of several canons. They were threatened with arrest and prison if they failed to vote for Beresztoczy on the next ballot. By this brutal means the communists forced the canons to elect Beresztoczy.

"Such communist tricks, however, were well known to Pope Pius XII. Beresztoczy was effectively displaced by the Pope's appointment of Bishop Andrew Hamvas as Apostolic Administrator of Esztergom. Unfortunately, this did not solve the problem, because under this timid bishop's administration, the Esztergom Archdiocese was allowed to fall into the hands of the leftist 'peace priests.'

"Monsignor Beresztoczy had been put in charge of the 'Priests Peace Movement' on August 1, 1950. Using brute force, the secret police recruited some 150 priests to attend the first meeting of the 'peace movement'. The Bishops Forbade their priests to take part. The communists used their priest-collaborators to publicly attack the bishops conference. In spite of all such attacks, the communists never succeeded in recruiting any significant number of priests into the 'peace movement.'

"Following Cardinal Mindszenty's imprisonment in 1949, the communists had ordered the abolition of all teaching of religion in schools unless it was requested by individual parents. When ninety-five percent of them made the request, the communists turned to new tactics.

"Numerous religion teachers were fired as 'reactionaries'. Students were warned that if they received religious instruction, they would not be admitted to higher education, universities would be closed to them. They would not be able to secure either scholarships or public financial aid.

"Meanwhile, all non-Marxist youth organizations were dissolved including the boy and girl scouts and the YMCA. All text books in schools were rewritten to conform to Marxist Ideology. Students in state colleges were forbidden to go to church or receive religious instruction. Religious publishing houses were nationalized. Only communists were permitted to publish books or periodicals designed for ideological training of youth.

"The communists expelled the religious not only from their schools but also from hospitals, orphanages and homes for the aged. The communists then turned to violent tactics to force the bishops to begin church-state talks on communist terms.

"In a night raid on June 9, 1950, the secret police arrested 1,000 priests, monks, brothers, and nuns and put them in concentration camps, including some sick, disabled, and elderly. The communists said, 'Their presence is a danger to public order and security.'

"Then, to break all remaining spirit of resistance by the bishops, the communists in a second night raid on June 18, seized another 1,000 religious and sent them also to concentration camps.

"In July, a government decree ordered the dissolution of almost all religious orders. The monasteries for men were reduced from 187 to 6. Out of 456 convents for nuns, all but two were closed. The eight remaining institutions were restricted to a maximum twenty-five members each.

"Out of a once proud total of 11,000 men and women who belonged to religious orders, only 200 could remain. Of the once proud total of 3,122 Catholic schools, only eight remained. All the monasteries, convents, seminaries, and novitates had to be abandoned by December 31, 1950, the date set for government confiscation of all their property.

"In the summer of 1951, the 'peace priests' took over the offices of vicar general and chancellor in every diocese. A representative of the national bureau for church affairs sat in every Episcopal residence and kept the seal of the diocese as well as the key to treasury and archives.

"No one could see the bishop without his permission. He exercised a veto over the bishop's every decision and every meeting in the diocese.

"The bureau finally forced the entire administration of the church into the hands of the 'peace priests' who always subordinated the interests of the church to those of the government. Thus the bureau enslaved the church and made it a vehicle of total communist control over the minds and morals of men."

No. 47—July, 1974 Rudolph M. Unger

Chapter 48

"Some of the most dramatic and amazing events of the 20th century took place during the last several days of October and the first several days of November, 1956. My eyewitness account is recorded in this letter which I wrote to mother Mindszenty."

So wrote Father Joseph Vecsey, Cardinal Mindszenty's secretary, in his book "Mindszenty The Man" co-authored with Phyllis Schlafly. Excerpts from the letter follow:

"Dear mother Barbara, it is with greatest joy that I tell you that I am home in Budapest and writing you on behalf of the cardinal!

"On October 25, hearing about the revolution, I made my way from Vienna to the Austro-Hungarian border, where tents and supplies had been set up by the Red Cross and by International Catholic Charities. I could hardly believe my eyes. The barricade was down, the red star on the soldiers' caps had been replaced by the Hungarian tricolor, and traffic was proceeding normally.

"I saw a truck with four soldiers approach. They confirmed the unbelievable – that in Budapest and the larger Hungarian cities, workers and students were actually fighting government troops and soviet army units!

"I heard the news that, on the threshold of victory, the newly formed revolutionary government had called Cardinal Mindszenty to the capital. Hungarian revolutionary troops had liberated the cardinal from the hands of the secret police in Felsopeteny.

"When I arrived in Budapest, the cardinal spotted me immediately. Before I could even greet him, he said, 'Thank you so much for the many services you have rendered my mother.'

"A representative of the new free Hungarian government told the cardinal that the Russians promised to leave Hungary, gave their consent to free elections, and stated they did not object to Hungary's neutrality. The cardinal advised the government not to believe these communist statements, but to plead its own cause immediately at the United Nations.

"Another representative of the new free government remarked: 'The

Soviets are barbarians without consciences, and therefore we cannot trust their promises.'

"At this moment, the people in Budapest are filled with joy. The whole free world is thrilled about the cardinal's liberation. He has received a telegram from Pope Pius XII, saying:

'The news of your liberation fills our soul with happiness. At this moment there is great joy not only in your own nation, but in the entire Catholic world. With a grateful heart we give thanks to the Lord...His grace has shone brightly on your faith and fortitude...our heartfelt wish is that the Catholic faith, so tested by errors and bloodshed, may be renewed again.'

"After eight years imprisonment, you can imagine how thrilled the cardinal was to be freed by the Hungarian people he loves so much. He told me how much he enjoyed those first hours he spent with the soldiers who freed him in their barracks. 'They were all so happy with high hopes for a better and brighter future,' he said.

"They decided that he should go to Budapest and he asked them, 'But, my sons, what will guarantee that I will arrive safely in Budapest?' Major Pallavicini, the head of the liberators, replied, 'Only our lives. Nothing but our lives.' The cardinal replied, 'My sons, I trust you. We will go.'

"Upon his arrival in Budapest, after mass in his chapel, he told the people, 'A magnificent heroism has liberated our country. Such a fight for freedom is without parallel in history. Our young men deserve every honor. I offer my gratitude and prayers for the glorious patriotism of our soldiers, our workers and our farmers.'" (End of letter)

"After a meeting with his bishops, including Archbishop Grosz, the cardinal addressed the Hungarian nation by radio:

'With the help of divine providence, I am the same man I was before I was imprisoned. Though prison has taken its toll of my physical strength, I stand by my convictions with the same spirit and mind I had eight years ago. I have always spoken frankly and forthrightly, saying what I believe to be right and true, and I continue in plain spoken language today.

'Every civilized nation has sided with us and is trying to help us. This is a great tribute to the moral force exerted thruout the world by one very small country.

'Hungary has one special distinction. In 1,000 years of history, no nation has suffered more for freedom. Again and again we had to fight for our survival and to man the ramparts of western freedom.

'Our whole future depends on the attitude of the 200 million strong Soviet Union and on the intentions of its army stationed within our borders. We are informed that the Soviets are sending reinforcements to these units. Only an enemy nation attacks another nation. We have not attacked Russia. A nation which is a mere bag of bones is fighting desperately for its freedom. Our national survival is at stake. The flower of our nation's youth is today battling in the front lines of a life and death struggle for freedom.

'Our people are fighting for freedom because they want to be free to decide their own destiny, to elect their own government, and to keep for themselves the benefits of their own economic production. Our first concern is our daily bread and the very survival of our nation. We also expect, in all justice, the restoration to the church of its freedom. We put our trust in Divine Providence.'

"The next morning, November 4, 1956, the Hungarian free radio announced: 'Soviet troops have attacked Budapest at dawn with the clear intention of overthrowing the free democratic Hungarian government. Our troops are fighting the soviets for right and freedom.'

"Later in the day, the last desperate cries of free Hungary went out over teletype and radio: 'Please tell the world of the treacherous attack against our struggle for liberty...Help! Help! Help! SOS! SOS! SOS! ...We have almost no weapons – only light machine guns, rifles. The people are jumping at the tanks and throwing in hand grenades. The Hungarian people are not afraid of death. It is only a pity we cannot stand for long. What is the United Nations doing? Give us a little encouragement.'

"Finding asylum in the American Legation in Budapest, Cardinal Mindszenty informed President Eisenhower, 'Shipwrecked in the fight for Hungarian freedom, I have found a haven, thanks to your generosity. While a guest in your legation, I am at the same time a refugee in my own homeland. Your country's hospitality has saved me from certain death.'

"After President John F. Kennedy met Nikita Khrushchev in Vienna in June, 1961, it became very noticeable that various groups were busily trying to induce the cardinal to leave Hungary. But he steadfastly refused to accept safety and freedom for himself as long as his Hungarian people were denied their freedom of religion. His recurrent theme was:

'For 1,000 years, our blood and our soil have defended the peace, the civilization, the culture, and the wealth of the western world. This is why you could remain within the gates of life. Hungarian blood flowed in streams while Michelangelo quietly conceived the dome of St. Peter's. While London enjoyed Shakespeare, Hungarians stood guard over the very gates of Rome, London, and Paris.'

"By 1971, the atmosphere in the American embassy in Budapest had lost its original cordiality and the new U.S. Policy calling for 'an era of negotiation' rather than 'an era of confrontation' made Cardinal Mindszenty no longer a welcome guest. The new mood in the U.S. State Department was that an old anti-communist such as Cardinal Mindszenty should, like old soldiers, 'simply fade away.'

"The de facto policy of the present U.S. Administration is to do business with the communist imperialists. The hallmarks of the new policy – negotiations, accommodations, detente, rapprochement, trade deals, financial credits, and treaties – are out of tune with Cardinal Mindszenty's half century of accurate analysis and uncompromising opposition to communism.

"On Christmas day, 1971, he reminded the world: 'What I have previously condemned as evil and destructive, still is. And I will always be faithful to the principles which are necessary for the survival of Hungary and the freedom of its people.'"

No. 48—August, 1974 Rudolph M. Unger

Chapter 49

Sister Adelaide was a nun who was assigned to be the traveling companion to Cardinal Mindszenty's mother on her frequent and often futile trips from Mindszent to Budapest to try to see her imprisoned son.

In the appendix to the book "Mindszenty The Man" by the cardinal's secretary, Father Joseph Vecsey, and co-author Phyllis Schlafly, appear excerpts from Sister Adelaide's dairy. Portions of it follow:

"June 20, 1950 – The night before last, some 1,000 religious were hauled away from their convents by the secret police. I escaped this fate only because I had gone with mother Barbara to Mindszent. According to my superior's previous instructions, I changed into secular dress and came back home to stay with my widowed mother in Budapest.

"July 2, 1950 – Today I went to VAC to see the sisters from my convent who had been taken there by the secret police. About 500 nuns from various religious communities are crowded into the bishop's residence. Many of them sleep on straw on the floor. They are not allowed to leave the building and they are in the dark as to their future.

"May 15, 1955 – It is a long time since I have written in my diary – almost three years. In prison we were not allowed to have any paper or pencil. To be at home! What a joy to be with mother, to walk around freely, to open and close doors with my own hands, even to be able to turn on and off the lights.

"I have not seen mother Barbra since 1952. That year life for nearly all religious became desperate. Many of our sisters could get jobs only as factory workers or as cleaning women and cooks in private homes. The only job one of our nuns could find was shoveling scrap iron at a steel plant. Another nun became a street sweeper. Both had degrees in higher education.

"Sisters in other countries invited us to continue our religious lives in freedom in the west – but that would mean taking the risk of trying to escape across the border. I received an invitation from a convent in another country. With two other sisters and a trusted guard, I started on a journey which was to take us north into Czechoslovakia and then west across the border into Austria. We were advised to take this route because the Czech border was not mined as heavily as the Hungarian border.

"In a small canoe, we crossed the Danube River into Czechoslovakia during the night. We took a train to a small village, hid out in a peasant's house for several days, and then took a train to Bratislava. There we were joined by 16 other people for the most dangerous part of our journey.

"Our companions were an elderly couple with their daughter and five year old grandson, a woman with two daughters, ages 12 and 15, another couple with their 18 year old son, a young couple with a one year old son who was given a sleeping pill to keep him quiet, and four other adults who desperately wanted to reach the free world.

"After sunset, we left the city on foot. We were unpleasantly surprised to find the meadows and fields covered by fresh snow. Fortunately, our guide was able to find the route he had planned. Most of the time we followed each other in single file, or two by two.

"Our guide led us forward in the pitch blackness of a night that seemed to have no end. From time to time, we heard dogs barking in the distance and we would immediately stop. Twice we dropped flat on the ground to hide from passersby or from border guards.

"Just before midnight, we arrived at a triple woven barbed wire fence. Our guide pulled the wires apart to help each of us crawl through. After crossing some railroad tracks, we rested for a bit, as we were tired from hiking thru the fields, which were kept freshly plowed to make it easier for the border police to catch people trying to escape.

"Our guide told us, 'Within ten minutes we will be in Austria,' pointing in the direction of an Austrian village. We could see a light in the far distance. The guide went ahead to find the Austrian guards he was supposed to know. Obeying his instructions, we followed him single file in a long stretched out line, leaving plenty of space between each person. We had walked only a couple of minutes when Sister Marie stopped and said, 'I can't go any further. I am too tired. Leave me here. At least you can escape.'

"'You can't stay behind,' I told her. 'It's a matter of life or death.' I offered her my arm and tried to help her but she just couldn't walk.

"Meanwhile, a full moon had lighted the countryside. I looked around for our third sister to help me. At that moment, I saw that the family in front of us had stopped and knelt down. We did likewise, just as our guide had instructed us before we began our flight.

"Just then, a flare went up high in the sky above us. From behind us, somewhere to our right, a spray of bullets came our way. At the first fusillade, Sister Maria, who was kneeling at my right, cried out, 'I'm shot.' She fell to the ground, her arms stretched out toward me. I hugged the ground beside her in the snow and, instinctively, made an act of contrition.

"A second flare went off, and all I could think of was that I was not ready to die. Suddenly, I had a passionate desire to live. There were two more volleys of shots, and bullets fell like hailstones all around us. Maria cried out in pain three times before I could clamp my hand over her mouth so she would not betray our position.

"But it was too late. In a matter of moments we were surrounded by the Czech border police. Their guns pointed directly at us and their police dogs were held at leash length. While I was still on the ground, the police chained my hands behind my back, then pulled me up to my feet. I asked them to help Maria up. They shone their flashlights on her face, took a look, and made a negative gesture. She was dead. They left her there.

"I was surrounded by three of the guards. They led me toward another group a few yards away. Then one of the guards put out his foot and tripped me so that I fell in the snow with both my hands tied behind my back. As I looked around, I saw a sight I shall never forget.

"Behind us lay the elderly couple, their daughter and grandson, and a bachelor who had carried the boy on his back. The two women were dead. The grandfather was lying on his back, moaning in his death agony. The boy had been wounded in the back. The bachelor lay with his hands bound behind his back. His left leg was bleeding profusely. We were blindfolded and taken to the Bratislava city jail, where we were interrogated. We were tried and imprisoned. Each of us ceased to be a person and was known only by a number.

"During this year in prison, only Divine Providence helped me retain my sanity and humanity. After four months some thirty priests were transferred from another jail to ours. One told me that some of them managed to offer mass secretly and he promised to bring me the Blessed Sacrament the next day. As I meditated and offered adoration in anticipation, I had the great consolation to know that Christ was my companion not only in the peaceful convent, but even in this wretched prison.

"One of my companions in prison was a 72 year old widow who had escaped deportation in 1951 by swimming across the Danube into Czechoslovakia. That was the year the Hungarian government carried out mass deportations from the larger cities in order to eliminate the educated non-communist middle class. She was one of more than eighty Hungarians I had met in prison who had tried to escape from Hungary through Czechoslovakia into Austria.

"She desperately had wanted to reach her children in West Germany. For several months, she tried to find a guide who would lead her across the border into Austria. She spent many nights sleeping under the bushes in public parks, in the waiting rooms at railroad stations. Finally she found a man who agreed to help her for a certain price. After pocketing his fee, he led her straight into the hands of the Czech border police!

"My most depressing recollection was the period when I was confined to a cell whose only window overlooked the prison yard where executions of political prisoners were carried out each Tuesday and Friday morning at 5:00 a.m. I would always pray for the doomed as they were hanged.

"These prison experiences helped me to realize that everything on earth has value only in the light of eternity. Whatever cannot be made to serve our passage to eternal life, is not worthy of our attachment. We must always be ready to give an account of our actions.

"My release from prison came at daybreak. I walked through the empty streets of Kalocsa to the cathedral. Its doors were not yet open. I knelt on the step in front of the locked gate and thanked God for helping me to survive."

No. 49—September, 1974 Rudolph M. Unger

Chapter 50

Rhetoric and literature today, as down through history, is replete with someone or another's master plan to create Utopia, heaven on earth. The bright geniuses who beget all these phantasms miss the mark. Why? Because they lack common sense.

Man's need and the answer to that need does not lie in some grandiose, supercalifragilistic plan. It lies in something very simple, something within the reach of every human being. It reflects the simple wisdom of God.

In 1965, the writer submitted two letters dealing with this idea to the "New World," the Chicago Catholic Archdiocese newspaper. Not surprisingly, neither letter was published. The writer believes the points they raise are as germane today as they were then.

The first letter (March 24, 1965):

"Father Robert M. Kearns of the Archdiocese's urban affairs office, one of the recent political adjuncts to the chancery, recently rose to the public defense of priests and nuns on the firing line in Selma, Alabama, by quoting what he said was a statement approved at the Ecumenical Council.

"The statement read:

'Because the human race today is joining more and more into a civic, economic, and social unity, it is more necessary that priests by combined efforts and aid under the leadership of the bishops and the supreme pontiff wipe out every kind of separateness so that the whole human race may be brought into the unity of the family of God.'

"The first part of this quote is not a statement of fact and is unrelated to reality. Rather it is a statement of the vain hope of pseudo-liberals, in and out of the church, for their illusory vision of one world.

"This vision is the proclaimed and unretracted goal of the communist party, which is an instrumentality of the devil. The only manner in which mankind ever will see one world is under totalitarian rule, for it is a totalitarian concept, obtainable only by totalitarian means...be they labeled communist, socialist, fascist, or even that non-existent contradiction – the Christian welfare state.

"And the second portion of the above quote is certainly a statement of totalitarian intention – 'to wipe out every kind of separateness.'

"The quarrel of the pseudo-liberals is with God. He didn't consult them before he created human nature. God made man diverse. And diverse he shall stay, one man or all men not withstanding.

"The pseudo-liberals hate diversity and difference. They abhor independence and freedom. For these give the lie to, make a mockery of, their own pretensions to moral and intellectual superiority.

"In their blind, arrogant pride, they presume they can pervert man's nature by ultimately making all men identical via the creation of one race, one language, one culture, one religion, and one all encompassing leviathan to impose this solidarity.

"Thus, they conceive, they would arrive at the millennium by having wiped out all distinctions in mankind.

"Where they to arrive at this point in their unobtainable quest for the great never-never land, induced by addiction to intellectual conceit, they would find to their chagrin that their journey in search of mankind's oblivion would just have begun.

"They would then have to begin the task of eradicating the independent mind and free will of every human creature dwelling on the face of the earth.

"The family of God, having been created by God, can be unified only by God's method and not that of man or the devil. Man, inspired by the devil, seeks to impose his own will on his fellow men by the use of political, economic, and social force, power, control, which is irreconcilable with human nature and therefore doomed to failure.

"Whereas God conquers and brings the members of His family into communion with His love, truth, and beauty, which correlate with the freedom, independence, and uniqueness He put in each of His creatures.

"God respects the individual human He has seen fit in His eternal wisdom to create. It is a shame so many members of mankind do not."

The second letter (August 7, 1965):

"May I share with your readers some wisdom I recently read?:

'How far wide of the mark we have gone in our times searching for remedies for the unhappiness of man!

'We have piled up gifts before man like peace offerings before the idol of an angry God, remotely hoping that some one or the other would please him.

'On the positive side we have talked of better housing, better food, more education, more culture, more leisure, more health – all of them good. But was it not evident from the first that thousands of men and women who had all of these things were desperately unhappy?

'So we went to the negative side, saying it was not something that men lacked, but something they already had which was making them unhappy. We took away the notion of sin, of God, of a soul, of a free will, even of an intellect. We took away all restraint from the passions, all responsibility from actions, all meaning from life, and was man made more happy?

'We failed, utterly, miserably. And we will continue to fail until we are willing to face the awful but inspiring truth that the will of man is the sole sufficient cause of unhappiness of man. Awful because it puts the responsibility directly into our hands. Inspiring because it puts the destruction of unhappiness within our power.

'The bad will of man is the sole sufficient cause of sin. This is the root of human unhappiness. Other things may make life unpleasant, uncomfortable, extraordinarily difficult, but not necessarily unhappy. We can find happiness amidst the most abject poverty, in squalor, in sickness, in ignorance, in terrible physical fatigue, in back breaking labor. But happiness is not to be found in the heart of a sinner.

'The remedy for unhappiness is good will. It was most fitting that the message of the angels 'Peace To Men Of Good Will' should have been delivered to ignorant shepherds. It should have shocked us into the realization that good will is independent of the circumstances of life, that good will is the ultimate foundation for peace even in this life of ours.

'For where can there be peace where there is no happiness and where can there be happiness without the cause of happiness? God would not put us at the mercy of circumstances which for the most part are out of our control.

'Human happiness was intended for every man, put within the grasp of every man, independent of the world he lived in, independent of the activities of other men, of devils, even of angels.

'It was to flow from the good will of the individual man.'

"The above excerpt is from the late Father Walter Farrell's 'A Companion To The Summa.' He, of course, was merely elucidating St. Thomas Aquinas.

"Aquinas, of course, is little known and passe in our modern society. Even, unfortunately, throughout much of holy mother church."

As another wise man rarely read by moderns wrote:

"If you can keep your head when all about you are losing theirs…If you can trust yourself when all men doubt you…If being lied about, you don't deal in lies, or being hated, don't give way to hating…

"If you can dream – and not make dreams your master. If you can think – and not make thoughts your aim. If you can meet with triumph and disaster and treat these two imposters just the same. If you can bear to hear the truth you've spoken twisted by knaves to make a trap for fools, or watch the things you gave your life to, broken, and stoop and build 'em up with worn-out tools…

"If you can force your heart and nerve and sinew to serve your turn long after they are gone, and so hold on when there is nothing in you except the will which says to them – 'hold on!'

"If you can talk with crowds and keep your virtue, or walk with kings, nor lose the common touch. If neither foes nor loving friends can hurt you, if all men count with you, but none too much.

"If you can fill the unforgiving minute with sixty seconds worth of distance run, yours is the earth and everything that's in it, and – which is more – you'll be a man, my son!" (Rudyard Kipling)

No. 50—October, 1974 Rudolph M. Unger

Chapter 51

One man trying to control another, one group trying to regulate another, one government trying to dominate another. My power over your freedom. I master, you servant.

That's the story down through history, the reason for, the cause of the friction that mars the harmony of man.

Unity? Oh yes, by all means. But on my terms, my conditions, not yours. After all, ultimately, it is, of course, a question of who is the better, the greater, the more qualified, the more moral, the more intelligent, the stronger, yes – the really key word – the most powerful.

When this mentality is capable of exerting itself on an international scale, then it becomes a matter of imperialism, of empire. And this mentality wears many garbs – from the most cruel, blatant, to the most benign, benevolent. From atheistic to Christian.

In an article in the "Intercollegiate Review" in 1966, entitled, "Imperialism: The Threat To Existence", Leo Paul de Alvarez, a political philosophy teacher at the University of Dallas, described the various types of empires down thru history.

The excerpts from his article which follow are confined to two types, two – perhaps they are really one – which frequently, generally, are not even considered by many to be imperialism. On the contrary, many believe them to be the ideal, the ultimate fulfillment of Christian Democracy.

What these believers – and they reside in the highest seats of spiritual and secular authority and power – forget, are the words of Christ:

"Render unto Caesar the things that are Caesar's and unto God the things that are God's" and "My kingdom is not of this world."

Alvarez wrote:

"Each of these great empires makes the claim that it alone possesses authority, imperium, over the peoples of the world. Further, the expansion of the empire, that is, imperialism, is considered simply a legitimate exercise of power.

"One may summarize the essence of empire in one phrase – it is the pretension to universality and uniqueness.

"Universality signifies that the empire claims to be the political representative of all mankind. There are no legitimate alternatives to oppose its claim.

"The claim to legitimate rule is based, furthermore, upon a heresy derived from the revealed faiths.

"The realization that mankind is one was a great spiritual event in history. To reach through the boundaries of one's community to the idea that there can be a common bond with men of other communities requires the conception that all men belong to 'a higher community.'

"This higher community must transcend all political communities – it must thus be a spiritual community. But the discovery of the transcendent community throws a shadow on the status of the political community. Can a man who is open to the transcendent community give his full allegiance to the earthly community to which he belongs?

"The solution that remains for the political community is to appropriate for itself the symbols of the transcendent order. The tension between the citizen's loyalty to the political order and to the transcendent order is resolved.

"The temporal community is the earthly incarnation of the transcendent order. Such is the pretension of the world empire. The world empire appropriates the symbols of the order of the soul. It places itself forward as the earthly reproduction of the divine order.

"There is the empire that bases itself upon a revealed faith, upon the discovery of a personal God – a God who speaks with man. The man to whom he speaks is truly a chosen man. His task is to communicate the new truth revealed to him to other men.

"The community he forms is a chosen community for no other community has revealed truth. That truth, of course, is a truth for all men. But there can occur a profound misunderstanding of revelation, and the community that considers itself chosen may seek to establish itself as a political rather than a spiritual community.

"The empire declares itself the mediator between God and man. It now has a two fold task – to spread the new truth and to defend its purity. Hence we call empires of this type, orthodox empires.

"Examples of such empires are the Holy Roman Empire, Byzantium, the Russian Orthodox Empire, and the Muslim Caliphate.

"The empire is the political expression of the human desire to incarnate the eternal in the secular. It is the political imitation of the universality of the spiritual realm.

"The empire is a doomed human enterprise with a paradox at its very heart – the attempt to express adequately the universality of the divine in a particular political structure.

"Incredible pride is therefore inherent in the idea of the empire. Incredible pride because it supposes that the political order that exists in 27 B.C., or 220 A.D., or 800 A.D., is the only possible order mankind can articulate.

"A failure to understand that there is an abyss between the divine universal order and finite political orders has occurred.

"Imperialism is a destructive demonic force. St. Augustine emphatically makes this point in the opening books of his 'City of God' when he condemns the Roman empire.

"The universalization of a particular political order leads inevitably to the destruction of all other political orders. A reduction of existence takes place, a narrowing of existence...only the universalized particular is allowed existence.

"Put in an abstract manner, we lose touch with the horror of empire. We fully comprehend, however, the horror of something like Nazism. It proclaimed that only one race deserved existence. A particular race was declared the universal race. A deliberate policy of reducing mankind to this one race followed. What the results were we all know.

"The meaning of universalizing a particular political order can perhaps be better understood if I take another contemporary example.

"A powerful movement exists today whose purpose is to establish a world community. I have noted a tendency in the literature of this movement to argue that one form and only one form of political order is good for mankind – and that is democracy.

"Now the establishment of a world democratic community that would embrace all the presently existing peoples of the world would be the establishment of a form of empire.

"All that will be done by the formation of a world democratic community is to pretend that the form of government that certain men of the past 300 years have considered good – for not all have agreed that it is good – is one that is eternally good.

"A movement to establish a world democratic community and a movement to establish an empire based upon race are in principle not different. One imperialism is, of course, much more bearable than another, as Roman imperialism was much more bearable than Assyrian imperialism.

"One imperialism may be morally on a higher plane than another, as democratic imperialism is on a far higher moral plane than Nazi imperialism.

"They are, however, all imperialisms, and, make no mistake about it, they all inflict immense destruction upon mankind – though, again, one imperialism may be far more destructive than another.

"An empire poses a threat worse than threat of physical death to the members of other communities. It tells them that what they are, their very being, is a meaningless one.

"The empire desires to take all men and mold them in its own image – and it is this threat to the meaning of their existence, that arouses the deepest hatreds of the peoples conquered by the empire.

"Imperial domination causes great psychic shock. The shattering blow of imperial domination causes first great apathy, a stunned silence, and then a fierce and total rebellion. Let the hand of imperial domination lift for a moment and the total rebellion in the soul of the conquered explodes into overt acts of violence and war."

No. 51—November, 1974 Rudolph M. Unger

Chapter 52

Where in our time is God's Moses, saying to the communist imperialists, and to all the other statist imperialists, of every form, – "The Lord God sayeth, 'Let my people go!'"?

Prophets down through history have frequently been without honor in their nations in their time. Why? Because they speak the truth and their countrymen do not want to hear it nor believe it.

Whittaker Chambers was such a man in America in the 20th century. Why was he not recognized and appreciated? The following excerpts from his "Witness" tell why. They, likewise, explain why America and Western Christian Civilization are dying.

He wrote:

"The communist vision is the vision of man without God. It is the vision of man's mind displacing God as the creative intelligence of the world. It is the vision of materialism.

"It is an intensely practical vision. The tools to turn it into reality are at hand – science and technology, whose traditional method – the rigorous exclusion of all supernatural factors in solving problems – has contributed to the intellectual climate in which the vision flourishes.

"The vision is shared by millions who are not communists. They are part of communism's secret strength.

"The crisis of communism exists to the degree in which it has failed to free the peoples that it rules from God. The crisis of the western world exists to the degree in which it actually shares communism's materialist vision, is dazzled by the logic of the materialist interpretation of history, politics, and economics.

"The 20th century is the first in which a decisive part of the most articulate section of mankind has not merely ceased to believe in God, but has deliberately rejected God. It is the century in which this religious rejection has taken a specifically political form.

"At every point, religion and politics interlace, and must do so more acutely as the conflict between the two great camps of men – those who reject and those who worship God – becomes irrepressible. Those camps are not only outside, but also within nations.

"The most conspicuously menacing form of that rejection is communism. But there are other forms of the same rejection, which in any case, communism did not originate, but merely adopted and adapted.

"One who breaks from and fights communism must do so amidst the deafening chatter and verbal droppings of those who sit above the battle, who lack the power to act for good or evil, because they lack any power to act at all, and who, in the day when heaven was falling, were, in Dante's words, neither for God nor for Satan, but were for themselves.

"Such a fighter is taught by experience that there is a gulf fixed between the reality he must warn against and the ability of the world to grasp his warnings.

"When my information in 1939 about the communist conspiracy inside the government in Washington – given to Adolph Berle, assistant secretary of state, – was dismissed laughingly by President Roosevelt, with astonishment I took my first hard look at the New Deal.

"All the New Dealers I had known were communists or near communists. None of them took the New Deal seriously as an end in itself. They regarded it as an instrument for gaining their own revolutionary ends.

"I began to realize that the inner drift of this great movement known as the New Deal was prevailingly toward socialism, through the mass of those who, in part directed, in part were carried along by it, sincerely supposed that they were liberals.

"I saw that the New Deal was only superfically a reform movement. I had to acknowledge the truth of what its more forthright protagonists, sometimes unwarily, some defiantly, averred – the New Deal was a genuine revolution, whose deepest purpose was not simply reform within existing traditions, but a basic change in the social, and, above all, the power relationships in the nation.

"It was not a revolution by violence. It was a revolution by bookkeeping and lawmaking. In so far as it was successful, the power of politics has replaced the power of business.

"This is the basic power shift of all the revolutions of our time. This shift was the revolution. It was only of incidental interest that the revolution was not complete, that it was not made by tanks and machine guns, but by acts of congress and decisions of the Supreme Court, or that many of the revolutionists did not know what they were or denied it.

"But revolution is always an affair of force, whatever forms the force disguises itself in. Whether the revolutionists prefer to call themselves Fabians, who seek power by the inevitability of gradualism, or Bolsheviks, who seek power by the dictatorship of the proletariat, the struggle is for power.

"Now I began to see how it was that so many Communist were clustered in government and how it was possible for them to operate so freely with so little fear of detection.

"At the basic point of the revolution—the shift of power from business to government—the two kinds of revolutionists were at one. They shared many other views and hopes. Those many who sincerely abhorred the word communism, in the pursuit of common ends found that they were unable to distinguish the communists from themselves.

"These men, who honestly could not see that what they firmly believed was liberalism added up to socialism, could scarcely be expected to see what added up to communism.

"Any charge of communism enraged them precisely because they could not grasp the differences between themselves and those against whom it was made. But as the struggle was for revolutionary power, that was the point at which they betrayed their real character. For they reacted not like liberals, but with the fierceness of revolutionists whenever that power was at issue.

"Every move against the communists was felt by the liberals as a move against themselves. The communists knew that they had only to shout their innocence and cry 'witch hunt' for the liberals to rally in all innocence to their defense.

"I did not know, I could not have dreamed of the immense scope and power of Alger Hiss' political alliances and his social connections, which cut across all party lines and ran from the supreme court to the Quakers, from governors of states and instructors in college faculties, to the staff members of liberal magazines.

"He had used his career, particularly his identification with the cause of peace thru his part in organizing the United Nations, to put down roots that made him one with the American upper class, enlightened middle class, liberal and official life. His roots could not be disturbed without disturbing all the roots on all sides of him.

"I had attacked an architect of the U.N. And the partisans of peace fell upon me like combat troops. I had attacked an intellectual and a 'liberal'. A whole generation felt itself to be on trial – and with pretty good reason too.

"From their roosts in the great cities, and certain college eyries, the left wing intellectuals of almost every feather swooped and hovered and gave vent to hoarse cries and defilements.

"I had also accused a 'certified gentleman' and the 'conspiracy of gentlemen' closed its retaliatory ranks against me.

"The simple fact is that when I took up my little sling and aimed at communism, I also hit something else. What I hit was the forces of the great socialist revolution, which, in the name of liberalism, spasmodically, incompletely, somewhat formlessly, but always in the same direction, has been inching its ice cap over the nation for decades.

"My opinion of the revolution is not at issue. It is a statement of fact that need startle no one who has voted for that revolution in whole or in part. And consciously or unconsciously, a majority of the nation has so voted for years."

No. 52—December, 1974 Rudolph M. Unger

Chapter 53

Life is a riddle which man is ever trying to solve. Proof?

Well, believe it or not, in the diversity of life there is a unity, a relationship among the bits and pieces that creates a harmonious whole. Just like a jigsaw puzzle.

It is something that is not readily apparent to us. It is a big part of that paradox of life which generally befuddles our dim minds. To God it is clear as crystal, or, a completed puzzle; for He perceives the pattern of the whole.

To us it is frequently clear as mud. All we see is the bits and pieces and we have to keep searching for the relationship between them that makes them whole.

This month's offering will be an example of that inter-relationship of seemingly unrelated things. There follow comments by two men with totally different backgrounds, writing 22 years apart on two subjects which on the surface seemingly have no relationship.

And that's what each of them is talking about – in different ways – that is the common thread that runs through the seemingly unrelated articles – relationship.

The relationship of man – to his God, to his fellow man on a personal basis, and the collective projection of that relationship on a nation to nation basis.

And relationship is perhaps the toughest single job man has.

We will proceed from the general to the particular. See if you see the relationship between the two articles. Then see if you perceive their relationship to recent articles that appeared in this newsletter and current ones appearing in the sister epistle.

The first article was written as part of a debate on world government in the University of Notre Dame student magazine "Scholastic", on February 15, 1952, by the late Waldemar Gurian. Gurian, a political science professor, was a refugee from Nazi Germany and was regarded as one of the world's foremost authorities on communism.

"World government is regarded by many as necessary in order to establish lasting peace," wrote Gurian. "They believe that there must be wars as long as national sovereignity exists. Wars can disappear only if these sovereign governments are replaced by one government, for this world government could not start a fight against itself.

"This argument is impressive – but it proves erroneous as soon as we analyze it. Will all nations and territories be always satisfied with the policies of world government?

"Even if the world government is successfully established, there is no guarantee against revolts or revolutions. The claim of such men as Mortimer Adler, R.M. Hutchins, and G. Borgese that lasting peace will be the necessary result of world government is wrong.

"Further, it ought to be realized that world government cannot be set up as a federal organization. It can be created only by a political group with overwhelming power. This Hegemonial group must be strong enough to impose its will upon the whole world and to maintain permanently its superiority of power.

"World government is possible only as world tyranny, operating in the same way as the totalitarian rule of the communist minority over the masses in the Soviet Union and its satellites.

"Finally, how could world government be established today without a world war? For the Soviet Union would accept only a world government under control of its communist leadership – the soviet system must be wiped out before a world government under control of the United States could be erected.

"By the way, the people of the United States would reject an American world domination, which would demand armaments on a gigantic scale and make the United States into a permanent garrison.

"Therefore, I regard world government not as a means to establish peace; just because I am for a policy having peace as its aim, I am against world government. Those who demand world government as the single sovereign power in the world, are working (against their conscious will) for war.

"Sometimes the term 'world government' is used to characterize the necessity of a moral unity of mankind. This demand is quite different from the request for an organized political world government. Working for such a moral unity means truly working for peace.

"Realistic policies which try to establish closer cooperation among nations to overcome for example, the outdated conflicts between European nations by trying to establish a United Europe, must also be clearly distinguished from the Utopian perfectionist claim for organized world government.

"The Utopian perfectionism is unrealistic because it does not see the human nature as it exists, and, believes that institutional gadgets can bring about paradise on earth.

"The demand for world government is a typical expression of that pseudo-legal and pseudo-moral approach which, according to the wise American diplomat, the U.S. Ambassador to Moscow, Mr. George Kennan, is the greatest threat to a sound American foreign policy aiming at securing peace, as well as at safeguarding national interest, and achieving the maximum of justice possible under existing conditions."

In an article entitled "Freedom And Responsibility", Dr. Harold Blake Walker, the superlative religion columnist for the Chicago Tribune, on February 10, 1974, wrote:

"To those of us who believe in freedom, it is disturbing to notice that two-thirds or more of the world's people in the developing countries appear willing to exchange freedom for order, or, for order in tandem with economic growth and national prestige.

"The assumption seems to be that progress requires ultimate external restraint and coercion to limit the freedom of men to speak and to act as individuals.

"We in the western world have inherited faith in freedom, a firm belief that progress comes as a result of individual initiative and struggle. Traditionally we have assumed that in the Providence of God, reason will triumph over unreason, and truth over falsehood.

"We have been willing to risk the interplay of competitive forces with a minimum of external regulation.

"Now and then we have doubted our own faith, wondering if law and order could be maintained in a free society. Under stress, we have been tempted to exchange freedom for order, as if freedom might be too great a luxury to be endured in a disrupted society.

"At the moment, we seem to be uncertain of ourselves. Arthur Bremer, who shot Governor George Wallace, suggested a disturbing mood when he remarked, 'I would have liked it if society had protected me from myself.'

"In the past, society has sought to protect us from ourselves with moral sanctions, established conventions simply perceived and accepted by consensus.

"In a higher sense, morality is a matter of the spirit. Socrates called it 'integrity of soul.' It goes beyond customs or social regulations and involves inner integrity, respect for the rights of others, and caring concern for persons.

"It is only as society helps to inspire inner integrity in persons that society is able to protect us more adequately from ourselves and to undergird social order. Edmund Burke back in the 18th century wrote:

'Men are qualified for civil liberties in exact proportion to their disposition to put moral chains on their own appetites. Society cannot exist unless a controlling power upon will and appetite be placed somewhere. And the less of it there is within, the more there must be without. It is ordained, in the internal constitution of things, that men of intemperate minds cannot be free. Their passions forge their fetters.'

"The weakening of those inner moral chains that protect both ourselves and society has been coincident with the decline of religion in our time. Having forsaken both Sinai and Golgotha as symbols of the highest, we have underminded the ethical foundations on which freedom rests. If we wish both freedom and order, we must affirm once again, 'In God We Trust.'"

No. 53—January, 1975 Rudolph M. Unger

Chapter 54

Our age is an age of conceit. It acknowledges and tolerates nothing that is not of itself. It shuns history and tradition. It deprecates the knowledge, experience, and wisdom of those that have gone before.

The zeitgeist, that is, the spirit of the times, is the great motivating and guiding force which determines what men will be like. It is the focal point, the focus, the fulcrum on which everything turns.

For ours is an intelligent, educated, sophisicated, emancipated, beneficient age, the likes of which the world has never before seen. And all those who have existed before, by comparison, are crude, ignorant, provincial, and incompetent.

Contemporanity…that is the criteria, that is the standard, by which all and everything is compared, judged, accepted or rejected. If it is not of us, of our creation, of our doing, if it doesn't have our fine hand in it, it isn't worthy of consideration.

The zeitgeist, the God of contemporanity, has infected not only the world. It has also left its diseasing touch on the church. With the death of Pius XII, the new leaders of the church couldn't hasten quickly enough, in a spirit of "We know better and we love better", to throw open all the pandora boxes that Pius and his predecessors had labored so to keep shut, knowing the perfumed, insidious, narcotizing contents within.

The area where the damage is most obvious and most pervasive is, of course, in the liturgy. The new order is in. The old order is verboten. And, brothers and sisters in love, you better believe that!

Still, here and there, there still remain a few flickering candles, striving valiantly to keep the light of tradition burning in the darkness of our antisepticized cathedrals and churches.

One such is Father Blase Schauer, a Dominican priest in Santa Fe, New Mexico, who was granted by Archbishop James P. Davis the use of his empty Immaculate Heart seminary to set up a parish and a pastoral liturgist institute. His work there was described by Father Gerald A. Buckley, another Dominican, in an article in the "Catholic Currents" newspaper on June 1, 1973.

"During the summer the parish becomes an institute where Father Schauer gathers the finest pastoral men he can find and turns them loose on priests and seminarians who have come to the ancient city, out of curiosity or conviction, to learn from his program," began Father Buckley.

"Father Schauer is one of the foremost pastoral liturgists in the country. Yet he is something of a maverick whom many of his colleagues choose to ignore.

'They have never forgiven me,' he said, 'since that national liturgical bash a few years back when I challenged a whole board of breast-beating 'experts.'

"He was referring to the national liturgical convention in Kansas City in 1967. The theme of social relevance dominated everything and American liturgists initiated their game of footsies with Harvey Cox secularism by launching a thousand balloons into the atmosphere.

"Father Schauer committed the ultimate sin. He insisted publicly upon the sacred dimensions of the liturgy and the priesthood. Unwilling to answer him rationally, the convention directors flicked their hands and dismissed him as a pitiable mossback, a sourdough triumphalist kook from the western desert.

"In an age that has canonized the hesitant and the confused, Father Schauer has the self assurance and fighting qualities of a game cock, his self assurance comes from nothing less than a solid mooring in sacred scripture, the theology of St. Thomas Aquinas, and the writing of psychologists like Jung and religious anthropologists like Eliade.

'Jung tells us of the Catholic's greater psychic strength because the rich symbolism of his worship keeps his keel even,' noted Father Schauer. 'Eliade reminds us constantly of the deep need for the sacred in our lives – sacred persons, places, things, actions. Get rid of this dimension, as modern secular man has done, and you are a sick man.'

"As for St. Thomas, Father Schauer reads him constantly.

'I see the need for St. Thomas today more than ever,' he comments. 'Thomas probes the essential, the universal. Priests and seminarians are intrigued by sociology. What could be more superficial, more ephemeral than sociology. Where is the wisdom to it? We have got to reassume the role of spiritual leaders, not remain feathers to be whisked along by the latest existentialist sneeze.'

"Father Schauer had studied music at Berkeley and Columbia, and for a while had drifted away from the faith. 'We arty people were expected to be Bohemian,' he recalled with a smile, 'and some of us deceived ourselves into thinking we were.'

"A singular episode, one that would have a lot to do with Father Schauer's future outlook, recalled him to the faith. It was the sight of a man unashamedly crossing himself and offering grace before a meal in a Manhattan restaurant.

'The deep symbolism of that sign of the cross, expressed so publicly, rekindled in me the fire of my own heritage – the profound faith of my German and Italian ancestors, and the deep Catholicism of the very soil of Spanish New Mexico where I grew up,' he remarked.

"Having won his degree in musical criticism, he joined the Dominican order in 1950 at the age of 30. Strangely enough, his appreciation for theology did not come during his seminary years, but later, when he was out in the apostolate.

'Book learning has always been sterile for me,' he said. 'A priest has got to apply his long training to appreciate it. Even resent the term, pastoral liturgist, if a liturgist isn't pastoral, he isn't a liturgist.

'Every priest has got to be a liturgist. He has got to stand between the people the church has committed to him and their God. He has got to help the people in their longing to achieve a sense of God's transcendence and holiness.

'As a pastor, I am for my people. As a teacher, I want priests. They are the ones who have got to learn. Unfortunately, we never draw enough of them.

'To help a priest understand and appreciate the deep riches of his traditions is not the 'in' thing.'

"Today, Father Schauer views the American church with sadness. 'When modern man lost his sense of symbol,' he notes, 'he lost his sense of celebration. Look how we push our commemorative holidays now to the 'long weekend'. We don't give a hoot about the meaning of the holiday itself. It is just time off.

'Catholics have lost the sense of the saints' days. This includes the priests. We have been in the grip of a madness, but I think the worst is over. We shall start rediscovering. We shall have to.'

"The Dominican includes such traditional devotions as the rosary, the daily angelus, and benediction of the Blessed Sacrament in his parish services. Gregorian Chant has become a part of every larger feast, as has the use of incense.

'It is amazing how the people, especially the young people, take to Gregorian Chant,' he said. 'Nothing keep us in better contact with our ancient rootings.'

"He recalled in his student chaplain days at New Mexico state university, where his work won him the award for the nation's best Newman program, he used to travel to various campuses spreading his ideas and raising funds.

'The Protestants and Jews would give me a better reception than Catholic colleges,' he noted. 'They had gone the route. They wanted back into the sacred.'

"Father Schauer insists on being called 'father' by his congregation. 'It is a small thing, but an important symbol,' he remarked. 'Once we let ourselves be called 'Jack' or 'Blase', the deep implication of what we are becomes blurred, and the people don't know what we are. And then we don't know!'

"As for sisters and priests who have given up their religious garb, he says, 'I feel sorry for them. They are schizophrenic. They don their garb only to demonstrate politically. Otherwise, they don't want to stand for anything. They want anonymity. Then they go on talking about 'personal fufillment' but hide their dedication.'"

No. 54—February, 1975 Rudolph M. Unger

Chapter 55

The age of the martyrs is not at an end in the church. Amid the words of peace, the deeds of evil go on. While we in the United States have been spared the ultimate test, a vast, faceless, nameless, numberless array of our brothers are and have been suffering and dying for faith and for freedom in Europe and Asia.

Our recent portrayal of the struggle of Cardinal Mindszenty and the Hungarian people is but the tip of the iceberg that we in the western world see.

It was ever thus in the ebb and flow of the struggle between good and evil and it will be ever thus. Christ foretold it when he told the apostles:

"Behold I send you as sheep in the midst of wolves...And you shall be hated by men for My name's sake. But he that shall persevere unto the end, he shall be saved.

"The disciple is not above the master...if they have called the good man of the house Beelzebub, how much more them of his household...fear not...every one that shall confess Me before men, I will also confess him before My Father who is in heaven...he that shall lose his life for Me shall find it."

We do not have to go to other continents to find persecution. Less than fifty years ago, in the lifetime of many of us, we need only look south of the border in Mexico in the 1920s'.

In "The Life Of Father Miguel Pro" by The Reverend M.D. Forrest which recounts this persecution, the author remarks, "The names of Carranza, Obregon, and Calles will forever stain the pages of Mexican history.

"Under Carranza, soldiers perpretrated atrocities equal to those unspeakable outrages committed in Ireland by the Cromwellian Militia...Although he did not wage a bloody persecution, Obregon harassed the church unceasingly in a cunning, insidious manner ...In 1924 Obregon was succeeded by Calles, under whose regime a fierce persecution, claiming many martyrs, of whom 150 were priests, was waged from 1926 to 1929."

Father Pro had only been a priest for two years and three months when, at the orders of Calles, a firing squad executed him on November 23, 1927, at the age of 36.

But as Father Forrest wrote, "A classmate of Father Pro told me that the young Jesuit had done the work of seven priests during his 16 months apostolate in Mexico City.

"And another young Mexican Jesuit said that Father Pro was a martyr in a twofold sense of the term, for he had undergone severe physical suffering for many years and had borne it with heroic patience and even cheerfulness.

"This had included three severe operations within six months, including one that had to be performed without anaesthetic, and in midst of which physical sufferings, as Father Pro had written, 'God our Lord willed to send me the hardest trial for my heart – the death of my holy and beloved mother.'"

The scene was set for the supreme sacrifice by Father Pro and the other seven score priests, Father Forrest noted:

"When Calles in July, 1926, promulgated a new law, which laicized (or rather, rendered atheistic) all education, dissolved all religious orders, forbade priests to criticize, even in private, the government or the laws of the country; restricted public worship to the interior of churches, put all public worship under the supervision of the secular power, and declared all churches, monasteries, convents, and other religious buildings to be the property of the state.

"The bishops of the Mexican Republic, a week before the satanic decree of Calles was to go into effect, issued an official statement to the Catholics of the nation:

'Since the conditions imposed render impossible the continuation of the sacred ministry, we have decided, after consulting our most holy father, Pius XI, that, from July 31 until we determine otherwise, all public worship requiring the participation of priests will be suspended.

'The life of the church is that of its Divine Founder. Thus beloved children, the church of Mexico is today delivered up, persecuted, imprisoned, reduced to a state resembling death. But the Mexican Church also will, after a short period, rise again, full of life and strength, more vigorous than ever. Hold fast to this hope.'

"This episcopal proclamation, sanctioned in advance by the Holy See, by no means meant or implied that the bishops and priests were going to desert their people or leave them without the mass and sacraments.

"Quite the contrary, with a supernatural stubborness such as was displayed by the early popes, bishops, and priests during the ten great persecutions under the pagan Roman emperors; such as was manifested by the heroic clergy of England, Ireland, and Scotland during that long, dreary night of the penal laws; such as was still being shown by the courageous Russian clergy under Bolshevist despots, the Mexican clergy determined, even at the risk of imprisonment, torture, and execution, to stay with their beloved flock.

"The church in Mexico was driven underground by Godless tyrants. The ancient church of the Roman catacombs was renewed in a modern western republic. The radiance of the early Christian martyrs shone upon the faithful people of Mexico.

"A month before his martyrdom, Father Pro wrote a poem, excerpts from which follow:

'Our lovely temples bare and dismal stand, no chant of choir, no bells resound afar, dread silence hovers over our native land...no roses fill the church with fragrance sweet, no lighted candles on the altar glow, our naves are now as silent as the sombre night. All seems oblivion, sadness, sleep, and death ...souls trembling with the thought of 'morrow's grief, souls crushed beneath the present cross of pain,...the very breath of hell floats in the air. The cup of crime is filled by tyrant's hand. And through the hideous gloom no dawning fair of hope is seen to glimmer over the land. The barque of Peter on the stormy sea seems well-nigh wrecked by man's inquity... by our martyrs' blood for thee shed joyfully, return O Lord in haste to Thy dear sanctuary.'

"Father Pro had established 'eucharistic stations' thruout Mexico City. These were houses of reliable Catholics who were willing to incur any risk for their own faith and the salvation of others. In these houses he said mass and distributed communion to 200 to 300 persons a day.

"Masses were regularly celebrated, sick calls were promptly attended, baptism was administered, confessions were heard, sermons were preached, and even retreats conducted. And all this Father Pro did despite the vigilance of police and the espionage of detectives.

"He organized a company of 300 young men whom he trained as religious lecturers, hundreds of traveling catechists were organized, special attention was given to instructing children in the faith.

"Father Pro distributed religious leaflets, secretly printed, wherever he went. Once he and others used 600 balloons to disseminate thousands of such leaflets. With begged alms he was able to house and pay the rent for 96 impoverished families.

"On November 18, 1927, Father Pro and his two brothers, Humberto and Roberto, were arrested and falsely accused of conspiring in an assassination attempt on then General Obregon five days earlier.

"Calles ordered the execution of Father Pro and Humberto without even the semblance of a trial. 'I do not want forms, but the deed,' he ordered.

"At 10:20 a.m., November 23, 1927, Father Pro was taken from his dungeon to the place of execution. Leaving the cell, he turned to his brother and two other men who were to be shot moments after him and said, 'Goodbye my brothers, until we meet in heaven.'

"In the execution yard, he knelt, took from his pocket a crucifix, which he kissed and held in his right hand, and rosary, which he held in the left.

"He commended his soul to God and, refusing to be blindfolded as he stood erect, said calmly, 'Lord, thou knowest that I am innocent.' He then made the sign of the cross over the spectators and said to the firing squad, 'May God have mercy on you. May God bless you.'

"Stretching his arms in the form of a cross, he said, 'With all my heart I forgive my enemies.' He then said, 'Viva Cristo Reyi', 'Long live Christ The King.' The volley was fired and the beloved Father Pro, idol of the people of Mexico City, fell dead."

No. 55—March, 1975 Rudolph M. Unger

Chapter 56

What is it that makes a saint out of this mortal coil of ours? What is it that enables some even to rise to the heights of the martyrs?

What is it that motivates a young, vibrant, life-loving man like Father Miguel Pro to counter and overcome that most powerful instinct in our natural makeup – self-preservation – to give up life itself for something greater than life itself?

Where stems this power, whence springs this ability, which has been displayed by millions of the most valiant souls over the centuries, from small children to venerable elders?

The Australian priest, the Reverend M.D. Forrest, in his biography of the Mexican martyr, presents some of the sources of this nobility of the human spirit.

"Father Pro's parents were Miguel Pro and Josefina Juarez," began father Forrest. "Uncontaminated by modern paganism, they had a large family, being blessed with 11 children. Of these, four died in infancy, two became nuns, two were martyred, and three were married.

"Love of God and of home characterized the entire family. God came first in the life of each individual and in the family life. The bright light of Catholic faith illumined the home and the law of God and the church was unfailingly kept before the minds and hearts of the children by saintly parents.

"The family rosary was recited every night. Devotion to the Sacred Heart, to Mary Immaculate, to St. Joseph and the practice of the nine first Fridays were observed. Great attention was paid to the various festivals of the church.

"At Miguel's baptism, water from the river Jordan was used. In his tender years he overindulged in a certain Mexican fruit and was stricken with a severe malady.

"The doctors declared that he would either die or live on as a complete imbecile. For a year the child lived on, unable to speak, scarcely recognizing his parents, and then his condition became acute and he was at death's door.

"His father, profoundly moved and beside himself with grief, took the boy in his arms, held him as an offering before an antique picture of Our Lady of Guadalupe and from the recesses of his heart cried, 'My Mother, give me back my son.' The child was cured.

"A few years later, returning from hunting near his mining town, Miguel took a short cut, slipped, and caught his foot in the track of the railroad which conveyed the heated remnants from the smelting works.

"Unable to free himself as one of the cars bore down on him, he called on Mary Immaculate, promising sacrifices in her honor if she would deliver him to safety. His boot separated, leaving the sole behind, and he fled to safety.

'Since then,' he said, 'I made a compact with The Virgin that she would not let me go to purgatory and that I would be ever her faithful servant. Ever since she has been My Lady.'

"From his tenderest years, Miguel blended in his character a deep seriousness of thought with an irrepressible love of frolicsomeness. This spirit of gaiety and buoyancy was united in later life with deep piety, consuming zeal, and sublime heroism.

"Miguel Pro became one of those saints in whom grace leaves nature in possession of all those natural characteristics which are not sinful. And therefore, he was so beloved of the persecuted Mexican people to whom he ministered, in the face of the greatest danger, with irrepressible cheerfulness, loving interest and unselfishness, and indescribable zeal.

"His mother had the practice of visiting the sick poor mining families. With her children she visited them, taking food and medicine, and sending the children on errands for the incapacitated. Amidst great difficulties and personal privations, she finally established and maintained a free hospital for the sick and poor in the mining community.

"Miguel's frolicsomeness and faith were seen in the nocturnal excursions he would lead at 2 a.m. in 1910 to gaze on the Halley comet. Parading in the streets, he gave astronomy lessons to those who accompanied him.

"The enthusiasm of the group, engendered by the spirit of their leader, led a policeman to ascertain the cause of the gaiety in the middle of the night in the sleeping town. Seeing him, Miguel responded, 'We are peaceful people, but joyous' and he proceeded to quote verse for the perplexed officer.

"And then turning to the heavens, he spoke of, 'The blue heaven which would one day be his dwelling' a companion recalled, and, on witnessing the comet, he would exclaim, 'Praised be my Father God, who makes such beautiful things.'

"Years later, while catechizing in Spain during his study for the priesthood, he recounted how one day he had entered a Mexican church and heard a priest, in giving a sermon, remark, 'All this Jesus Christ did and suffered for us, and we, what are we doing for Him? He said that question, 'What have I done for Jesus?' was the turning point in his life and led him to the religious life.

"A Jesuit who knew him in the novitiate, recalled, 'Those who came in close contact with him could soon see that there were really two Pros. One of recreation and the other of prayer. One given to jokes, laughing, and singing, the other to self abnegation and silent suffering.'

"Upon his profession, Miguel wrote, 'Deceitful are the ephemeral pleasures and joys of this world. Our supreme comfort in this life is to die to the world that we may live with Jesus crucified.

'Let others seek gold and other earthly treasures. I already possess the immortal treasure of holy poverty on the cross of Jesus crucified. With the triple crown of poverty, chastity, and obedience, I can hope to pass beyond the fleeting confines of mortal man, by living poor on this earth and rich for heaven, united with Jesus crucified.'

"In the year following his ordination in Belgium, he wrote to others awaiting Holy Orders, 'On the day of my ordination, I asked one thing of God – to be useful to souls. For about a year now I have had the happiness of saying mass. I have not found a more rapid or efficacious means of living very closely united with Jesus than the holy mass.

'The joy that one feels is like nothing in this world. It is something higher, something spiritual and divine. There is something in me which I had never felt before, and which makes me see things in another manner.

'This is not the fruit of studies, nor of our holiness, nor of anything that has a personal or human seal. It comes from the priestly character which the Holy Ghost impresses in our souls. It is a closer participation in the divine life which raises us. It is a higher force which renders accessible the desires and aspirations which we had been unable hither to realize.'

"In writing of one of the secret retreats he gave during the Mexican persecution, Father Pro remarked, 'This group of 80 consisted of teachers and other government employees. They feared nothing, not even the devil. They denied the existence of hell, affirmed the mortality of the soul, gloried in self-sufficiency, and refused to submit to the sweet truths of our faith.

'I was more than repaid by seeing them all receive the sacraments. Now, you know my limitations. I could feel the grace of God alone working. All the force of my arguments, all my efforts, my thrusts, my explosions to make an impression were useless. I saw that the grace of God touched these souls through simple phrases which I coined at the moment. I counted more than a dozen very remarkable conversions. Blessed be my Father God, who is so wonderfully good.'

"The following prayer, which Father Pro often said, he was to literally fulfill: 'In my life I wish for the scoffing and mockery of Calvary. I desire the slow agony of Thy Son, O My Mother. The contempt, ignominy, infamy of the cross.

'Oh, charity of God! I plunge within Thy breast. My all in all art Thou, rich fount of every grace. Wound me as Thou dost will, I care not for the rest, to Thee I've given all. Myself I now efface.'

"On September 21, 1927, two months and two days before his execution, he said mass in a convent and asked the nuns to pray that God would accept him as a victim for Calles, for priests, for the good of the fatherland. A nun recalled that 'During the entire mass he was under great emotion and at the end he said, 'I know not whether it is imagination or it has actually occurred, but I feel clearly that our Lord has evidently accepted my offer.'"

No. 56—April, 1975 Rudolph M. Unger

Chapter 57

Jean Ousset, a French writer, in noting the problems that beset the church in our age, comments that the situation isn't really unusual.

To prove his point, he then lists all twenty centuries of the church's history along with the heresy or heresies that afflicted the faithful in each of them. He says:

"We imagine today that in all these heresies the opposing parties were well defined, the faithful on the one side, the heretics or schismatics on the other, but for those who experienced them it was a 'dark disorder' with nobody knowing which side to take.

"The parish priest was on one side, his curate on the other. There was disagreement among the bishops. Saints like St. Athanasius were a tiny minority."

St. Athanasius? Who was he? Defender of the faith, champion of orthodoxy, true pillar and intrepid champion of the church, model of bishops, are among the definitions we find in the various reports on his life.

"A principal instrument after the apostles by which the sacred truths of Christianity have been conveyed and secured to the world," was the analysis of Cardinal John Henry Newman.

Thomas Molnar in his "Ecumenism or New Reformation?" states that "The Church today faces a crisis comparable only to the times when Arianism all but conquered it from within" and notes that in the struggle "In Athanasius the church was immensely fortunate to find an intrepid champion."

The following portrayal of this giant, this father of the church, is variously drawn from "Lives of Saints" by two Franciscans, Fathers Thomas Plassmann and Joseph Vann; "A Saint Of The Week" by the Dominican, Father Desmond Murray, and the "Penguin Dictionary Of Saints" by Donald Attwater.

"Persecution was the lot of St. Athanasius, the great defender of the faith. For nearly fifty years his mighty figure dominated the battlefield of the church. Of him, St. Gregory Nazianzen wrote, 'He was the true pillar of the church. His life and conduct were the rule of bishops, and his doctrine the rule of the orthodox faith.'

"Athanasius was the bishop of Alexandria in Egypt for 46 years, from 327 to 373 A.D. he spent 17 of these years in exile, having been banished on five separate occasions because of his vigorous opposition to the Arian Heresy which had been condemned at the council of Nicaea in 325.

"Cardinal Newman declared that in the troubles that followed the council of Nicaea, the laity were firm champions of Christian orthodoxy and the bishops were not. Among the exceptions, Athanasius was outstanding.

"Small in physical stature but of towering spirit, his contemporaries tell us that he proved a lodestone of good influence to heretics and a tower of strength against the persecutors of the church.

"Possessed of keen intelligence and sterling virtue, he was a doctor in Holy Scripture, Canon Law, and Civil Law, and educated in Greek Literature and Philosophy, and Rhetoric. He was a prolific and influential writer of Apologetic, Dogmatic, Historical, and Exegetical treatises.

"He took his spiritual novitiate under St. Anthony of Egypt, the great hermit, with whom he spent four years in the desert and whose biography he wrote.

"The condemnation of Arianism at the council of Nicaea in 325 A.D. was a victory of the minority, a victory largely due to the persuasive power of Athanasius, who was present at the council as an aide to Alexander, his predecessor as bishop at Alexandria, whom he succeeded two years later at the age of 29.

"It was in 323 A.D. that Arius, another African priest, began preaching the heresy that God The Son was not co-eternal with God the Father, was not of the same substance as the Father, and was created by the Father.

"The heresy was condemned by a synod of bishops and Arius was deposed along with eleven priests and deacons of Alexandria. But Arius continued to propagate his ideas and enlisted the support of Bishop Eusebius of Nicomedia and other Syrian prelates. In Egypt he had already won over many of the metaphysicians as well as Meletius, bishop of Lycopolis and leader of a dissident group.

"Theology being the topic which most deeply engaged men's minds, the Arian controversy interested all classes of the population. The heretical propositions were publicized in the form of songs set to popular tunes, and these were chanted in the forums and carried by sailors from port to port.

"It is probable that Athanasius composed the encyclical letter announcing the condemnation of Arius. It was at the famous council of Nicaea, the church's first general council, called by the Emperor Constantine to determine matters of dogma, that the sentence against Arius was confirmed and the confession of faith known as the Nicene creed promulgated and subscribed.

"Said at the mass, the creed states, '…I believe in one Lord, Jesus Christ, the only begotten Son of God, born of the Father before all ages; God of God, light of light, true God of true God; begotten, not made, of one substance with the Father, through whom all things were created…'

"The rest of Athanasius' life was a testimony to the Divinity of the Saviour.

"After he became bishop of Alexandria, the Meletians made common cause with the Arians, and the movement, temporarily discredited by the council of Nicaea, was soon again rampant in Egypt and Asia Minor.

"In 330, the Arian Bishop of Nicomedia, Eusebius, returned from his exile and before long had persuaded the aging Constantine to write to Athanasius, bidding him readmit Arius into communion, in the interests of unity.

"Eusebius sent an ingratiating letter in defense of Arius, but Athanasius held to his conviction that the church could have no communion with heretics who attacked the Divinity of Christ. Then Eusebius wrote the Egyptian Meletians urging them to impeach Athanasius for personal misconduct.

"At his trial before the emperor, Athanasius cleared himself. Then his enemies accused him of murdering a Meletian Bishop and this time Athanasius was banished but kept in touch with his flock by letter.

"Constantine then died and his empire was divided amongst his three sons – Constantine II, Constantius, and Constans.

"Eusebius completely won over Constantius, within whose portion of the empire Alexandria was situated. New scandals were invented and Athanasius was now accused of raising sedition, promoting bloodshed, and keeping for himself corn intended for the poor. And Athanasius, who had returned after Constantine's death, was again deposed, this time by a church council which met at Antioch and ratified an Arian Bishop for Alexandria.

"Athanasius went to Rome to await the hearing of the case by the pope. A synod was summoned but the Eusebians who had proposed it failed to appear. The result was a complete vindication of Athanasius.

"After eight years absence he returned to Alexandria, but after four years of comparative peace, Constans was murdered in 350. Thus was removed the most powerful support of orthodoxy, and, Constantius, now total ruler, set out to crush the man he now regarded as a personal enemy, Athanasius.

"At Arles in 353 he obtained the condemnation of Athanasius from a council of Gallic bishops. Two years later at Milan, Constantius met with opposition from the Italian bishops, but when he gave them the choice between condemnation of Athanasius and exile, by far the greater number yielded.

"The few stubborn bishops were exiled, including the new Pope Liberius. He was sent into isolation in Thrace until, broken in body and spirit, he too gave his consent to the Arian decrees.

"Athanasius held on for another year with the support of his own clergy and people. Finally one night, soldiers broke into the church where he was keeping a vigil, but his people surrounded him and swept him to safety, but for six years he was again in exile.

"After Constantius died in 361 Athanasius returned, but within a few months the new emperor, Julian the Apostate, banished the saint again as, 'A disturber of the peace and an enemy of the Gods.' Julian's successor, Jovian, ended the banishment in 364 but the next year, Valens, his successor caused the worn and aged Athanasius to flee a fifth time. Four months later, Valens relented and Athanasius was joyfully received by his flock in Alexandria who had refused to accept any other bishop. And there he died in peace on May 2, 373, 1602 years ago."

No. 57—May, 1975 Rudolph M. Unger

Chapter 58

In scripture, in the book of Jeremiah, it says, "They healed the breach of the daughter of my people disgracefully, saying, 'Peace. Peace.' And there was no peace...Thus saith the Lord, 'Stand ye on the ways, and see, and ask for the old paths, which is the good way, and walk ye in it and you shall find refreshment for your souls.'"

And Christ, in St. Matthew, said, "Beware of false prophets who come to you in sheep's clothing but inwardly are ravening wolves. By their fruits you shall know them...A good tree cannot bring forth evil fruit; neither can an evil tree bring forth good fruit."

The writer has a favorite phrase which goes:

"The great evil of our age is that mimicking, mocking caricature of charity which goes about the world beating its breast in the name of love."

The Gods of our age are – unity, equality, peace, and security.

More than fifty years ago a prophetic speech was made in Rome by Archbishop Jean Arthur Chollet of Cambrai, France. Speaking before The International Eucharistic Congress on May 27, 1922, he compared the peace of Christ with the peace of the world.

"I will meditate with you for a few minutes on the great law of peace," he began. "That law which wishes that peace, like all gifts, descend from on high; which wishes that the essential condition of peace of men among themselves be the peace of men with God. Because there is no peace for the wicked. ("Glory to God in the highest, and on earth, peace to men of good will.")

"There is a peace of the world which differs from the peace of Christ. It is Jesus Christ who warns us of this. He told the apostles, 'My peace I give to you.' Not 'peace' but 'My peace.' And he added immediately, 'I do not give it to you as the world gives it.'

"The peace of Christ clearly supposes the presence and the intervention of the savior. He acts there, He is the bond. In like manner, the apostolic peace, the peace of the church, supposes the presence and the intervention of the church.

"This peace of Christ and of the church involves:

"(1) A respect for human freedom which must be drawn to faith and love, not by violence, but by the convincing power of the light and the attraction of grace.

"(2) An apostolate based on zeal which spreads the knowledge of God, of Jesus, of the church, and draws human consciences to their authority and to their laws.

"Love of and respect for our brothers initiate peace.

"Contrast this with the peace which the world pursues fruitlessly.

"The peace of the world seeks to establish itself among men by building on the foundation of equality. It proceeds by concessions and by silence. It makes concessions to error and to evil. It cloaks the truth and good with silence. It puts the true and the false, the good and the evil, on an equal footing and accords them the same rights. In this way it thinks that it can appease all protests and reign without any trouble.

"There are religious minded men who pray to God and seek to serve Him, but at the same time challenge either the divinity of Christ or the authority of the church. They do not accept the truths which the church teaches, nor the sacraments of which she is the administrator, nor the heirarchy which is the framework of the church.

"However, these people are brothers and must be loved. There are some in the church who wish to extend their hand to them, to come to some understanding with them, to bring about some collaboration. What do they do to effect this?

"They turn to the true sons of the church and ask them to consent – while preserving their personal convictions – to keep them quiet, to cloak them with a profound silence in order not to sadden or alienate the dissident brothers.

"They wish to put all beliefs on the same level and propose a common work, an elaboration of a credo from which would be deleted all the articles challenged by one faith or another, and in the profession of which all would concur. This would be a poor, weak credo which would quickly disappear.

"Now, one soon becomes aware that besides all these religious minded men there are others whom one is obliged to call honest people and who do not believe in God, nor profess any religion, nor feel the need of any religious sentiment. These are also brothers. One loves them. One wishes to stretch out his hand to them, to come to some understanding with them, to bring about some collaboration.

"Then, one turns to the religious minded men, one asks them to consent—while preserving their personal convictions—to keep them quiet, to cloak them in a profound silence in order not to sadden or alienate their unbelieving brothers. One will be united outside of all profession of religious principles on a social level. One will work in common to save the social order by material means.

"But soon, looking beyond this large group, one perceives that besides the partisans of the social order, there exist other men who reject the bases on which this social order rests. They wish neither the idea of country nor family. They reject authority and private ownership. At all events, these are brothers. One wishes to love them, to extend a hand to them.

"To achieve such an enviable result one returns to the defenders of the social order. While remaining faithful to their convictions, let them cloak them in profound silence. Let them refrain from speaking of country and family, of authority and private ownership.

"Then, it will be possible to agree on a common ground, i.e., a material, a commercial one.

"Thus the veil which cloaks the religious and social principles becomes each day wider and thicker. Some truths which demand an explicit and public profession disappear from the language. One no longer speaks of them. But it is a law of human psychology that the ideas of which one does not speak fade very quickly.

"The convictions that these ideas inspire become weak. After having disappeared from the language, they disappear from the human conscience.

"What remains then?

"There remains appetites, ambitions, and passions. There remains the need for riches, for honor, and for pleasure. There remains jealousy and lust. In a word, there remains the human animal. There remains all that which divides, all that which arouses evil hate, all that which unleashes unforgivable wars.

"One has sought peace by methods which were not those of the Prince and of the God of Peace. One has not found peace and thus is confirmed the word of the sacred books—'They proclaimed peace but there was no peace.'

'They have even projected a very strange light on this formula which could very well be a law of history—'If you wish war, foster peace,' (si vis bellum, para pacem), the peace according to this world.

"One day, King Abimelech came to Bersabee to visit the old Isaac. He said to him 'I have seen that God is with you. And because of that, I have come to propose an alliance. My people have not done you any harm. We have left you enjoy the prosperity which the blessing from on high has brought you. I ask that, in turn, you do no harm to us.'

"Isaac agreed to the proposition of Abimelech. He offered him a banquet and shared bread and wine with him. They then exchanged solemn promises and peace reigned.

"The proofs of the assistance given by God to Isaac, the gratitude for the benefits due to this assistance, the mutual respect for their persons and their property, the sharing of the same banquet, such are the reasons which underlay the ceremonies of peace between Abimelech and Isaac.

"The same means can assure peace among men—let them all recognize each other as sons of God. Let them see in their history the hand of God and the action of His beneficient Providence. Let them respect each other in their persons and in their goods. Let them sit down at the holy table where they will take in common the Eucharistic bread and wine. Thus will they fulfill their destinies in peace. They will enjoy the prosperity and happiness which the blessing of the Lord procures for them."

No. 58—June, 1975 Rudolph M. Unger

Chapter 59

The fallacious, unhealthy tendencies which Archbishop Chollet saw developing in the church more than a half century ago have blossomed forth into a full blown, ugly, cancerous reality in our time.

Long in developing and now deeply rooted, these malignant tentacles have attained a tenacious grip and will not be easily eradicated from the footholds they have so assiduously and cunningly gained.

The depth of the crisis they have engendered in the church was well delineated recently by a leader of one of the church's religious orders.

The forthright, unequivocal diagnosis of the disease was made by the Reverend Christopher J. O'Toole, presently southern provincial of the priests of the Holy Cross and, from 1950 to 1962, superior general of the congregation of the Holy Cross.

Writing last December in the magazine of the University of Notre Dame on the crisis in Catholic universities, Father O'Toole wrote:

"Somewhere along the line, Catholic universities have either compromised or underplayed their Catholicity and are now endeavoring to identify themselves in the contemporary academic arena.

"Despite an academic defense of their position, Catholic universities have, in fact, become secularized. Hence, the urgent problem arises—how can these institutions become what they are supposed to be?

"Instead of focusing our attention on the structure called 'university' let us look at the living element within it—the student. Since we are talking about Catholic universities, our students will be, for the most part, Catholic.

"Now, what intellectual and spiritual formation for these students does the church expect from Catholic universities? The answer is brief and clear—'That the students of these institutions may become men truly outstanding in learning, ready to shoulder society's heavier burdens, and to witness the faith to the world.' (Vatican II)

"Not only is the graduate to be learned, but he is to be so thoroughly Catholic that he will have the knowledge, will power, and spiritual stamina 'to witness the faith to the world.'

"I submit that in the present organization of Catholic universities a student of this type will emerge not because of the university's program, but in spite of it. Why?

"Mainly because the university does not or cannot provide that unified intellectual, moral, spiritual formation that will allow him to develop not only as a scholar, but as a saint (and the word saint is used in its basic meaning—Holy).

"Some say that this suggestion is utopian, unrealistic. On the contrary it is very realistic because it conforms to the nature and person of the Catholic student who, through baptism, shares in the life of the Trinity.

"We cannot separate into compartments the intellectual, moral, and spiritual life of the student. He is a unified being and consequently, along with his intellectual growth there should go a corresponding growth in his spiritual life.

"The more learned he becomes, the more saintly he should be. It is true that knowledge and virtue are not synonymous, but it is also true that learning and virtue (or holiness) should grow apace.

"What do we see today in Catholic universities? On the intellectual level, particularly in the humanities, we find students exposed to every kind of "ism.' We find professors who teach that we cannot arrive at objective truth. Others who maintain that our settled condition is agnostic. Still others who deny spiritual realities and the basic principles of both reason and faith.

"We find professors of ethics and morality who are cut adrift from self-evident principles and who justify all moral conduct by 'situation.' Even among the clergy engaged in teaching, we encounter those who practically defy the official teachings of the church.

"They deride pronouncements of the Holy Father, pontificate upon the church's loss of credibility because she refuses to bend to the utterly secularistic and humanistic trends of our day, and insulate the university from any ecclesiastical interference under the guise of autonomy and academic freedom.

"Can anyone in his right mind imagine that students, no matter how high their ideals both intellectual and spiritual, can remain unscathed in this atmosphere?

"What can be done to counter this fragmentation of knowledge, this intellectual mixtum-gatherum supplied by doctors of philosophy and theology? How can we bridge the gap between the positive sciences which aim at certitude and the humanities which are shot through with relativism?

"How can we liquidate this segregation of the intellectual from the spiritual so that the student's growth may go forward in a unified manner? There are several things we can do, but the prospect of doing them is dim, given the mentality of many Catholic university administrators and professors.

"One of the first things to be done is to avoid 'dumping' a student into a sea of 'isms' before he has had an opportunity to acquire some point of reference. If one of the central items in a Catholic university is philosophy, this obviously must be philosophy in the Catholic tradition.

"Once a student has been versed in logic, epistemology and metaphysics; once he realizes that it is possible for him to arrive at objective truth, even though that truth may not be complete; once he has, so to say, a base of operation, then he will be in a position to integrate into his thought everything worthwhile he may discover in other systems.

"It is true that philosophy plays a greater role in the humanities than in the positive sciences. Nevertheless, care must be taken that students preparing for a B.S. degree in one field or another have a basic philosophic outlook which will prevent overspecialization at the expense of education.

"Equally important as the student's intellectual formation is his moral and spiritual formation.

"His growth in secular knowledge should be accompanied by growth in sacred knowledge—a knowledge which does not remain platonic but which governs daily living and stamps the student as a genuine Catholic.

"Once a student comes to realize that his life is not compartmentalized, that his intellectual life is not something separate from his spiritual life, then the meaning of the phrase 'Catholic education' will dawn upon him.

"He will realize that growth in Christ is not merely counsel but a command. He will learn by experience that the spiritual life he leads has an effect on his secular studies. For this type of student the Eucharist (mass) is a <u>must</u>. He needs it for his spiritual growth as he needs food for his physical growth.

"Why, then, the falling off in attendance at the liturgy? Why the neglect of the sacrament of penance? Why the looseness in moral practice?

"Because effective leadership is lacking. What is the student to think when he finds ordained ministers of God, who are supposed to radiate the spirit of Christ, unable to agree upon the meaning of prayer, unable to guide him with sureness and conviction along the path of morality, or who manifest uncertainty about what is right and what is wrong in the domain of sex?

"What is he to think when he sees priests practically defying the Holy Father, if not insulting him? How can he understand permissiveness in the face of patent wrongdoing?

"He is asking for bread and he is offered a stone. He is seeking priests and professors through whom Christ and the spirit of the gospel come through; persons who possess that charism that can only come through close personal union with Christ; persons whose speech and conduct shed about them true Christian joy and serenity and reveal unshakable convictions.

"Only when we have overcome the segregation of the spiritual from the intellectual in student life will the student understand the genuine character of a Catholic university."

No. 59—July, 1975 Rudolph M. Unger

Chapter 60

Over most of the years that the writer was privileged to travel to see and enjoy the bounty of God's Providence, he kept a log in which he recorded his experiences and his impressions.

Following is an excerpt from one of those logs:

"Sunday, September 27, 1970—

"It got down to 20 degrees in West Yellowstone by the time the sun rose on this glorious Sunday.

"The car had plenty of frost on it as I drove to church—Our Lady of the Pines.

"When mass becomes an experience that depresses rather than uplifts and elates one, then it is a terrible commentary on the times—times inside the church that try men's souls.

"The priest who said the mass was from Bozeman, Montana. Well, he turned out to be a real mod. Perhaps today was declared Christian unity Sunday by the Pope, I don't know.

"But all we heard was the glories of ecumenism as preached by the Great High Priest—John XXIII. The priest didn't even read the scripture responses, as they are now called—the epistle and gradual. But instead read an excerpt from the Vatican II council on the glories of Christian togetherness.

"And the priest said, the reason for all this... he got a request from Lutherans who would like to share use of the church.

"The priest said here was a glorious chance for the parish to live the spirit of Christian unity. He recommended they share the church with the Lutherans.

"He said he talked to the bishop, who said by all means, as long as he explained to the parishioners, there is a difference between the two religions. Of course there are differences, the priest said, and always will be and we cannot deny that.

"Nevertheless, he asked that the Catholic Church share its church with the Lutherans—who economically!—Ah materialism—could never afford to build their own.

"He, however, wouldn't want to do this unless the majority favored it and if anyone didn't approve, they should talk to him after mass. Of course, the impression was clearly left, that he intended to proceed with his idea unless opponents stepped forward to disapprove.

"He made a great deal of the friendship time, the fellowship time, following the Our Father and came down himself to talk to the strangers, one of them, of course, being me.

"He offered his hand and I didn't give him mine. He asked me where I was from as he noted my missal. I was deliberately cold. I answered only as much as courtesy indicated. I am sure he got the message.

"Two women up front dressed similarly in blue coats turned out to be nuns. After mass I saw the three of them leave a restaurant. He, of course, was dressed as a civilian, being a democratic sort of one of the people folk.

"They drove, as I did, into Yellowstone and he and I took pictures of the same swans. I noted that at the mass he had five separate books to refer to. I think this is an excellent example of why the devil has used ecumenism to hornswaggle the church leaders and hornswaggle them he has.

"As only he can, waving the white flag of Christian unity and ecumenism to steer the church away from her obligation to convert men to the one true faith.

"So now a Catholic priest, with the approval of his bishop, urges his parishioners to give aid in the propagation of a heresy—which is what Lutheranism is. This is the 'renewed' church?

"They speak of love and know not what love is. They speak of unity and know not what unity is. There is no love without truth. There is no unity without truth. It is the basis of both.

"He who builds on false foundations shall find his structure will collapse of its inherent contradictions and this is what is going to happen in the current flight from obligation and reality—to wit, the ecumenical movement. Love is based on God's law, not on the wishes of men.

"On this glorious day in Yellowstone, I found the God who was difficult to see in the church this morning.

"The unchanging God, the ever constant God—in that same glorious sun, that same blue sky, that same towering awesome majesty of the mountains, that same color of evergreen, that same fall dress in the other vegetation; the same sparkling, flowing rivers, the same sweet fragrances of life's growth in that same sweet smelling, clear, clean air, uncontaminated by modern man, the arrogant fool!

"Fishermen were prominent today on Yellowstone's wonderful rivers where fish are still caught as they historically have been and no substitute has been made, and funny, man never gets tired of going back to the same nature to stand in the same sun to catch the same fish.

"But, strangely, it is now believed by those who control that that same man won't go to that same old liturgy which God has used for centuries to catch what he told Peter and the apostles to catch.

"In the late afternoon sun, I made the long, glorious climb northeast out of Yellowstone up over 10,942 foot Bear Tooth pass. This drive in the high country of the Absaroka Mountains unveiled perhaps the grandest panorama of mountains that I have ever seen.

"I thought several times I was at the top of the pass as I constantly stopped to shoot pictures of:

"Snow clad peaks, of sunny mounts, of deep, wide valleys, of surrogated, silhouetted ranges, of brilliantly glimmering sunlight down a road of snow—frocked trees, of a big, beautiful bull moose enjoying his supper, of the ethereal spirit of the high country in the last glimmers of sunlight, of quiet lakes eloquently picturing snow clad mountains mantled in the last rays of the sun, of the brilliant God of the sky flashing his day's final brilliance, of a whole grand indescribable array of snowy white peaks standing eloquently silent and darkened in the day's end, of snow bordered roadway as it serpent-like wound its way to its ultimate summit atop the darkening, white, still, clear ethereal world—like which there is nothing else in creation.

"My last shot—the final picture of the last of my twenty-four rolls of film, was the scene at the summit, 10,942 feet…cold, white, darkening, earthly terminus beneath the golden afterglow. A climax to a day I shall never forget, thanks be to an ever thoughtful God…

"Finally, after a fifteen mile steep, winding descent down and around chasms of darkness, I cleared this mammoth range and shot eastward sixty miles along straight-as-an-arrow farm road toward Billings, Montana, with a big, beautiful, sparkling star at the end of it to guide the way.

"Those last miles approaching my destination, I was pulled along the way by the Marian hour from Our Lady of the Prairies in Powers Lake, North Dakota, up near the Canadian border.

"Out of this little farm hamlet in the middle of nowhere, comes the praise and recognition of the Mother of God that is increasingly difficult to hear and find in the great glory of the Roman Catholic Church's great centers.

"The small group of persons, children and adults, prayed the rosary in several languages. A priest, whose name was not given, but who sounded somewhat like Alan Ladd, gave the meditations on each of the glorious mysteries. And after each decade, God was asked to have mercy on sinners.

"The priest also gave superb remarks before and after the rosary—the kind we rarely hear in the Catholic Church today.

"In prelude, he spoke of the world today—the coming of the respectability of evil and the ostracization of good; the tolerance of the former and the belittling of the latter, and why all this was so—a world turning from God and God's prayer.

"In the epilogue, he zeroed in eloquently on the lack of modesty in modern women and the role this plays in the growth of sexual crimes…

"Hours later, after supper and this writing, there ended this climax day of this four week western swing into America's Northern Rockies… certainly a day to remember with joy as long as the memory of man can remember—Deo Gratias!"

No. 60—August, 1975 Rudolph M. Unger

Chapter 61

The following letter was sent to a member of the American hierarchy by the writer on May 2, 1974:

"May I preface my remarks with the comment that I greatly admire your writings. I am extremely pleased that you have decided to retire from your Episcopal post and have decided to devote your full time to writing.

"As far as I am concerned, you are one of the few hopeful lights in the church leadership. The church, like the world, is undergoing a crisis of leadership and as a result the children of the church are undergoing a crisis of faith.

"I find very few among the leaders who hold any apparent and obvious brief for the great unnumbered and unheard in the ranks of the faithful, who lament what has happened in the church since Pius died.

"You are one of the few who give any hope to such as we. I believe Paul himself has called us 'malcontents.'

"You may not realize but you perform an important apostolate within the household of the faith. The leadership generally is concerned about the left leaning radicals in the church and with all those outside the church.

"But few show any concern for, or even admit, that there is a great number within who have been shell shocked, are reeling, and are desperately looking for something or someone, who will help them to hold on to the barque of Peter as the storms of change batter the venerable craft.

"The leadership has bent everywhere it can to the rebels and to those outside. The only place it hasn't bent is where it can't. But as to the conservatives, nary a crumb of concern is expressed.

"God only knows how many souls are able to keep their sense of balance and keep from falling off the barque by the lifeline, the pillar, that is yourself.

"I have for several years authored two monthly newsletters in a small effort to give some hope, some help to some of that vast number of unheard, shattered souls in the ranks.

"It isn't easy, because I find little encouragement from what I read and hear, from the pronouncements and actions of the hierarchy. And so it helps, personally, a great deal to read your writings. And God knows everyone needs support. And communication of ideas and ideals is support. It is hope!

"I am sorry for this long prior digression before coming to the item that led me to write in the first place.

"It was your article which began, 'Whatever became of Christian humanism?'

"I could easily say that I agree with ninety-five percent of it, which in a sense I do.

"But more deeply, I must pick a bone. What became of Christian humanism is what might have been expected. Look around the church today and you will see the fruits of it everywhere.

"Christian humanism was a clever diversion proffered to the church leadership by Lucifer in his never ceasing, ever searching way of sidetracking it and the church from its prime job.

"The job of the church is Christianity, not Christian humanism. As I once told a friend, humanism is a way-station which will lead either to Christianity or to secularism.

"And I think a look around in the shambles of the church today readily indicates which way it went and perhaps Maritain, who you refer to in your article, bears part of the responsibility, as Thomas Molnar indicates.

"And perhaps his last testament, 'The Peasant of Garrone', indicates that Maritain himself in his last days realized what has evolved from that vaunted Christian humanism.

"It is a very clever foil, bearing the marks of Lucifer, for he is the cunning, subtle one, who always mixes his devious offering with a heavy or tasty portion of half-truths. The sugar disguising the arsenic.

"Thereby the headman from Hades has been able to soften up, muddle,—enervate—to me that is the key word in all of this strategy of his. Not head on, not kill, but slowly, subtly, one step back... two forward, co-existence, negotiation, compromise, sweet talk, the carrot and the stick, until the opponent is so confused, so tired by the long fight, that he has lost, almost without realizing it, his initiative, his punch, his firepower, and most importantly, and the devil's goal—his will to resist, to fight, to attack, to take the initiative, to win.

"And today, rising out of the growth of this indigestible fruit, Lucifer offers us another, further tantalizing, seemingly reasonable, possible route, which again leads the church to take her eye off the mark…his whole strategy—the path of ecumenism…which is the spiritual parallel of the secular disease—co-existence.

"I have always envisioned the great evil of our times as being—that mimicking, mocking caricature of charity which goes about the world beating its breast in the name of love.

"And—Christian humanism, ecumenism, and co-existence—are among its most alluring garbs.

"And so I propose to you another question, posed in several ways, for consideration for your answer in some future column:

"Whatever became of Catholicism, of Catholic action, of the church militant, of apologetics, of unabashed and unapologetic pride in being fortunate enough—through God's love—of having and being able to share the one, true, Catholic, apostolic faith?

"Whatever became of conversion, of honest, forthright, open, unhypocritical, non-milk toast proselytism…of the Lord's command to 'Go out and teach ye all nations, baptizing in the name of the Father, Son, and Holy Spirit'?

"What became of religion as the relationship between God and man, whatever became of approaching our brothers with the truth, goodness, and beauty and knowledge of God that God blessed us with, rather than today's approach with 'sweetness' and hesitancy and image consciousness?

"Whatever became of the glorious spirit described in that stirring, uplifting, encouraging song of Father Lord's that we sang with joy and unapologetically in our school days:

'On earth's battlefield never a 'vantage we will yield as onward we fight for Christ the Lord…heads lifted high, Catholic action is our cry and the cross (of sacrifice, truth, reality) our only sword.'?

"No wonder the world, the flesh, and the devil are winning…just good old 'outdated', non-mod Thomistic cause and effect.

"Another favorite analogy of mine:

'Have you ever seen two men in a prize fight ring and one wants to fight and the other doesn't? Any question who will win?'

"But, now to haul in the reins, and say in parting—God bless you. May

He fill you with wisdom, constancy, courage, and a long productive, fruitful life. For God's children need you."

"Oh God, our refuge and our strength, graciously look upon thy people who cry to thee…in thy mercy and kindness hear the prayers which we pour forth for the conversion of sinners and for the freedom and exaltation of Holy Mother the church. Through Christ our Lord. Amen.

"Saint Michael, the Archangel, defend us in the battle, be our protection against the wickedness and snares of the devil. Rebuke him, God, we humbly beseech thee. And do thou, O Prince of the Heavenly Host, by the Divine Power, drive into hell Satan and the other evil spirits who roam through the world. Seeking the ruin of souls. Amen.

"Most Sacred Heart of Jesus, have mercy on us."

No. 61—September, 1975 Rudolph M. Unger

Chapter 62

In England, the Roman Catholic Church was supplanted by the Anglican or Episcopal Church during the reign of the Tudor monarch, Henry VIII.

Some aspects of how this tragedy of the English speaking world came to be are fairly well known in our day. Others are not so well known. Some of these will be found in the following excerpts taken from the chapter on "The English Reformation" from Father Philip Hughes' book, "A Popular History Of The Reformation."

"Pertinent to what was now about to happen in England were the activities of a handful of clerical graduates of the University Of Cambridge from about 1520-21 when Pope Leo X condemned the errors of Luther and excommunicated him.

"At Cambridge there was a group of students in theology who were sympathetically interested in Luther's theories. They read his books and met to discuss them at the White Horse Inn, a tavern of easy access from the backs of the colleges where most of them dwelt. The inn soon became known as 'Little Germany.'

"From this little group of Cambridge men, obscure in the 1520's rather than from any other one source, was to develop the whole of the English Reformation as the execution of a theological ideal.

"William Tyndale, Robert Barnes, Thomas Bilney, John Frith, John Lambert, and Rowland Taylor and the some-day-to-be Protestant bishops, Cranmer, Latimer, Ridley, Foxe, Shaxton, Coverdale, Parker and Cox.

"Inevitably, as the years passed, these groups came into conflict with authority. Already, in 1521, as part of the publication in England of Leo X's condemnation of Luther, there had been a great ceremonial burning of his books outside St. Paul's in London with all the bishops present. John Fisher, Bishop of Rochester, preached the sermon.

"In 1526, Tyndale, the first influence in the formation of the English Protestant mind, was preparing the first printed New Testament in English. Having fled as an accused heretic, he worked in Germany, for a time in Luther's own town of Wittenberg. And his views developed in the closest possible relation to the new theology.

"We know nowadays, from the studies of the scholars, that quite a lot of Tyndale's work is nothing more or less than a word for word translation of Luther. In Tyndale's pamphlets, and he was a superlative master of the simplicity of the English language, is set out in all its plainness the key doctrine of the Reformation:

"That the one thing necessary for man in order to save his soul, the one essential act on man's part, is not repentance, is not charity, but confidence in God. Not confidence that God will save a man if the man does his best, but confidence that God has already saved him, independently of anything a man has done or will do.

"In the lengthy list of Tyndale's heretical writings, one can see what an extraordinary medley of anti-clerical, anti-Catholic, anti-social, and anti-intellectual ideas were already flooding the English mind in 1530.

"Here are a few—faith only doth justify us; saints in heaven cannot help us thither; the commandments be given us not to do them but to know our damnation and call for mercy to God; beware of good intents, they are damned of God; every man is a priest; purgatory is of the pope's invention; God bindeth us to that which is impossible; keeping of virginity and chastity of religion is a devilish thing.

"St. Thomas Aquinas savoureth nothing of the spirit of God; the New Testament of Christ will not suffer any law of compulsion, but only of counsel and exhortation; we have as great right and as much right to heaven as Christ; the good Christian shall not defend himself by justice in no manner; he that is rich may not use or spend his goods as he wills; men of war are not allowed by the gospel; matrimony is as gold, the spiritual estates are as dung; thou canst not perish or be damned whatsoever thing thou shalt outwardly either do or else leave undone; we owe nothing to any man saving only love.

"When William Warham, the archbishop of Canterbury, died in 1532, Henry VIII's choice fell upon a priest who until lately had never left the scholarly precincts of Cambridge—Dr. Thomas Cranmer, a one time habitue of the gatherings at the White Horse Inn.

"At the time of his appointment by Henry, Cranmer was serving as ambassador at the court of Charles V, Holy Roman Emperor and King of Spain. With his appointment, the Reformation made its first entry into English public life.

"Protests against the appointment were sent to Rome from Charles' ambassador in London, warning the Holy See that it was notorious that the elect, Cranmer, was a Lutheran.

"It was at this time (1533) that Henry went through a form of marriage with Anne Boleyn. At Rome there was no opposition to Cranmer's appointment. The bulls were granted and he was consecrated. Cranmer pronounced the king's marriage with Anne as good and lawful. He crowned her queen in Westminister Abbey.

"Pope Clement VII then quashed the proceedings of Cranmer's marriage court, excommunicated those who had taken part in them, and excommunicated the king. And, at long last, the pope made up his mind to try the case he had called into his courts now four years ago. In 1534 the pope declared that Henry's marriage to Catherine, his wife of twenty-one years, was valid and binding.

"Parliament, upon the behest of Henry, passed a series of acts which forced all Englishmen to swear under oath, among other things, that the King was the supreme head of the church in England.

"With a handful of exceptions the whole country, secular and religious, agreed to take the oath. For a great proportion of enforcing the oath, the principal means was Cranmer.

"In the last six years of Henry's reign, from 1541 to 1547, one of the two leading personages in public life in England was Cranmer, influential always by reason of the king's unfailing personal affection for him.

"When Henry died, and with him his theological differences with the Lutherans, and Edward VI took the throne, the course was set for the complete protestantising of the Anglican Church. Cranmer, at last, came into his own. What he now achieved has lasted to this day.

"The lent of 1547 was ushered in by Barlow and Ridley, the latter of the White Inn Group, preaching against the very idea of lent. They also denounced the veneration of images as idolatry. Soon mobs began destroying the images.

Cranmer was the chief author of 'The Homilies'. Here, in clear and unmistakable language, are all the foundation doctrines of Protestantism:

"That the bible is the only source of true knowledge of God; that by Adam's sin the very nature of man has been corrupted irremediably; that justification is through faith alone; that there are only two sacraments—

baptism and the supper of the Lord; that a man's good works are without effect as to his salvation. There is also much scornful, fiercely written denunciation of the pious practices traditional for centuries among Catholics.

"There was published 'The Order of Communion' which called for a separate service, not in Latin, but in English to be added to the mass on communion days. It was an adaptation of a Lutheran rite and it delivered a powerful blow against the sacrament of penance, saying that communicants, if they were in a state of sin, need not confess before receiving communion, saying also that the absolution in the communion rite was sufficient.

"The whole collection of Catholic liturgical service books was abolished. In their place came the Book Of Common Prayer, with Cranmer credited as the author. Cranmer had for the theology of which the mass was the expression, as passionate a hatred as though it were a living enemy.

"Cranmer used the practice of ambiguity which Luther had promoted. 'Concessions' have had to be made, Cranmer explained, (these concessions, however, were to be temporary, he added), 'Lest the people, should be deterred by too extensive innovations.' In the communion service, whatever indicates or implies a belief that what is going on is a sacrifice to God of the Body And Blood of Jesus Christ, truly present on the altar, was cut out.

"Not only the communion service, but the ordination rite had been disassociated by Cranmer and his associates from the idea of a sacrificing priesthood. There still remained, however, in every church, the silent reminder of sacrifice—the altar. All altars were ordered destroyed.

'The form of a table shall move the simple from the superstitious opinions of the popish mass unto the right use of the Lord's supper. For the use of an altar is to make a sacrifice upon, a table to serve men to eat upon,' was the explanation. The very words 'altar' and 'mass' disappeared."

No. 62—October, 1975 Rudolph M. Unger

Chapter 63

Twenty-eight years ago this month, November, 1947, Pope Pius XII, of happy and holy memory, wrote an encyclical on the sacred liturgy entitled, "Mediator Dei." Following are excerpts from the letter.

"The church prolongs the priestly mission of Jesus Christ mainly by means of the sacred liturgy. She does this in the first place at the altar through the sacrifice of the cross. She does it next through the sacraments. And finally she does so by prayer.

"We note with satisfaction the renewed scholarly interest in the sacred liturgy, but while we are pleased with the wholesome results of this movement, duty obliges us to give serious attention to this 'revival' as it is advocated in some quarters and to take proper steps to preserve it at the outset from excess or outright perversion.

"We observe with considerable anxiety and some misgiving certain enthusiasts over-eager in their search for novelty, who are straying beyond the path of sound doctrine and prudence. Not seldom they interlard their plans and hopes for a revival of the sacred liturgy with principles which compromise this holiest of causes and sometimes even taint it with errors touching Catholic faith and ascetical doctrine.

"The worship rendered by the church must be, in its entirety, interior as well as exterior. It is exterior because the nature of man as a composite of body and soul requires it to be so. Divine Providence has disposed that 'While we recognize God visibly, we may be drawn by Him to love of things unseen.' Besides, every impulse of the human heart expresses itself naturally through the senses.

"The outward acts of religion are designed to rouse the heart to veneration of the sacred realities and to raise the mind to meditation on the supernatural. They serve to foster piety, kindle charity, increase our faith, deepen devotion. They provide instruction for the simple folk, decoration for divine worship, and continuity of religious practice. They make it possible to tell genuine Christians from their false or heretical counterparts.

"But the chief element of divine worship must be interior. The sacred liturgy requires that both of these elements, exterior and interior, be intimately linked with each other.

"There are certain recent theories touching so called objective piety which tend to belittle, or pass over in silence, what they call subjective or personal piety. They feel that all other religious exercises not directly connected with the sacred liturgy and performed outside of public worship should be omitted.

"The conclusions drawn from them respecting the two sorts of piety are false, insidious, and quite pernicious.

"If the private and interior devotion of individuals were to neglect the august sacrifice of the altar and the sacraments, it would indeed be sterile. But when devotional exercises and pious practices have the express purpose of directing human acts to God, of leading men to the difficult path of perfection, then such practices are not only highly praiseworthy but absolutely indispensable.

"Unquestionably liturgical prayer is superior in excellence to private prayers. But this superior worth does not at all imply contrast or incompatibility between these two kinds of prayer. Both merge harmoniously and tend toward the same objective—until Christ be formed in us.

"The church grows, develops, adapts and accommodates herself to temporal needs and circumstances, provided only that the integrity of her doctrine be safeguarded.

"The temerity and daring of those who introduce novel liturgical practices, or call for the revival of obsolete rites out of harmony with prevailing laws and rubrics, deserve severe reproof.

"It has pained us grievously to note such innovations are actually being introduced, not merely in minor details, but in matters of major importance as well. We note in point of fact, those who make use of the vernacular in the celebration of the august Eucharistic sacrifice. Those who transfer feast days to other dates. Those who delete from prayer books the sacred texts of the Old Testament, deeming them inopportune for modern times.

"The use of the Latin language is a manifest and beautiful sign of unity as well as an effective antidote for any corruption of doctrinal truth.

"It is neither wise nor laudable to reduce everything to antiquity. Thus one would be straying from the straight path were he to wish the altar restored to its primitive table form. Where he to want to exclude black as a color for the liturgical vestments. Where he to forbid the use of sacred images and statues in churches. Where he to order the crucifix so designed that the divine redeemer's body shows no trace of His cruel sufferings. Where he to disdain and reject polyphonic music or singing in parts.

"Some disapprove of masses offered privately and without a congregation. They are mistaken in appealing in this matter to the social character of the Eucharistic sacrifice. This sacrifice: necessarily and of its very nature, has always and everywhere the character of a public and social act, inasmuch as he who offers it, acts in the name of Christ and of the faithful, for the church, for the living and dead. This is so, whether the faithful are present or are not present.

"When we stand before the altar, priests and laity, it is our duty to transform our hearts so that we may become acceptable to the Eternal Father.

"The prescriptions of the sacred liturgy aim, by every means at their disposal, at helping to bring about this holy purpose, including the vestments, the sacred rites and their external splendor. All these aim at enhancing the majesty of this great sacrifice, and raising the minds of the faithful, by means of these visible signs of religion and piety, to the contemplation of the sublime truths contained in this sacrifice.

"While a dialogue mass is commendable, if in accord with rubrics of the liturgy, it cannot replace the high mass which possesses its own special dignity due to the impressive character of its ritual and the magnificence of its ceremonies.

"It is to be observed also that they have strayed from the path of truth and right reason who make so much of these accidentals as to presume or assert that without them the mass cannot be fulfilled.

"Many of the faithful are unable to use the 'Roman missal' even though it is written in the vernacular. Nor are all capable of understanding correctly the liturgical rites and formulas. So varied and diverse are men's talents and characters that it is impossible for all to be moved and attracted to the same extent by community prayers, hymns, and liturgical services.

"Moreover, the needs and inclinations of all are not the same, nor are they always constant in the same individual. Who then would say, on account of such a prejudice, that all these Christians cannot participate in the mass, nor share its fruits?

"On the contrary, they can adopt some other method which proves easier for certain people. For instance, they can lovingly meditate on the mysteries of Jesus Christ or perform other exercises of piety or recite prayers which, though they differ from the sacred rites, are still essentially in harmony with them.

"Those err from the path of truth who do not want to have masses celebrated unless the faithful communicate and those are still more in error who put forward the captious argument that here there is a question not of a sacrifice merely, but of a sacrifice and a supper of brotherly union, and consider the general communion as the culminating point of the whole celebration... do not let a certain dangerous 'humanism' lead your flocks astray, venerable brethren.

"The sacred liturgy does not restrict the interior devotion of individual Christians, rather it fosters and promotes it. The church encourages such devotions as visits to the tabernacle, benediction, forty hours devotion, perpetual adoration, and vespers.

"It encourages knowledge of and imitation of the saints, most particularly Our Lady, and special prayers in her honor, among which the rosary has pride of place. It approves retreats, examination of conscience, meditation on spiritual things. Also, it urges adornment of churches and altars.

"All liturgical services should have sacredness, abhorring profane influences: nobility, which true and genuine arts should foster, and universality, which reveals the Catholic unity of the church."

No. 63—November, 1975 Rudolph M. Unger

Chapter 64

The following letter was written May 6, 1974:

Dear Pope Paul,

I have just been informed that at the order of Cardinal John Cody, archbishop of Chicago, the Latin Tridentine mass which had been offered every Sunday at Assumption Church on Chicago's near north side by the Servite Fathers, has been banned.

It was to my knowledge the last church to still offer the old mass in the Chicago area, and, it was one of my joys to be able on occasion to still participate in that superior rite, though I had to make a sixty mile round trip to do so.

My last opportunity was on Easter Sunday. How ironic. Easter had always in the church symbolized the resurrection and here we see it marking death.

The vengeance with which the church leadership has moved to wipe out the old way is much more akin to the totalitarianism which rules the communist world than the love of Christ with which Catholicism has always been associated.

That Cardinal Cody should take such a stand doesn't surprise me. That you, Christ's vicar on earth, should tolerate the destruction of the Latin Tridentine mass is beyond my comprehension.

No heresy could have been attacked and eradicated with greater vigilance and voracity than the way in which the church's leadership has moved to wipe out the Latin Tridentine mass along with the other practices of the pre-Johanninne-Pauline-Vatican II church.

As I wrote another member of the hierarchy this past week, one of the few who has retained any semblance of a good shepherd, "The Church, like the world, is undergoing a crisis of leadership and as a result the children of the church are undergoing a crisis of faith."

Pray tell, your holiness, what was the great evil, the great error, the great heresy, the great apostasy in the old mass and the old church that it has to be gored, decimated, annihilated, and its very recollection wiped out of the minds and hearts of the faithful? Pray, your holiness, tell me.

What is it that you leaders of the church today fear? What are you so afraid of? What is it in the old way that you find so obnoxious, so abhorrent, so despicable, so vile, so vomitonegrous?

The spirit of the hierarchy today toward the conservatives, the traditionalists in the church is:

Eradicate. Not a corner, not an inch, not a crevice, no nook, no cranny, no refuge, no oasis, no island, not an ounce. Wipe out, no mercy, no quarter—not one, not even one Latin Tridentine mass shall be allowed to the laity!

We have today a new order. And the old order is verboten! The only choices are—conform, shut up, or get out!

It is reminiscent of Shakespeare's "Out, out, damned spot!" of the Roman salting of the very soil of Carthage, so that surely never again would the world ever see any sign, any fruit, any remnant, any relic of the hated Carthaginian culture.

And this in the church which beats its breast in the name of renewal, reform, reconciliation, openness, dialogue, communication, tolerance, forbearance, understanding, compassion, negotiation, accommodation, compromise, and co-existence.

In my newsletter, "Counter-Reformation", in July, 1971 I wrote:

"It is said that the church of John, Paul, and the Second Vatican council is a church of love and tolerance.

"I say—nay, not so.

"You see tolerance? I see tyranny. You see an easing? I see a hardening. You see a more democratic spirit? I see a more authoritarian spirit. You see renewal? I see decay.

"You see growth? I see contraction. You see responsibility? I see dereliction. You see candor? I see duplicity. You see considerateness? I see cold, harsh indifference. You see a lamb? I see a wolf.

"You see greater freedom of speech and thought? I see brainwashing and thought control. You see a gentle hand? I see an iron fist. You see greater wisdom? I see arrogant stupidity. You see the Holy Spirit? I see a spirit dark and sinister.

"And nowhere is this dichotomy in the church professing to seek unity more bitter, more harsh, more painful, than in what has been done to the liturgy."

I then quoted in part from Christopher Derrick, the Englishman, who wrote:

"We now see demolition men moving in cheerfully to start their work. The intellectuals stand by, ready with exhortation, commanding a positive attitude and a docile acceptance of their own viewpoint.

"They arranged it all, it was by their standards and through their activities that the plan has been made to appear necessary, the old house anachronistic and absurd past any further toleration. And so as the wreckers move in, these men tell us to rejoice.

"Their plan, we are told, is a beneficent one. We ought to be grateful. We have no right, they say, to demand in the liturgy any richness that might also comfort and sustain us at the human and psychological and cultural level.

"Very meekly, one can make a plea for toleration. When Pope St. Pius V reformed the liturgy, imposing the Roman missal we now remember, he made kindly exceptions. In our day, the church is supposed to be less authoritarian and monolithic than in the past, more tolerant and flexible.

"The Second Vatican council said, 'Even in the liturgy, the church has no wish to impose a rigid uniformity in matters which do not implicate the faith or the good of the whole community.'

"Can these words be taken seriously? Are we going too far if we suggest that a certain practical toleration might be extended—even at some cost in uniformity—to those Catholics who love and revere the old liturgy. Are their 'pietas' to be simply slapped down by authority?

"If in the changes accomplished, they see a great deal of obvious loss and a small amount of highly questionable gain, are they so plainly wrong as to deserve no consideration at all?

"It seems that the old liturgy is to be stamped out completely and everywhere, just as though it were some remarkably pernicious kind of heresy. As things stand now, it seems that a priest who preaches frank heresy will be treated far more gently than a priest who has the sinful temerity to begin his mass with 'Introibo' and end it with 'plenum gratiae et veritatis.'

"If the good of the church 'genuinely and certainly' requires that the old liturgy has got to be totally abolished, the fact still needs to be demonstrated.

"In this age that claims to be so tolerant, may we hope for something less than one hundred percent remorselessness?"

Where Luther, Cranmer, and Calvin after all right? Where in reality, the Council of Trent, St. Pius V, St. Ignatius, St. Charles Borromeo, St. Peter Canisius wrong?

With leadership such as the church is saddled with today, she doesn't need any enemies.

May the loving God have mercy on His children for those divine qualities are increasingly rare commodities in His church today.

"See these Christians, how they love one another." "As I have loved you, so you love one another." "By their fruits you shall know them."

Yes indeed!

Rudolph M. Unger

8100 Woodglen Lane
Downers Grove, Illinois
60515, U.S.A.

cc: Cardinal Cody

No. 64—December, 1975 Rudolph M. Unger

Chapter 65

"A decade ago the Second Vatican Council opened the way for startling changes in the Catholic Church. Among the more conspicuous of those innovations has been the substitution of the vernacular mass for the Latin mass.

"Apparently most American Catholics now heartily disapprove of this reform."

So began an article in "Twin Circle", the Catholic weekly, last February 14, by Russell Kirk, an erudite observer of both the spiritual and secular world.

A man who, in his own words, "Became a convert to Catholicism during Vatican II, but not because of it."

"Many Catholics," Kirk continued, "desire Latin high masses (now very rare, in most dioceses), and also a choice, in their parishes, between alternate Latin and English masses.

"Resentment at the virtual abolition of the Latin mass runs high. A great deal was said about participation of the laity in the church's decision making at Vatican II. But the church hierarchy dealt arbitrarily and highhandedly with Catholic public opinion when it swept away the Latin mass for all practical purposes.

"The pope has declared more than once-that the Latin mass is not forbidden and indeed ought to be encouraged. But most bishops seem to turn a deaf ear to him.

"Why are most Catholics so strongly attached to the old Latin mass? A principal reason is an evocative link with nearly 2,000 years of Latin Christianity. It is the ancient language of the Catholic Church, transcending centuries and national barriers. It signifies that although whole nations and civilizations pass away, the Church abides.

"The Catholic communicant at the Latin mass senses that here is a symbol of the permanent things in an age of disastrous change.

"Also the Latin means that the Church is genuinely Catholic—that is – universal, worldwide. A Latin mass can be understood anywhere one travels, a vernacular mass cannot.

"African bishops generally are champions of the Latin mass, despite nationalism in Africa. For in Africa the 'vernacular' means hundreds of different languages and dialects, incomprehensible to those not reared in some particular African language or dialect. The Latin mass, then, is a bond joining together Catholics who otherwise would not feel like even thirty-second cousins, let alone brothers in Christ.

"Among lesser reasons for Latin's persistent popularity is that such a mass instructs communicants in a great language and literature which is the basis of all the modern romance languages and a considerable contributor to the English language.

"Until after Vatican II, American Catholic missals printed the Latin order of the mass with an English translation parallel so the Latin was quite comprehensible—no real obstacle to understanding the liturgy.

"If the present Catholic vernacular mass is unpopular, so is the 'priest's bible' that since Vatican II has supplanted the old Douai translation on the lectern. The grandeur of scripture has given way to a 'relevant' version expressed in the language of a luncheon club.

"The typical Catholic parishioner all too often also encounters a new priestly arrogance masquerading as 'progressivism'. The 'new breed' clergy, impatient of their parishioners resistance to innovation, thrust dubious changes after dubious changes upon the laity, treating them all too literally like sheep. Those hungry sheep look up and are not fed.

"So it is that attendance at mass falls off sharply in most dioceses; conversions drop alarmingly; priests and nuns, chafing at even the relaxed discipline, renounce their vows, and new vocations are too few.

"Nearly fifteen years ago I wrote an article 'Can Protestantism hold its own in modern America?' The troubles which I then found afflicting the Protestant churches now grip the Catholic Church even more mercilessly.

"I venture to predict that the Latin mass in some form will return to most or all Catholic parishes before very long and much more of the 'Old Church' too will be reasserted."

Three weeks following Kirk's article, on March 7, 1975, Archbishop Robert J. Dwyer, in his column in "Twin Circle", carried this article:

"The recent ukase of the Sacred Congregation For Christian Worship, headed by Cardinal Knox, with Archbishop Bugnini as secretary, practically forbidding the further use of the missal of Pope St. Pius V (The

Tridentine Mass) is bound to cause pain and dissension throughout the Catholic world.

"This in a year dedicated of all things to reconciliation!

"We publish here a translation of a comment on the subject by a well known French Dominican, Pere Henri Bruckberger, which appeared in a recent issue of the Paris Daily, "Figaro."

"Father Bruckberger, a distinguished historian and man of letters, was one of the heroes of the French underground during World War II.

"In the article he is undoubtedly very hard on the French hierarchy. He might now concede that it was only acting under orders from the sacred congregation.

"Our question, and it is a vital one, is whether the action of the congregation was ever formally sanctioned by the Holy Father himself. The Vatican, be it remembered, did not cease to be a prison with the signing of the treaty of conciliation in 1929!

"Father Bruckberger wrote:

'What is taking place in the church in France today? It is not the atheists, the anticlericals, the freethinkers, the Godless, who are seeking at all hazards to despoil the faithful of all that they hold dear.

'It is the bishops who are playing the role of the brigands.

'What is this all about?

'At the very time when the most bizarre of liturgical experiments are taking place almost everywhere in our churches, the most profane, even disgusting of exhibitions—even in our most venerable cathedrals—all with the approval and sometimes with the active participation of certain of our bishops, there is one rite, one sacred liturgy, one manner of offering the holy sacrifice of the mass which is absolutely forbidden.

'Practically under threat of excommunication!

'That is the traditional mass of Pope St. Pius V, the mass celebrated in the western church for nearly five centuries.

'So it is that the Cardinal Archbishop of Paris (Msgr. Marty) has seen fit to forbid the mass offered on Sunday in the Salle Wagram by Msgr. Ducauo Bourget, using that rite.

'Now what do our bishops take us for? Clod-hoppers? We too know something about the official documents. We know that the new missal of Pope Paul VI is simply <u>authorized</u>, not <u>imposed</u> upon us. We know that the Holy Father has never forbidden the celebration of mass according to the rite of Pope St. Pius V.

'We know full well that the Vatican Council and the Holy Father were in full agreement in holding to Latin as the official language of the church.

'We know that the pope is forever recommending the use of Latin and the Gregorian chant. We know that when Pope St. Pius V published his missal in the 16th century he specified, in the apostolic constitution accompanying it, that every priest, at any time, and under any circumstance, has the right to offer mass in that rite, all contrary sanctions being abrogated.

'And we know, finally, that in the Catholic church what one pope has solemnly decreed, can be undone by another pope only with the same solemnity. And so far as the missal of Pope St. Pius V is concerned, nothing like this has been done, nor is there the slightest likelihood that it ever will be.

'In his will, the late Georges Pompidou requested that his obsequies be in Latin, and since he was president of the republic, his wish was granted.

'Today, a parish priest may open his church to Mohammedans and Buddhists, to Tibetans and Patagonians, to Papuans and lower Slobovians, to freaks and deviants, to playboys and playgirls, to God knows what and who. But if that same poor parish priest takes a notion to offer the mass for which that church was built, or the laity wants to hear that mass, Episcopal lightning strikes! This, mark you, by bishops who talk to us so unctiously of ecumenism, of pluralism, of tolerance. Yes, for those outside the fold they are sweetness and light. But for us, their brethren, they weave crowns of thorns!'"

No. 65—January, 1976 Rudolph M. Unger

Chapter 66

"It is well known what strange work there has been in the world under the name and pretense of reformation. How often it has turned out to be deformation. Or, at best, a tinkering sort of business, where, while one hole has been mended, two have been made."

So wrote once a gentleman named George Horne and in the December 7 issue of "Twin Circle", Archbishop Robert J. Dwyer discussed this phenomenon as it recently has been applied in holy mother church.

"The liturgists of the post-Vatican II era, being Puritans of a stripe and density far surpassing John Knox in intolerance, have succeeded in stripping the church of the ministry of beauty and in depriving the faithful of the safety-valve of a controlled emotional outlet," began the archbishop.

"The result is not unlike that which followed the victory of Puritanism in England in the 17th century or in New England in the 18th, an outburst of emotionalism run wild and a widespread disillusionment and distaste for the institutional church.

"Civilized man requires the ministry of art. To deprive him of great literature, or sublime music, or splendid architecture, or the beauty of the plastic arts, is to maim and cripple him as a human being.

"He may survive for a while, 'living and half-living', but only by leading a kind of semi-barbarous existence...his soul starving for those things which ennoble him and lift him out of the primordial mire.

"Pre-eminently is this true of man as a religious being. For his worship of God, in addition to the adhesion of his intellect and the obedience of his will, he requires the best that the arts can bring to make his prayer take wing and his liturgy truly come alive.

"This has always been the case. Following his higher instincts, man has always enriched his acts of religion, his liturgy, by the employment of his artistic talent and genius.

"He has phrased his prayer in the noblest language his tongue can frame. He has lifted his voice in praise in music at once thrilling and purifying.

"He has made his temples or cathedrals the supreme expression of his power as a builder. He has endowed his images with the most perfect form his chisel can achieve. He has painted his saints as though sharing their vision of glory.

"When he has failed to do this, he has suffered and religion has suffered. As when he has turned to materialism or atheism. Or when he has tried to persuade himself that he can worship God adequately as a naked soul, face to face with the ultimate, and has found that he is merely talking to himself.

"This, we say, the liturgical Puritans have forgotten or ignored. They have reduced liturgical language, at least in the vernacular, to the utmost depths of banality, so that anyone in the least sensitive to the beauties of English prose or poetry must cringe every time he goes to mass or reads the sacred scriptures in the translation unhappily approved by the American bishops conference for the edification of the faithful.

"Where once our ears were attuned to the eloquent phrasing of the Douai version or the monumental work of the late Monsignor Knox, now they are assaulted by a version so pedestrian as to suggest that the presidential speech writers must have had a hand in the business.

"Music we have debased so crassly as to eliminate the last vestige of its sacred character. Worse, we have robbed it even of any kind of secular dignity, so that it is good neither for the sanctuary or the music hall.

"Church architecture has taken on all the endearing qualities of the local supermarket minus whatever it has of incidental interest.

"And in banishing by absolute fiat all decoration from the sanctuary we have outdone the 17th century Puritans at their own game. They at least had some appreciation of proportion, grace, and interior dignity. And they preserved intact the 'organ roll' of the King James Version of the bible.

"But what is of equal or even greater seriousness then the elimination of the ministry of art from the post-Vatican II liturgy, is the concomitant destruction of practically all of those liturgical or para-liturgical celebrations which for centuries gave a legitimate release of the emotions.

"We speak of such things as pontifical high mass, with its stately, slow-moving ceremony, its deliberate pageantry, its emphasis, not on the persons or personalities of the ministers, but on the tremendous significance of the action they were performing.

"The richness of vestments, covering for the time the poverty of our nature, the glory of the music proclaiming the praise of the most high, the eloquence of the Latin tongue, understood in substance by all present, and delighted in as rising above the very ordinariness of the vernacular.

"We speak of benediction of the Blessed Sacrament, with the altar ablaze with candles, to the awed wonder of our youthful eyes, a wonder which never fully wore off, however often the ritual was repeated in the days when we were a convent chaplain.

"We speak of the forty hours devotion and first Friday holy hours, of Lenten stations of the cross, of the rosary recited by the congregation, of vespers sung, however imperfectly, on a Sunday afternoon.

"We speak of the beauty of God's house and the place where his glory dwelleth.

"All gone now, all swept away, or so nearly as to make small difference. The liturgical Puritans have had their way, and the Holy See has not curbed their fanatic zeal. So the church is an empty supermarket, the altar a butcher's block, and the vestments are all being discarded by the now generation.

"One of the immediate and obvious results, of course, is the precipitous falling-off in mass attendance.

"Father Andrew Greeley's celebrated institute for exposing what's wrong with the church pronounces that this decline is primarily due to Pope Paul's encyclical 'Humane Vitae', a conclusion which is contradicted by the experience of every pastor in the land who has his finger on the pulse of the faithful. He knows that it is due to boredom, distaste, and a vague sense that that the glory has departed.

"But more…is not the wave of unbridled emotionalism now sweeping the church and threatening to loose her from her moorings a direct reaction to the iron hand of this liturgical Puritanism?

"Religious emotion must have an outlet. In itself, it is a legitimate expression of man's deepest feelings, which, if utterly restrained, break out in extreme and bizarre forms like the convulsionaries of Saint Medard in the 18th century Paris or the Penitentes of New Mexico.

"If the church fails to provide tested and sound outlets for religious emotion, it will seek some other vent, with results that can be extremely harmful to religion itself.

"For excessive emotional expression is always followed by an opposite reaction, usually in the form of disillusionment and disgust. Unmistakable signs of this reaction have already been widely observed here in America in consequence of the emotional hysteria which has been whipped up over the past decade.

"Nothing to be wondered at. The pattern is as old as man's religious experience.

"In frontier America of a century ago the emotional excesses of the camp meeting almost invariably were followed by lapse into religious indifference or even worse.

"The church as a wise mother has devised her liturgy and her para-liturgical services in such a way as to provide a safe balance, insisting always on the great primary objects of worship—the knowledge and praise of God and humble conformity to His will, with sufficient though not excessive outlets for the emotions.

"The liturgical Puritans have upset that balance. It will be a job to restore it."

"Blessed be God. Blessed be His Holy Name. Blessed be Jesus Christ, true God and true man. Blessed be the name of Jesus. Blessed be His most Sacred Heart. Blessed be Jesus in the most holy sacrament of the altar...blessed be God in His angels and in His saints."

No. 66—February. 1976 Rudolph M. Unger

Chapter 67

Father Robert E. Burns, a Paulist priest, wrote an article entitled "A Decade In Retrospect" in "The Wanderer" Catholic newspaper last May. In the next two issues we will present his measure of this tumultuous period in church history.

"In recent months, I have traveled quite extensively in this country of ours," he began. "I have talked with many Catholic pastors and Catholic parents. I am inspired by their strong faith, but everywhere I heard reports of the many young Catholics (mostly educated in Catholic schools) who no longer attend mass. In almost every case, the reason they gave is—'I don't get anything out of the mass.'

"Now this is rather strange because, as I recall, every liturgical innovation introduced (officially approved or otherwise) during the past ten years was always accompanied by the proclamation—'This will make the mass more meaningful to our people.'

"If all these innovations tended to make the mass more meaningful to our people, then why do so many young people now say—'I don't get anything out of the mass'?

"I do not doubt that, in the past, many Catholics felt that they got nothing out of the mass. Yet they attended mass regularly. Why? Because they realized that Sunday mass attendance (like Friday abstinence) was the law of the church and they wished to be obedient Catholics. Also they realized that as God's creatures they had a solemn obligation to worship Him.

"They knew that the mass is the official act of worship of the church. It is the 'perfect sacrifice of the new law' and the continuation of our Lord's sacrifice on Calvary. They attended mass because they loved the Catholic faith.

"How often they put up with boring sermons, Sunday after Sunday. How often they tolerated the rantings of cranky pastors who may have been afflicted with ulcers or the gout, but they realized that to a Catholic it is the mass that matters. The fact that so many people in recent years were so quick to discard mass bespeaks more than dissatisfaction with liturgical innovations. It bespeaks an underminding of their Catholic faith somewhere.

"In a large city which shall be nameless, there is a dedicated pastor who is under constant pressure from the diocesan liturgical committee because he is not moving fast enough in updating his parish. This priest has a very large parish and a large church. Sunday mass attendance at this church in recent years had increased somewhere between fifty and one hundred percent.

"It is no secret that this tremendous increase is due largely to the influx of fugitives from other parishes who are seeking the opportunity to worship God in a church which has preserved some degree of proper decor and in a service which has retained an atmosphere of reverence and devotion. It seems to me that this should send a message to someone in authority, but apparently it has not.

"I might say in passing that this good pastor has complied with all 'necessary' liturgical directives. Of course, he is considered backward by the new breed. Among other things, he cannot bring himself to wreck the beautiful main altar or to deprive the faithful of the consolation of receiving communion while kneeling at the beautiful marble altar rail. And, he will not tolerate communion in the hand.

"I have talked to many of the parishioners in this good parish and I shudder to think what will happen if the good pastor is forced to cave in or is transferred elsewhere.

"In another city, which shall be nameless, there is a Catholic high school filled to capacity with (mind you) a long waiting list. The old building is more than a century old, in a lower middle-class working neighborhood, although not a high crime area.

"Now here is a strange thing. In the same diocese, at least half a dozen Catholic high schools have closed in the past ten years because of decreased enrollment and mounting financial costs. Some of these schools were of relatively recent construction.

"Well, why wouldn't parents of children on the waiting list of the old school enroll them at one of the schools with plenty of openings?

"Are you kidding? More and more Catholic parents today have become selective. They realize that the same Catholic faith is not taught at every Catholic school today, as it was thirty years ago. They know that in too many of our schools, the new theology has replaced the true theology, the new morality has replaced the old morality. They also know something which apparently many Catholic educators do not know—that the new morality is the old immorality. Again, this should send a message to someone in authority, but apparently it has not.

"The past decade I believe was, among other things, characterized by the abuse of the 'imprimatur', which in many cases was rendered absolutely meaningless.

"The 'imprimatur' (a guarantee of sound doctrine) is granted by a bishop to some book or other literary work which in most cases he has not read (understandably so) and in some cases he may never have seen.

"Why then does he grant this 'imprimatur'?

"Well, he does it on the basis of the 'nihil obstat' (nothing objectionable) which was given by the bishop's trusted subordinate in Catholic education. But to put it very mildly and gently, the faith of some of these trusted subordinates today is highly questionable.

"For example, for some years the 'nihil obstat' in a New Jersey diocese was granted by a man who left the priesthood about six months ago. Four years ago (and I say this with all due charity) I was convinced that he had lost the faith and, particularly, that he no longer believed in the Divinity of Christ.

"If, instead of hiding behind an 'imprimatur' and a 'nihil obstat' when upset parents bring complaints to them, Catholic educators would try to reconcile textbooks with Pope Paul's 'Credo', the 'General Catechetical Directory' and the bishops' own 'Basic Teachings' document, perhaps fewer schools would be losing face with Catholic parents today."

Speaking of the Catholic faith as taught thirty years ago:

"Who made the world?—God made the world.

"Who is God?—God is the creator (maker) of heaven and earth and of all things.

"What is man?—Man is a creature composed of body and soul. And made to the image and likeness of God.

"What is a creature?—A creature is anything that God makes out of nothing.

"Why did God make you?—God made me to know Him, to love Him, and to serve Him in this world and to be happy with him forever in the next.

"What tells us that there is a God?—Our own heart and mind tell us that there is a God.

"Who tells us all we ought to know about God?—The Catholic Church tells us all we ought to know about God. (The chief truths, which the church teaches, are to be found in the Apostles' Creed.)

"Can we see God?—We cannot see God, because He is a spirit without a body.

"What is God?—God is a spirit, infinitely perfect.

"What is a spirit?—A spirit is a being that has understanding and free will, but not a body. A spirit cannot die.

"Had God a beginning?—God had no beginning. He always was and He always will be.

"Where is God?—God is everywhere. (God is present in a special manner in heaven, in the Blessed Sacrament, and in the souls of the just.)

"Can God do all things?—God can do all things.

"Does God see us?—God sees us and watches over us. (Divine Providence) (God knows all things, even our most secret thoughts, words, and actions.)

"Is God holy?—God is all holy. He loves what is good and hates what is evil.

"Is God just?—God is all-just. He rewards the good and punishes the evil.

"Is God merciful?—God is all-merciful. He forgives all who are sorry for their sins."

(The Baltimore Catechism)

No. 67—March, 1976 Rudolph M. Unger

Chapter 68

"If one were asked, what has been the single most influential movement in the church in America during the past decade, I think it would not be far off target to answer—the rise of the charismatic movement."

So wrote Father Robert E. Burns in his "A Decade In Retrospect."

"Like the late Bishop Vincent Waters of Raleigh, North Carolina, I have grave misgivings concerning this movement," Father Burns went on.

"Frankly, I don't see this 'baptism of the spirit' since our trusted friend, St. Paul, told us that there is 'one Lord, one faith, and one baptism.' I also have faith in the 'abiding presence of the Holy Spirit,' promised by our Lord to the church.

"Like Archbishop Robert Dwyer, I wonder where the Holy Spirit was during all those years before 1967, when two professors at Duquesne University received the 'baptism of the spirit' from the local Pentecostals and gave impetus to the Catholic Pentecostal movement.

"However, I have a theory of my own to help explain the phenomenal growth of this movement. The Pentecostal movement did not attract large numbers of Catholics when every parish church had regular benediction, holy hours, rosary devotions, and novenas.

"The Pentecostal movement was not attracting religious when nuns gathered regularly in the community chapel for meditation, community prayers, and devotions.

"In other words, I believe the charismatic movement has rushed in to fill a vacuum left by the elimination of traditional Catholic devotions in parish churches, convents, and other religious houses.

"Furthermore, I believe that the wholesale destruction of main altars and relegating the tabernacle to an insignificant part of the church edifice has played a big part in the elimination of Catholic devotion.

"In recent years, many people—in defiance of their bishops – have traveled regularly by bus to Necedah, Wis., Bayside, N.Y., and Santa Ana, Calif., where apparitions have allegedly taken place and messages received from on high.

"These folks return home feeling spiritually enriched. Why? Because they engage in devotions they have loved from childhood—devotions like benediction, rosary, processions in honor of the Blessed Virgin Mary, which have been eliminated from their parish churches.

"I am not commending their disobedience, but there is a lesson to be learned from their actions.

"Looking back over this decade since Vatican II, I feel (and many will agree with me) that the most decisive and precedent forming event that happened to the Catholic church in America was the controversy over Father Charles Curran, a dissenter from church teaching on contraception, at Catholic University in the spring of 1967.

"This controversy clearly demonstrated the awesome power of television in affairs of the church as well as those of society in general. Most people have no idea of the basic issue involved in this controversy, but they remember the touching scenes on TV showing new breed nuns carrying banners proclaiming—'We want our Charlie' and 'If Charlie goes we go.' (Too bad they didn't!)

"Well who would be foolish enough to allow himself to be humiliated and his image tarnished on TV? Better to capitulate at all costs than to undergo such humiliation.

"The lesson of Catholic University was not lost on others. A woman theologian at Boston College, noted for her pro-abortion articles long before the notorious supreme court decision, used the 'Curran technique' to save her job which was in jeopardy. And like 'beloved Charlie' she succeeded not only in saving her job, but also in obtaining tenure.

"The landmark 'Curran case' at Catholic University paved the way for the wholesale dissension by so-called experts from 'Humane Vitae' which certainly encouraged the pro-abortionists and inspired them to greater efforts, seeing that the ranks of the Catholics, their chief opponents, were so badly torn asunder.

"Another thing the Catholic University controversy clearly established was the untouchable status of the expert. As a result, the prestige of Father Charles Curran as a moral theologian today is so well established that he is free to attack any Catholic teaching, whenever and wherever he sees fit, and none dare call him a heretic—especially none who exercise authority over him.

"Experts of every variety—catechetical, theological, scriptural, liturgical, social, and what have you—are all deeply indebted to Father Charles Curran. Thanks to his courageous efforts in 1967, they are now free to express any opinion they desire, not only at theological, biblical, and canon law conventions, but at CCD gatherings, in textbooks, and in classrooms all over the country, and they need have no fear of being chastised for doing so.

"Will this trend of the so-called experts riding high, wide, and handsome, and ruling the day continue through the next decade and beyond?

"Apparently it will, unless someone in authority acquires the ability, the desire, and the courage to challenge the problem and meet it head-on.

"Julius Caesar, writing of his Gallic wars, said: 'Ambassadors are sacred.' "It could well happen that some future historian, writing of this past decade, the first after Vatican Council II, will say—'It was a time when experts were held to be sacred.'"

Regarding the Holy Ghost (Holy Spirit) the Baltimore catechism teaches:

"The Holy Ghost is the third person of the Blessed Trinity. He proceeds from the father and the son. He is equal to the father and the son. He descended upon the apostles on Pentecost, ten days after the ascension of our Lord into heaven. Christ sent the Holy Ghost to sanctify His church, to enlighten and strengthen the apostles, and to enable them to teach the gospel. He will abide with the church forever.

"What must we do to receive the Holy Ghost and His grace?—to receive the Holy Ghost and His grace we must belong to the Catholic church and receive the sacraments.

"Confirmation is a sacrament through which we receive the Holy Ghost to make us strong and perfect Christians and soldiers of Jesus Christ. Besides sanctifying grace, we receive in confirmation the seven <u>gifts</u> of the Holy Ghost.

"The gifts are—wisdom, understanding, counsel, fortitude, knowledge, piety, and fear of the Lord.

"The gifts help us to develop the virtues of faith, hope, and charity which we received in the sacrament of baptism.

"What is the relation of the seven gifts to the twelve fruits of the Holy Ghost and to the eight beatitudes?

"The virtues of faith, hope, and charity, influenced by the seven gifts, will produce the good deeds of a Christian life. These deeds are enumerated in the fruits and the beatitudes.

"The fruits describe acts in us similar to those of the active life of Christ. The beatitudes describe acts in us similar to those of the inner life of Christ.

"The fruits of the Holy Ghost are—charity, joy, peace, patience, benignity, goodness, longsuffering, mildness, faith, modesty, continency, and chastity.

"They are the chief but not the only good acts performed with the assistance of the Holy Ghost.

"The beatitudes are—the poor in spirit, the meek, those who mourn, those who hunger and thirst after justice, the merciful, the clean of heart, the peacemakers, those who suffer persecution for justice sake."

"Come Holy Ghost, creator blest, and in our souls take up thy rest. Come with thy grace and heavenly aid, and fill the hearts which thou hast made."

No. 68—April, 1976 Rudolph M. Unger

Chapter 69

The first line of the first newsletter more than five years ago was: "These are times that try men's souls!"

As evidence of the depth of this spiritual crisis which besets us, we offer the next two newsletters.

They will present a sermon—"The mystery of the cross, why it is so hated".

The sermon, reproduced from "The Remnant", a Catholic publication, was given by Archbishop Marcel Lefebvre last September 14 to the students at his seminary of St. Pius X in Econe, Switzerland.

And to provide you with further food for thought, keep in mind as you read his words, that the Vatican has withdrawn its sanction from this seminary, whose leader's only sin is that he is trying to keep alive a priesthood steeped in the traditional orthodoxy of the Catholic church.

Keep also in mind that in the sanctuary of the church of the archbishop of Chicago, one of the so-called reform leaders at Vatican II, and in the sanctuary of many other churches, there no longer hangs a crucifix nor is the Blessed Sacrament present.

Archbishop Lefebvre began:

"My dear brothers, the essential thing in your ascent to the priesthood is for you to remember that the mystery of the cross is of the greatest importance in our spirituality, in our Christian life.

"Throughout the history of the church, the saints—souls truly desirous of deepening their Christian life—have always found the means of doing so in the mystery of the cross.

"This was particularly true in the Christian middle ages. And in our own day one can still find traces of this deep devotion. It can be seen in the construction of those magnificent cathedrals wherein the cross dominates. It dominates the altar. The cross is the sign which serves to give the form to our churches.

"The love for the cross of our Lord Jesus Christ is manifested in the writings, in the very flesh of St. Francis of Assisi, St. Ignatius, St. Bernard, and other great saints.

"The mystery of our sanctification, of our justification, cannot be explained without the cross of our Lord Jesus Christ.

"And today, more than ever, we need to meditate upon this mystery, because at all times, and particularly perhaps in our own age, man wants to eliminate the cross.

"He does not want to look at it. He does not wish to have it before his eyes. Why? Because the cross represents sacrifice...Sacrifice! And yet it is only thereby—by the cross, by sacrifice—that the Christian soul can regain life.

"'Mors mortua tunc est,' the liturgy says. 'Death did then die, when he died who was the source of life.' 'Quando mortua vita fuit.' When he who is life died, then death itself died. Life triumphed.

"That is the entire summary of the spirituality of the cross. We must die to ourselves to find life. That is the spiritual life. That is our justification. Holiness is nothing else!

"It is very simple indeed—summed up in two movements of our soul—the hatred of sin and the desire for God.

"Die to sin in order to live unto God! That is the cross. It is nothing other than that! It is the symbol of death to sin in order to live in God!

"There is the entire explanation of the spiritual life, or our interior life. We must ever pursue the sinfulness within us, sacrifice ourselves, know how to die to ourselves, extinguish our evil tendencies, our evil instincts, our desires to do evil, our desire to disobey God.

"We must know how to destroy them in order to live in God, to liberate ourselves from sin. 'Liberati a peccatis, servi facti estis justitiae' says St. Paul. Delivered from your sins, you shall become the servants of holiness, the slaves of sanctity.

"Men speak today of 'liberation.' Everywhere they have this word so much on their lips—liberation, liberation, liberation! What liberation? Liberation from our Lord Jesus Christ! They want no more of our Lord Jesus Christ, no more of His cross, of His sacrifice. Why? Because His sacrifice reminds us that we must sacrifice ourselves.

"It reminds us that we must die to our sins to have life. And that, for men who seek rather their own pleasure and their own satisfaction, they can neither see nor understand. They want nothing to do with the cross. And that is why so many crosses have disappeared in our day.

"Now, where shall we find a living cross, the cross ever filled with that charity, with that holy spirit which we need to combat our evil tendencies so as to live the life of our Lord Jesus Christ?

"At the holy altar—in our churches—in the holy sacrifice of the mass!

"And that is why the holy sacrifice of the mass has so much importance and has always been at the center our sanctification, at the center of the preoccupation of the church.

"It is there that we find our Lord! This is not a cross which is simply a historical remembrance of the death of Christ. No, it is the living cross, Calvary renewed!

"The only difference between the altar and Calvary is that on Calvary, our Lord offered a bloody sacrifice, and, on the altar, He offers Himself in an unbloody manner. That is the only difference!

"It is truly Calvary that is renewed each time the priest ascends to the altar and offers the sacrifice of the mass. It is <u>there</u> that we must find the source of our sanctification—in the holy mass.

"And, all the words of the liturgy express precisely this desire of expiation, of the remission of sins. To expiate, to remit our sins is one of the principal ends of holy mass.

"And even to expiate the sins of the souls in purgatory! That is why the holy sacrifice of the mass has such great efficacy for the souls in purgatory!

"Alas, that is what the Protestants denied and still deny. That is what even priests ordained today, ordained recently, have a tendency to deny. This is very serious.

"We ought to have the conviction that in the holy sacrifice of the mass is the source of all the graces which we can receive. And that is why we have the need, why we feel the need, of keeping the holy sacrifice of the mass, of leaving it untouched, so precious is it.

"For we would otherwise risk to cut off the source of our graces. If we changed the spirit of the sacrifice of the mass, and if we came to make of it a simple communion, a simple thanksgiving, a simple meal, we would cause this source of grace—which is the sacrifice of our Lord Jesus Christ, His sacrificial oblation—to disappear.

"And that which the priest performs is a sacrifice. It is a sacrificial action which the priest performs on the altar. It is not only a recalling of the memory of the last supper, or of the memory of the cross.

"Oh no! It is much more than that! There is unfathomable mystery in the sacrifice of the mass.

"That is why we ought to be attached to it with our whole soul, with all our heart. Because it is there that we find indeed that which the love of God has done for us…that which the love of God has done for us."

"O my people, what have I done to you. Wherein have I afflicted you? Answer me. Because I led you out of the land of Egypt, because I led you through the desert for 40 years. And fed you with manna, and brought you into a land exceedingly good.

"I opened the sea before you, I went before you in a pillar of cloud, I gave you the water of salvation from the rock to drink. What more ought I have done for you than I have done?

"For this you have prepared a cross for your Savior. In my thirst you gave me vinegar to drink and with a lance you have pierced the side of your Savior.

"We adore Your cross, O Lord, and we praise and glorify Your holy resurrection, for behold, by that wood joy came into the whole world."

(Liturgy of Good Friday)

No. 69—May, 1976 Rudolph M. Unger

Chapter 70

"If there is a testimony of the love of God for us, it is certainly our Lord Jesus Christ crucified on the cross," stated Archbishop Marcel Lefebvre in his "The mystery of the cross, why it is so hated."

"What more could our Lord have done, what more could God have done, then to immolate himself on the cross for us, to redeem us from our sins?

"Shall we be insensible to the sacrifice of our Lord, of the Son of God?

"One can still find marked, on old crucifixes of another age, these words—'Can you say that I have not loved you, when you see love carved upon this cross?'

"Love carved upon the cross! That is the crucifix—love manifested, love alive…upon the cross.

"Thus one can understand the desire that all holy souls have felt ever to have the crucifix before them, to find in the crucifix the support of their spirituality, the source of their spiritual life.

"And how earnestly those souls desired to assist at the holy sacrifice of the mass, to participate therein, so as to re-live Calvary, to re-live what the Blessed Virgin Mary lived. And thus to unite themselves to the sufferings of our Lord Jesus Christ!

"Compassion! Our Lady of Compassion is the patroness of our religious. Why? Because Christian souls ought to suffer with our Lord. A soul that would not wish to suffer with our Lord would not be a Christian soul.

"And we should not only suffer with, but also, as it were, think with our Lord. That is to say, desire with our Lord to suffer for the remission of the sins of the world—all the injuries, the sacrileges, the sins which are so numerous in the world.

"And finally, we should complete the passion of our Lord Jesus Christ. St. Paul says this very thing—we ought to complete in our flesh the passion of our Lord Jesus Christ. And this, too, we should desire.

"Oh it is a desire that will cost us dearly…that will cost us dearly, that will make us suffer—for if we wish to complete the passion of our Lord

Jesus Christ it will be necessary to suffer with Him, to be immolated with Him.

"And it would be too easy to say—'Since I am a Christian, God will bless me and exempt me from all suffering. I shall lead a life without suffering, without sacrifice. Because I love God, God loves me, and therefore the good Lord should certainly not want me to suffer!'

"That is indeed but poorly to comprehend the mystery of the passion of our Lord Jesus Christ. If our Lord has shown us the example of suffering, then, on the contrary, we should always have the desire to suffer with Him, the desire to sacrifice ourselves with Him.

"And when the thorn of pain pierces us, we should be happy, and find in this sacrifice our joy, our happiness, in associating ourselves—as God wants us to associate ourselves!—To the passion of His son for the redemption of the world and for the remission of our sins.

"Is this not but another mark of love from God—His desire that we be united in suffering with our Lord Jesus Christ?

"<u>That</u> is the Christian life. That is the <u>Catholic</u> teaching. <u>That</u> is our faith, the object of our faith, the reality of our faith.

"That is what all Christian generations have understood. Those generations of holy fathers and mothers of families who suffered, who suffered in a Christian manner, who accepted their sufferings, who accepted their difficulties with joy, who were examples to their children.

"In suffering and in pain, they knew how to support them with our Lord Jesus Christ. These were the generations of Christian families which bore so many vocations. It was in <u>that</u> that vocations were born—in the example which their parents could give, of knowing how to live with our Lord Jesus Christ, to suffer with our Lord Jesus Christ, to pray with our Lord Jesus Christ. To assist at the holy sacrifice of the mass with such faith, with such piety, in the spirit of self-oblation as victims along with our Lord Jesus Christ.

"How beautiful it is, this Christian, this Catholic doctrine! How completely it transforms our life! How completely it transforms our life here below! And it is that which prepares us for life eternal!

"'O crux, ave, spes nostra'! We refer to the cross as our hope. For, in fact, the cross is only a road, a way – the way to eternal life, to glory.

"But it is necessary to pass by way of the cross. One must take up the cross and bear it after our Lord to arrive at eternal life! This via crucis should be ours throughout the course of our life, in order for us to arrive at life eternal.

"There, my dear friends, there is our faith. That is what you should be pursuing here. You should have the cross ever before your eyes. Your most precious desire should be to assist at, to participate in, the holy sacrifice of the mass.

"It should be this that fills your heart, your soul, with that balm that causes all the little difficulties you may have—in your studies, with your health, in the difficulties of community life—that causes all that to be eclipsed by the joy that you have in uniting yourself to our Lord Jesus Christ.

"The joy you have to live with our Lord Jesus Christ, the joy that one day, God willing, you will ascend the altar and offer the sacrifice of our Lord, that you will renew the sacrifice of Calvary, and that you will offer yourselves also as victims with our Lord on the altar for the redemption of the sins of the world.

"That you will preach this doctrine of the cross, that you will preach Jesus and Jesus crucified, as St. Paul says. Indeed St. Paul had no other preaching—'nisi jesum et jesum crucifixum.'

"That was the preaching of St. Paul. It will also be, I am sure, your preaching and as model of this participation, you will present to the world the most Blessed Virgin Mary, Our Lady of Compassion.

"In the Name of the Father, the Son, and of the Holy Ghost. Amen"

"Jesus hath many lovers of His kingdom of heaven, but He has few bearers of His cross. Many desire His consolation, but few desire His tribulation. He findeth many fellows at eating and drinking, but He findeth few that will be with Him in His abstinence and fasting.

"All men would rejoice with Christ, but few will anything suffer for Christ. Many follow Him to the breaking of His bread for their bodily refection, but few will follow Him to drink a draught of the chalice of His passion. Many honor His miracles, but few will follow the shame of His cross." (The Imitation of Christ. Thomas A. Kempis)

"I am the way, the truth, and the life. No man cometh to the father but by Me…if you love Me, keep My commandments…This is My commandment, that you love one another as I have loved you…greater love than this no man hath, that a man lay down his life for his friends.

"If the world hate you, know that it hath hated Me before you. If you had been of the world, the world would love its own. But because you are not of the world, but I have chosen you out of the world, therefore the world hateth you.

"The servant is not greater than the master. If they have persecuted Me, they will also persecute you…Amen I say to you that you shall lament and weep, but the world shall rejoice and you shall be made sorrowful, but your sorrow shall turn to joy.

"If any man will come after me, let him deny himself and take up his cross and follow Me. For he that will save his life shall lose it and he that shall lose his life for My sake shall find it …"

"For unto this are you called. Because Christ also suffered for us, leaving you an example that you should follow His steps…But if you partake of the sufferings of Christ, rejoice that, when His glory shall be revealed, you may also be glad with exceeding joy…If we suffer with Him, we may be also glorified in Him…The sufferings of this time are not worthy to be compared with the glory to come that shall be revealed in us."

No. 70—June, 1976 Rudolph M. Unger

Chapter 71

One of the greatest leaders bestowed on the Catholic Church in America was Cardinal James Gibbons, archbishop of Baltimore, whose long life spanned from 1834 to 1921.

Described by a non-Catholic authority as "The church's most persuasive spokesman to non-Catholic Americans, champion of democracy, and supporter of the separation of church and state," Cardinal Gibbons in 1876—100 years ago—wrote one of the classic works in Catholic American literature.

Entitled, "The Faith of our Fathers", it was reprinted hundreds of times and sold by the millions and is still read today, more than fifty years after his death.

Unlike the apologetic ecumenism that pervades the atmosphere today, the book was in the church's traditionally unabashed spirit of apologetics, or, in the cardinal's own words, "A plain exposition and vindication of the principal tenets of the Catholic church, the church founded by Jesus Christ."

He said its "Chief aim has been to bring home the truths of the Catholic faith to our separated brethren." The power of its argument is measured not only by its widespread reading in the United States, but also by the fact that it was translated into nearly every language of Europe.

We will deal here briefly with only two points he made in the book—"The use of religious ceremonies" and "Civil and religious liberty."

"True devotion must be interior and come from the heart," he wrote. "But we are not to infer from this, that exterior worship is to be condemned because interior worship is prescribed as essential.

"On the contrary, the rites and ceremonies enjoined in the worship of God and the administration of the sacraments are dictated by right reason.

"Man, by nature, is possessed of a soul and a body. It is, therefore, his privilege, as well as his duty, to offer to God the twofold homage of body and soul—to honor Him by internal and external worship.

"Genuine piety cannot long be concealed in the heart without manifesting itself by exterior practices of religion. Though the interior and exterior worship are distinct, they cannot be separated. The fruit of piety must be fostered by some outward observance or it will soon decay.

"Almighty God considered ceremonial so indispensable to interior worship that we find him in the old law prescribing in minute detail the various rites to be observed by the Jewish priests in their public worship. What is the entire book of Leviticus but an elaborate ritual of the Jewish church?

"And where shall we find a ritual so gorgeous as that presented to us in St. John's Book of Revelation? How glorious the pageant! How elaborate the detail!

"Strange would it be if God, who, in the dispensation past and that to come, is seen delighting in external majesty, should have deprived the church (the living link between the past and the future) of all external glory.

"The church performs these ceremonies from the highest motives of religion. Therefore, she has her solemn processions, her heavenly music, to soften the heart and raise it to God. She consecrates the cross, the banner of salvation; speaking not only to our head and heart by the word of God, but to our feelings and imagination by her grand and imposing rites."

Turning to the concepts of 'Civil and religious liberty, Cardinal Gibbons remarks:

"A man enjoys religious liberty when he possesses the free right of worshiping God according to the dictates of a right conscience. Every act infringing on his freedom of conscience is justly styled religious intolerance. This religious liberty is the true right of every man.

"A man enjoys civil liberty when he is exempt from the arbitrary will of others and when he is governed by equitable laws established for the general welfare of society.

"The Catholic church has always been the zealous promoter of religious and civil liberty. Her doctrine is, that as man by his own free will fell from grace, so of his own free will must he return to grace. Conversion and coercion are two terms that can never be reconciled.

"Whenever any encroachment on these sacred privileges were perpetrated by professing members of the church, far from being sanctioned by her, they were in violation of her authority.

"Among the innumerable historical examples of the church's defense of these sacred privileges, there is the beautiful admonition written by

Archbishop Fenelon of Cambrai, France, to the son of King James II of England:

'Above all, never force your subjects to change their religion. No human power can reach the impenetrable recess of the free will of the heart. Violence can never persuade men. It serves only to make hypocrites. Grant civil liberty to all, not in approving everything as indifferent, but in tolerating with patience whatever almighty God tolerates, and endeavoring to convert men by mild persuasion.'

"The only argument the church would use, is the argument of reason and persuasion. The only tribunal to which she would summon you, is the tribunal of conscience. The only weapon she would wield is 'the sword of the spirit, which is the word of God.'

"The church is, indeed, intolerant in this sense, that she can never confound truth with error. Nor can she admit that any man is conscientiously free to reject the truth when its claims are convincingly brought home to the mind.

"The church has not only respected the conscience of the people in embracing the religion of their choice, but she has also defended their civil rights and liberties against the encroachments of temporal sovereigns.

"The conflict between church and state has never died out, because the church has felt it to be her duty, in every age, to raise her voice against the despotic and arbitrary measures of princes. (Communist imperialism)

"As a Protestant American reviewer well said, 'It was a blessing of Providence that there was a spiritual power on earth that could stand like a wall of brass against the tyranny of earthly sovereigns and say to them—'Thus far shall you go, and no farther. This is not lawful for thee.'

"The greatest bulwark of civil liberty is the famous Magna Charta, the foundation, not only of British, but also of American constitutional freedom. Who were the framers of this memorable charter?—Archbishop Langton of Canterbury and the Catholic barons of England, who, on the plains of Runnymede in 1215, compelled King John to sign the paper that was the death blow of arbitrary power and the cornerstone of constitutional government.

"In this nation, Washington, the father of our country, told Catholic Americans—'I presume that your fellow citizens will not forget the patriotic part which you took in the accomplishment of their revolution, and the establishment of their government; or the important assistance they received from a nation in which the Roman Catholic faith is professed.'

"It is in a spirit of just pride that we can affirm that hitherto in the United States, no Protestant house of worship or educational institution has been destroyed, nor violence offered to a Protestant minister, by those who profess the Catholic faith. God grant that this may always be our record.

"From my heart, I say—America, with all thy faults, I love thee still. Perhaps at this moment there is no nation on the face of the earth where the church is less trammeled and where she has more liberty to carry out her sublime destiny than in these United States.

"For my part, I much prefer the system which prevails in this country, where the temporal needs of the church are supplied by voluntary contributions of the faithful, to the system which obtains in some Catholic countries in Europe, where the church is supported by the government.

"The church pays dearly for this indemnity, for she has to bear the perpetual attempts at interference and vexatious enactments of the civil power, which aims at making her wholly dependent upon itself.

"I do not wish to see the day when the church will invoke or receive any government aid to build our churches, or to pay the salary of our clergy, for the government may then begin to dictate to us what doctrines we ought to preach.

"No amount of state subsidy would compensate for the evils resulting from the government censorship of the gospel, and the suppression of apostolic freedom in proclaiming it. And moreover, in proportion as state patronage would increase, the sympathy and aid of the faithful would diminish.

"May the happy condition of things now existing among us always continue—bishops and priests bestowing their voluntary labors, and, in return receiving the free will offerings, the devotion and gratitude, of a filial people."

No. 71—July, 1976 Rudolph M. Unger

Chapter 72

Have you ever heard of Michael Ghisleri? It isn't likely that you have. But dear brothers in Christ, pray that God in His loving Providence may once again allow a Michael Ghisleri to ascend to the throne of Peter in this—our desperate age!

For the age in which he reigned saw one of the most desperate crises in the nearly 2,000 years history of the one true church. The worst perhaps since Arianism held sway 1,200 years before. And the likes of which perhaps was not again seen for another 400 years, until this—our unfortunate age.

In fact, the similarities, the parallels between the interior and exterior crises faced by the church in this our day and his day are uncannily alike.

Michael Ghisleri reigned only six years as Christ's vicar on earth under the title of St. Pius V. But he was one of the greatest popes in the two millenniums of the church's existence. In that short period he broke the backs of both the church's exterior enemy—Mohammedanism—and its interior enemy—the Protestant Reformation.

Today, the church stands desperately in need of another Ghisleri as its leader to break the backs of these two heresies' modern counterparts—communism and ecumenical—ironical renewal.

Michael Ghisleri didn't want the job. In fact he had to be taken physically by his fellow cardinals before he finally consented to accept the august position.

Nor was he a popular choice. To which his response was that if joy had been lacking at his election, he hoped there would be regret at his death. And regret, indeed, there was.

He was the first pope to be canonized a saint in nearly 300 years, not since St. Celestine V back in the golden age of the church, the 13th century. And there has been only one canonized in the 400 years since—St. Pius X.

St. Pius V was a leader of character and courage. He was tough. He was single-minded. His concern was not for what men thought. His concern was for what God thought.

That is why he became a saint. That is why he was a good shepherd. Three years ago a brief history of his life was written. In the foreword to that book, by Robin Anderson, Cardinal Alfredo Ottaviani, that pillar of orthodoxy in the church, whose influence is sorely missing from the present scheme of things in the Vatican, wrote:

"This book does something truly opportune, giving an account of the virtue and merits of St. Pius V, great saint, glorious defender of Christian standards, valiant guardian of the treasures of truth, justice and sanctity, which the church was born to spread through out the world.

"And this is all the more opportune in our age when materialism, communism, humanism and atheism have joined together as adversaries of the Christian way.

"Rome, the church, the entire world needed a man of the temper, holiness and energetic action such as were proper to him."

And so, for such a man do the needs of Christianity, Christendom, and the world, cry out again today.

"A man in whom the light of everlasting truth can never fail, such a light was St. Pius V," as Cardinal Ottaviani wrote.

A dozen years after Columbus discovered America, "Michael Ghisleri was born in Bosco Township in the Piedmont region of Northern Italy in 1504," Professor Anderson wrote.

"He was first called Anthony but later took the name of Michael, prince of the heavenly hosts, whom he chose as his patron. His parents were peasants of deeply Christian faith.

"As a boy, he had a special love for the Mother of God and he wanted to be a priest but his people were too poor and he was set to mind flocks of sheep.

"As he was doing so one day, he met two Dominican priests who were struck by the boy's piety and intelligence, and eventually he was allowed to take the habit of their order. By age 20, following studies at Bologna University, he was appointed professor of philosophy.

"He was ordained at 24, but when he journeyed to the parish church of his birthplace to say his first mass, he found it burnt down and his home half desecrated by imperial troops.

"In the days to follow he was a highly successful teacher and was four times elected prior, but he practiced mortifications to keep himself from becoming vain over his success with his students.

"His reputation for sanctity soon spread far beyond his monastery. His government was gentle but severe. His health was often poor. Everywhere at the time there was strife, rebellion, and discord. Heresy, open or concealed, was spreading continually.

"Ghisleri was named inquisitor by Rome for Northern Italy where the Protestant Reformation had found its way and where many of the Lombard clergy had been affected.

"He proceeded against a bishop, known to be surrounded by heretics, and led to the bishop's being deposed and exiled. Later, when a prelate at the Vatican had remarked that perhaps he had been too severe, Ghisleri replied:

'Nothing can be too severe for those who attempt to hinder the ministers of religion in their rightful duties by means of civil power.'

"For the bishop had sent armed forces to try to capture Ghisleri who had escaped them and returned to Rome.

"Pope Julius III promoted Ghisleri in the fight against heresy. He did all he could to clear up doubts and dispel error and his kindness and help caused many a change of heart, repentance, and conversion.

"Cardinal Caraffa upon becoming Pope Paul IV made him a bishop and general inquisitor of all Christendom. He later raised him to cardinal, but Ghisleri continued to wear the rough white habit of the Dominican order.

"Relentless as was the war he waged against heresy, he nevertheless sought to dissuade the authorities from taking too rigorous action and came to the defense of the Archbishop of Toledo, imprisoned by the Spanish inquisition.

"In 1559, Paul IV was succeeded by Pius IV, of very different character and far less strict. The final stage of the Council of Trent was concluded under him. Though he continued to make use of the inquisition, which had been re-instituted by Paul III to cope with the Reformation, he was easy going in regard to heresy. He too confirmed Ghisleri in the inquisitor office, but by appointing him bishop for a distant diocese, he virtually exiled from Rome one who had been among Paul IV's chief counselors and almost the only cardinal of strong and resolute character.

"But he was soon summoned back to Rome, largely at the instance of Cardinal Charles Borromeo, archbishop of Milan, who had made his uncle the pope realize the desirability of having Ghisleri near him. Ghisleri's counsels were indispensable in bringing the Council of Trent to a close.

"Ghisleri had often to speak to the pontiff with extreme firmness, although by doing so he risked losing favor and confidence. He was the only-adviser who dared try and dissuade Pius IV (but without success) from making two young princes cardinals, one of them a boy of thirteen.

"But when it came to disagreeing with the pontiff over having his favorite nephew paid several thousand ducats out of the papal treasury, he did finally fall into disgrace and might have been confined in Castel St. Angelo had not Cardinal Borromeo again spoken in his behalf.

"In this period he fell ill from the first attack of a sickness which would bring about his death in a few years and thus could not leave Rome. In the meantime, Pius IV fell ill and died. Thus, by God's Providence, Ghisleri never left Rome again.

"The ensuing conclave met unsuccessfully for three weeks seeking to choose a successor. Cardinal Borromeo persuaded Cardinal Farnese to renounce his aspiration to the papacy and join him and the others in choosing Ghisleri. Led by Borromeo, the cardinals went to Ghisleri who refused.

"The cardinals, against his will, took him to the Pauline Chapel, where he again refused and finally assented to ascend the throne of Peter. Thus the world in 1566 obtained a pontiff of holiness and firmness of character, sorely needed by the world."

No. 72—August, 1976 Rudolph M. Unger

Chapter 73

In recounting the reforms made in Rome and the Papal states by St. Pius V as their temporal ruler, Robin Anderson in his biography of the great pontiff wrote:

"The profound impression made by the white robed Dominican friar, once a shepherd, now supreme pastor of the universal church, was noted in report after report of the ambassadors in Rome.

"The Spanish ambassador affirmed that for 300 years the church had not had a better head, adding 'this pope is a saint.'

"He eliminated the anniversary banquets of his coronation and ordered the money instead to be used for charitable works. His first act after being crowned was to dismiss the papal court jester, and no pope has had one since.

"As temporal sovereign of Rome, Pius set out to bring greater order, health, and beauty to the eternal city. Among his first acts were the repairing of sacred buildings, of aqueducts and walls, renewing fortifications, opening workshops and factories to provide employment, and creating free schools.

"Provision was made for beggars, imprisonment for debt was forbidden, the papal treasury was drained for the poor, the pope himself living on a bare minimum; merchants and dealers were forbidden to use the images of saints as trade marks and shop signs.

"When plague broke out after famine he organized a relief committee, going himself on foot to bring comfort to the suffering and dying. He was tireless in ransoming Christian slaves from the Turks and his charity to English Catholics exiled for their religion was boundless.

"Disreputable taverns were closed, he persuaded a group of virtuous women to devote themselves to the reform of the city's courtesans, and he took steps to prevent further pollution of the Tiber River.

"Counselors warned the pope to pay heed to what he was about for fear of provoking the few practicing Catholics that remained into defying or shunning his authority. But Pius did not change. He said rather than allow licentiousness in the holy city he would transfer his court elsewhere.

"In all these works the pope's right hand was his nephew, Cardinal Bonelli, also a Dominican. Pius had made his relative a cardinal and given him this responsibility only when his belief had been shaken in the disinterestedness of Cardinal Farnese and others, some of whom depended on temporal princes and minded more their own than the church's interests.

"The young cardinal, chosen for his trustworthiness, ability, and austere character, though only 25, was not allowed to hold any benefices, make gifts to relatives or receive any.

"When it was suggested to Pius, who had a horror of nepotism, that he give preferment to other relatives, he replied God had called him to serve the church, not have the church serve him. This firmness towards the members of his own family still further increased the Roman people's respect for the new pope.

"Even in temporal administration, though aided by Bonelli and later by others when the work grew overwhelming, it was evident that the real direction of affairs was kept firmly in the pope's hands.

"The Spanish ambassador wrote—'Rarely indeed in a pope has the monarch so given place to the priest. One thing only he has at heart, the salvation of souls. This is what determines his entire policy.'

"As inquisitor, Pius had been familiar with the affected righteousness concerning religious art of the Protestant reformers, in reality destroyers of true culture and beauty.

"Aided by Cardinal Borromeo and Philip Neri, Pius engaged the best artists in painting, sculpture and architecture to capture the radiant ideals of the Catholic faith.

"The building of the new St. Peter's went ahead under his direction. He also ordered work begun on the church of St. Mary of the Angels, built above the chapel in the Umbrian Plain where St. Francis Assisi died.

"Pius' day began with mass preceded by long meditation and followed by long thanksgiving. Out of love for the Blessed Sacrament, he would never allow himself to be carried at the Corpus Christi procession, but went on foot bearing the monstrance. Daily he would be seen walking in the city, saying the rosary."

Regarding St. Pius V's spiritual reforms, Professor Anderson wrote, "The deplorable state in which he found the church on becoming pope might have seemed ruinous but for Christ's promise that the gates of hell will never prevail.

"Repeated yielding and compromises on every front had allowed Protestantism to spread, with its negation of the supernatural, the priesthood, and the sacraments.

"It appeared to triumph in more and more places, affording proof that it was not so much authoritarianism as laxism that, by refusing to issue clear commands and set fixed limits, engendered false creeds, individual rebellion, and contestation.

"Not only had feeble resistance to the innovators been offered by emperor and Catholic sovereigns, but also, in spite of Trent, false hopes had continued to be entertained—it seems even by Pius V's very predecessor—of winning Protestants by making concessions to them regarding the rite of communion and ecclesiastical discipline.

"The guiding principle in all that Pius V undertook was the exact and rigorous application of the decrees of the Council of Trent.

"And it was thanks to his determined energy that these decrees did not remain a dead letter, as those of some previous councils, such as Constance and the 5th Lateran.

"He reminded the cardinals that not least among the causes of spreading heresy was the lax and unedifying life led by many of the clergy. He refused a request of the imperial envoy in Rome that the red hat be conferred on a certain prelate. The cardinals he did create were chosen for their merit and attitude, regardless of political or national considerations.

"Some of his former Dominican conferees who began to appear in the Vatican were told to stay in their monasteries and the same independence was shown by Pius towards the Jesuits and other orders, from whom he wished to remain free from undue influence.

"His first care was for the reform of the clergy and he noted, 'It is an established fact that bad priests are the ruin of the people and that odious heresy, introduced by force, has no other aim than corrupting the faithful.

"Absentee bishops were ordered to return to their dioceses and govern their flocks. Bishops were strongly exhorted to fast and pray, to lead their people by penitential example, and to fight heresy courageously.

"In bringing God's ministers back to essentials, Pius warned them against having any part in temporal affairs that could endanger their spiritual health. Recital of the Divine Office was everywhere rendered obligatory.

"Parish priests in Rome were ordered to have parents send their children to Sunday school for instruction in Catholic doctrine as laid down by the Council of Trent.

"Hundreds of bulls show with what vigor and precision Pius unflaggingly watched over and defended the deposit of faith.

"When Emperor Maximilian, as a solution for the dearth of vocations, had advocated abolition of priestly celibacy, and was supported by certain cardinals, Pius unequivocally reaffirmed celibacy. He also warned religious of the obligation of wearing clerical dress and religious habit.

"Ecclesiastical seminaries were not thought of until the Council of Trent ordered the setting up in every diocese of special training colleges for the formation of future priests. Pius pledged himself most particularly to the carrying out of the Tridentine decrees in this respect.

"He turned himself to the task of sending missionaries to the vast, new territories of North and South America, Africa, Asia, and India. He urged them to organize native communities apart from whites as a means of deterring the latter from abuse of power. He insisted the missionaries educate the people in self-government and aim at training a native clergy.

"Sixty apostolic constitutions and bulls were directed by him at eradicating abuses in the religious orders and to bring them back to the spirit of their founders.

"A culminating act of Pius' spiritual reforms was his declaring St. Thomas Aquinas a doctor of the church and making Aquinas' Summa Theologica obligatory teaching in the universities to counteract doctrinal deviations and false theologies."

No. 73—September, 1976 Rudolph M. Unger

Chapter 74

"Some thirty-five years before St. Pius V became pope, Emperor Charles V at the Diet of Augsburg in 1530, had rejected the 'confession' of Protestantism and ordered the restoration of Catholic worship in Germany," recalled Professor Robin Anderson in his biography of the great pontiff.

"Yet only a quarter of a century later, after the 'interim' declared by Charles, with concessions to the Protestants, pending the resumption of the Council of Trent, Catholicism and Protestantism were officially recognized by the 'Peace' of Augsburg in 1555.

"Every ruler was granted the right to decide which religion was to be practiced in his territory. (Religion thus became a matter of power, not faith.)

"When Pius ascended the throne of Peter in 1566, Protestantism was continuing to gain ground in most of the German provinces. Luther had died in 1546, but Calvin, who did not die until 1564, had meanwhile built the heresiarch's revolt into a codified religion.

"Elizabeth, whose hereditary right to the English crown was not recognized by Pius IV, had caused schism to pass into official heresy and apostasy by having parliament declare her supreme, in spiritual as well as temporal matters, by imposing the new religion of '39 Articles Of Faith' and a liturgy, altered out of recognition, upon the nation and Ireland.

"France was virtually in the hands of the unscrupulous, Machiavellian regent, Catherine de Medici, mother of young King Charles IX, and the Huguenots were threatening the country's religious and civil unity.

"Switzerland was in the grip of Calvinism. Scandinavia was largely lost to the church. Poland was on the verge of schism.

"The forthright, unworldly, and, humanly speaking, undiplomatic character and policy of Pius V, must have made many in the Roman curia and diplomatic circles wonder how the new pope would handle the European situation.

"The King of Poland was pressing the Holy See for a dissolution of his marriage on a pretext not unlike that of Henry VIII of England, that his queen could not bear him a male heir. Several Polish bishops with ambitious aims and infected by Protestantism backed the king.

"Pius sent Cardinal Commendone, the highly skilled Vatican diplomat, to Poland and he encouraged the Polish bishops to hold fast to orthodoxy and avoid a schism such as led to the English persecution. The Jesuits aided in saving the nation from a break with the church and Commendone did not leave until the king, whose wife had meantime died, promised he would remain true to the Catholic faith.

"In England, Pius at first, as had his predecessor, Pius IV, hoped for Elizabeth's conversion, but once finding she was not to be trusted, became tough with her.

"He required that all Catholics avoid attendance of Protestant services. The effects of this order were positive. Priests began reporting an end to considerable wavering. More and more Catholics, mostly of the older generation, refused to take part in Anglican worship, professing their faith courageously before magistrates and willingly accepting penalties and imprisonment. But they expressed fear for their children and the younger ones listening to heretical preaching.

"In February, 1570, after spending days in prayer and fasting, Pius V finally put his signature to the bull placing Elizabeth under the ban of the church, declaring her guilty of heresy, and thereby incurring excommunication.

"The Emperor Maximillian urged the pope not to promulgate the bull but Pius' mind was made up. Rome had waited more than a decade during which one appeal after another had reached Elizabeth in vain.

"Crowned according to Catholic rites, she had sworn to govern as a Catholic monarch. But almost immediately violating her coronation oath, and repudiating the pope's authority, she had begun to destroy the Catholic faith and persecute the church.

"Pius said his purpose in the bull was to give courage to the English Catholics. He said they had requested justice against Elizabeth and he in conscience could not refuse.

"The bull may have made cowards of some and confirmed others in cowardice. But many more were given the necessary strength to stay away from the Anglican rites despite the cruel penalties.

"Regarding the other great enemy of the church met forthrightly by Pius, Cardinal Henry Newman wrote, 'The Turkish successes began in the middle of the 11th century. They ended in the 16th when St. Pius V came to the throne of the apostle.

'The Battle of Lepanto on October 7, 1571, arrested for ever the danger of Mohammedan invasion in the south of Europe—and Lepanto was won by prayer.'

Professor Anderson elaborated, "Since the 7th century, the holy places of Palestine had been in the hands of the Mohammedans, and the Seljuk Turks, after capturing Jerusalem, threatened Constantinople and the eastern empire.

"The crusades of the 11th to 13th centuries, despite their flaws, did keep the west from invasion and staved off the conquest of the east. But in 1453, Constantinople finally fell, signaling the end of the Byzantine Empire, which for centuries had providentially barred Mohammedan entrance to Europe from the east.

"In 1470, the Turks over-ran Greece. In 1480, they landed in southern Italy. Many popes had endeavored but failed to unite Europe's sovereigns against the enemy from the east.

"St. Pius V was the pope to whom fell the task of carrying out, at long last, the ideal that culminated in the greatest naval victory of history.

"Mahomet II had boasted to the world that he would top St. Peter's Dome with the crescent moon and wind the pope's head in a turban. The failure of Emperor Maximillian's attempt in 1566, Pius' first year as pope, to wrest some Hungarian territory from the Turks weakened Catholic morale and resistance.

"The first check to Turkish sea-power had come the year before, 1565, with the valiant defense of Malta against tremendous odds under the leadership of Jean de la Valette. Upon becoming pope, Pius encouraged de la Valette to hold on and sought help for him from Spain, Portugal, and the Venetian Republic. He obtained money and architects to rebuild Malta's defenses.

"From the start of his pontificate, St. Pius V, whose thoughts were not of war but of peace, had nevertheless seen the need for a common call to arms on the part of European sovereigns and peoples, as well as the prayer and penance necessary to defeat the enemy.

"'By the penance of believing peoples, God's anger may be appeased and there will be hope in His all powerful aid,' the pope proclaimed.

"The pope sounded to Europe the alarm of the Turkish menace and after much arduous negotiation he united the forces of Spain, Venice, Genoa, and the other Italian states; the Knights of Malta, and the Holy See, to do naval battle with the powerful Turks.

"Don John of Austria, son of Emperor Charles V and half brother to King Philip II of Spain, though only twenty-four, was agreed upon by the allies to be the commander of their fleet.

"The Pope ordered extraordinary prayers, day and night, and penitential processions in which he took part. He fasted three days a week and spent long hours each day in prayer. The Turkish sultan declared that he feared the prayers of Pius V more than all the forces at the emperor's command.

"In 1569, Pius had enjoined the prayer of the holy rosary as the most effective means against heresy. Now he put the forthcoming battle for Europe under the protection of Our Lady Queen of the Most Holy Rosary.

"On October 7, 1571, the allied Christian fleet under Don John engaged the Turkish fleet in battle near its base of Lepanto in the Gulf of Corinth. By 5 p.m. The greatest sea battle in Christian history was over.

"The Turks lost 30,000 men, 8,000 were taken prisoner, and all but 45 of their 270 ships were sunk or captured. The Christians lost 7,500 men and 12 ships. Thousands of Christian galley slaves were freed.

"At 5 p.m., Pius rose from his work in the Vatican, looked out a window to the east, and turning said, 'The Christian fleet is victorious!' And began to weep in thanksgiving. Two weeks later, delayed by sea storms, came the confirmation of the victory.

"The Te Deum was sung in St. Peter's, the Pope credited the victory to the intercession of Our Lady, and the Roman senate proclaimed 'Now bravery triumphs, love reigns, and piety flourishes.'"

No. 74—October, 1976 Rudolph M. Unger

Chapter 75

"The renewal achieved by Pius V based on the Council of Trent, was completed by his publication of the Roman Catechism, or Catechism of Trent, followed by the revision of the breviary and the missal," noted Robin Anderson in his biography of the great pontiff and saint.

"The decrees of the Council of Trent were the greatest in 1,200 years, the greatest since the Council of Nicea had countered Arianism.

"The Council of Trent gathered up the hitherto dispersed forces of true reform, inspired and led by martyrs and saints such as St. Thomas More, St. John Fisher, St. Ignatius Loyola, St. Cajetan, and St. Angela Merci.

"The new Protestant theologians and most of the German universities had actively worked against the church. Since these reformers identified their doctrines with national interest, freedom of conscience, and human progress, the average Catholic was often deceived.

"First, Pope Pius entrusted the Jesuit, St. Peter Canisius, with refuting the Protestant theologians, who were striking at the heart of the Catholic faith—the real presence of Christ in the Eucharist, and the priesthood. Canisius consulted with St. Philip Neri.

"This work was followed by others which, as Pius V, who was not in the habit of mincing words, said, served, 'To confound the lies of heretics.'

"Most importantly, there followed, in compliance with Trent, another broader, more general compendium of Christian doctrine stated in clearest terms to safeguard the faith of Catholics. St. Charles Borromeo played a considerable part in seeing this work through, as he also did with revising the Roman breviary and missal.

"The Trent Catechism was issued in 1566 and Pius issued a bull to assure that the Catholic bishops would indeed base their teaching on it and in turn have it taught.

"Pius then turned to revising the breviary, or Divine Office, which members of the clergy are bound to say daily under pain of mortal sin.

"Various versions of the breviary had sprung up and this had caused a confusing and disintegrating influence, which Pius said had led to scandal by allowing indecorous rites to be used in the divine worship.

"The revised breviary brought the psaltery and scripture back into their own as they had been before the introduction of novelties and arbitrary individual deviations.

"Persuaded that the work of the Council of Trent, which had condemned the heresies of the time and proclaimed the church's true teaching, should be completed by a demonstration of the unity of dogmatic tradition in the east and west, and of the middle ages with antiquity, Pius decreed—

"Inclusion for the first time in the public worship of the universal church of the four Greek Doctors—St. Athanasius, St. Basil, St. Gregory Nazianzen, and St. John Chrysostom—side by side with the four Latin doctors—St. Augustine, St. Ambrose, St. Jerome, and St. Gregory The Great.

"However, Pius forbade Latin priests to say mass in Greek and Greek priests to say mass in Latin.

"The clergy of most countries welcomed the revised breviary. Though it was subsequently altered by two popes, who were therefore criticized by St. Robert Bellarmine, St. Pius X brought it back almost wholly to the text laid down by St. Pius V.

"Revision of the breviary was necessarily followed by that of the missal. There had existed for a long time some variety of mass rites in the west, but none of these departed substantially from the old Roman rite, which had taken on definite and final form early in the 5th century, with the building of the first Christian churches after the mass had emerged from the catacombs and public worship became possible.

"But divergences of relatively recent growth—from one nation to another and even from diocese to diocese—had become an unsettling factor, if not a threat to unity of faith, worship, doctrine, and morals.

"The Protestant innovations, among others—substitution of liturgical Latin by the national idiom in the mass and sacred rites, had at length seriously compromised unity. And Luther had said that when the mass should be overthrown the papacy itself would be overcome.

"As counteractant and safeguard, Trent had ordered everywhere to be kept the ancient rites in the original languages—Latin in the west, Greek in the east, and a few other eastern liturgies admitted and approved by Rome for centuries.

"The disorders and disunity disfiguring the church had allowed the disaster of heretical reforms to overtake Christendom and by combating and clearly condeming these false doctrines, Pius V dealth a death blow to the malady.

"The opening words of his bull—Quo Primum Tempore—posted upon the portals of St. Peter's on July 29, 1570, announced Pius V's intentions in unequivocal terms as far as the liturgy of the mass was concerned:

'As it is most fitting that the church should have one way of praising God, and one rite for the celebration of mass…'

"He therefore laid down one mass for all, to have universally binding force—In perpetuity (with the exception, as with the breviary, of rites continuously in use, and approved by the Holy See, for at least 200 years. These ancient rites were not merely allowed but encouraged to continue.

("Thus the Ambrosian, Carthusian, Dominican and one or two other variants of Latin rite peaceably continued, along with the ancient eastern liturgies—The Byzantine, Alexandrian, Antiochian, Armenian, and Chaldean.)

"Unity and purity of faith, worship, doctrine, and morals were thus safeguarded by uniformity of rite and language in the west, as in the east, with due exceptions in regard to sure tradition and antiquity.

"It was furthermore of the greatest benefit to the universal church that any alterations whatsoever in the liturgies were reserved to the Holy See, preventing future intrusions of irresponsible, self-authorized and incompetent reformers.

"The Roman missal of St. Pius V was, then, no new creation or departure from former practice, any more than his breviary. Rather was it a re-establishing of the church's most ancient, approved tradition, an elimination of accretions and innovations, while avoiding their replacement by other novelties.

"The revised missal was welcomed, as the breviary, by clergy everywhere. There is no record of any widespread distress caused to priests or laity by Pius V's Roman missal.

"And it was the ancient Roman rite, revised and made uniform by Pius, that the English people demanded in the risings throughout that country against the changes forcibly imposed by Henry, Edward, and Elizabeth.

"It was the constant uniting of spiritual contemplation and active works by Michael Ghisleri that was the source of the radical and far reaching spiritual and temporal reforms Pius V was able to bring about in but six years—for the church and Christian civilization.

"Whether fighting heresy within or enemies without, he was all the while, by his own self denial, penances and piety, drawing more and more people back to the faith and practice of true religion.

"Never passively resigned to the present course of events—the 'historic moment' as some today like to call it—he knew no half measures in his dealings.

"Living with the utmost frugality and least possible regard for his own health and comfort, his goodness, humility, and generosity went to heroic lengths.

"Characteristic of him was the gratitude he showed in many ways to all who had benefited him. Loving and prizing truth above all else, he had a horror of insincerity and feigning.

"Such was the holiness of Pius V that his worst foes were often overcome by it. God attested to this great holiness of the church's head by miracles even during his lifetime.

"The intermittent pains he had long suffered from 'stones' at length grew almost unbearable, but he chose to suffer rather than submit to surgery.

"After Holy Week ceremonies on Good Friday, 1572, he was obliged to take to his bed. On the last day of April, aware his death was approaching, he asked for the last sacraments. He desired to die in his Dominican habit.

"On May 1, in great agony, he uttered, 'Lord, increase my pain, but may it please thee also to increase my patience!' And then he died. St. Teresa Avila, many miles away in Italy, told her nuns to mourn, as the church had just lost her most holy pastor. Pius was beatified in 1672 and canonized in 1712."

No. 75—November, 1976 Rudolph M. Unger

Chapter 76

It is 404 years since St. Pius V, that flaming comet of God, went to his eternal reward after having saved the church and Christendom from their enemies within and without.

How different the response of the church and Christendom to the enemies within and without in our age's crisis.

In the 16th century it was "Stand fast and fight for principle."

In the 20th century it is "Bend and compromise and avoid a fight if at all possible."

In April, 1975, in two editorials in the National Catholic Register, the late Archbishop Robert J. Dwyer, who was one of the few clear and unequivocal voices for orthodoxy in the heirarchy today, pointedly described the difference. In the first editorial, entitled "The Decline Of The West," he wrote:

"As the First world war dragged on to its inglorious and inconclusive end in November, 1918, a German scholar, Oswald Spengler, professor at the University of Munich, published the two massive volumes of his essay on historical necessity—"The Decline Of The West."

"Spengler's main thesis was that western civilization, basically Christendom, based on money power, was just about played out and that the succession must inevitably bring in some form of absolute dictatorship.

"The rise of Hilter's Nazism, little more than a decade later, seemed to many at the time to vindicate handsomely the accuracy of Spengler's insights.

"But one need not expound so involved and recondite a theory to account for the phenomenon which now is overwhelming and overpowering the west, half a century later.

"The bankruptcy of liberalism, the catastrophic collapse of the public morality, the stark loss of confidence in the democratic process, the feverish eagerness to capitulate to absolutist tyranny, all these cry out with a voice of thunder that the west is finished—kaput!

"The old Gods seem to be fading as the economic and moral twilight deepens. The music of the masked ball grows wilder and wilder as the dancers twist and contort in a mad sexual orgy:

'But at my back I always hear time's winged chariot hurrying near. And yonder all before us lie deserts of vast eternity.'

"No question but that the west is in fearful decline. No question but that westerners, many if not most, have well nigh lost Faith of any kind, whether in God or in man; lost Hope in the conceivable redemption of our times; lost even Love in the perversion of sex and the glorification of utter selfishness.

"We could be said to be as close to total moral collapse as the Babylon of Belshazzar's feast, when Mene, Thekel, Upharsin were written on the wall, or as Rome when the barbarian hordes were thundering at the gates.

"Is this indeed the end, then, and are we to go down to dusty death in our 'stiff, dishonored shroud'?

"Spengler's doctrine of historical necessity or Marx's equivalent dialectic materialism would say— yes— with absolute finality.

"But in spite of all the evidence, some valid, more propagandist, we answer—no—even more absolutely and with the ultimate finality of God's word.

"For we are free men, with the freedom wherewith Christ has made us free. We are redeemed by His blood and it is within us to be again sons of grace. But this only by dint of a supreme, almighty effort.

"No more of this death wish, this despair of life, this readiness to capitulate to the powers of evil.

"Somehow the west must shake off the nightmare that enthralls it, rise up in new strength, take up the cross of Christ once more, with a glad shout—'In Hoc Signo Vincamus!'"

In his second editorial—'On Poles and Polarization'—the archbishop wrote:

"'Don't polarize the church! Whatever you do, don't rock the boat!'

"For the past decade these warnings have been posted with all the flaming urgency of storm signals at sea or tornado warnings in Kansas.

"Anyone who polarizes is a public enemy, guilty of the most heinous of crimes. 'A plague on both of your houses' is the only safe standard to follow—the way of balance, the middle path, avoiding either extreme of liberalism or conservatism.

"And on the face of it, for many, perhaps most, it has seemed the soundest advice, the wisest counsel. And so we have gone along, sedulously avoiding anything and everything that hints of extremism, all that indicates a determination to stand fast for the absolutes of faith.

"Bishops and superiors have been pliantly permissive, theologians have assured us that this is the wave of the future.

"And where do we find ourselves? In a gray, murky fog of confusion, where nothing, whether dogma or moral principle, is fixed and firm; where everyman and his brother claims for himself the blessed liberty of judging dogmas for himself and determining morality according to the situation at hand; where the teaching and disciplinary authority of the church is shrugged off as a relic of medieval superstition.

"But if anyone dares to get up and 'tell it like it is' he is immediately shouted down as 'polarizing' the church.

"What is strangely forgotten or ignored in this whole business is the plain, unalterable fact that Christ himself polarized the church, once and for all.

"He set her up as a sign of contradiction. What is polarization, after all, but taking a final stand, of proclaiming the absolute, eternal, unchangeable truth; establishing an infallible, indefectible authority?

"He Himself took such a stand—'He who is not for Me is against Me. He who gathereth not with Me, scattereth.'

"He gave to His church the sole commission to teach all men and to Peter as its head the very power of the keys.

"If this is not polarization, then words have no more meaning than what Humpty Dumpty arbitrarily decides to assign to them.

"Yes, let the darkling suspicion be dragged out into the open—that those who decry polarization the loudest are the very ones who are bent, knowingly or unwittingly, on destroying the church, robbing her of her divine character, making her over into some form of a debating society instead of our accredited teacher and our rock of salvation.

"And it might not be a bad idea, the next time you hear one of these anguished spirits lamenting the obscurantism of the Holy Father, or denouncing the loyal hierarchy and laity for polarizing the church, to ask, mildly,—on what pole he or she is sitting."

In his "Witness", Whittaker Chambers wrote:

"Two faiths were on trial—the two irreconcilable faiths of our time: communism and freedom. Human societies, like human beings, live by faith and die when this faith dies.

"In this century, within the next decades, will be decided for generations whether all mankind is to become communist, whether the whole world is to become free, or whether, in the struggle, civilization as we know it is to be completely destroyed or completely changed. It is our fate to live upon that turning point in history.

"Few men are so dull that they do not know that the crisis exists and that it threatens their lives at every point. It is a total crisis—religious, moral, social, political, economic.

"The power of the communists, whose nature baffles the rest of the world, because in a large measure the rest of the world has lost that power, is the power to hold convictions and to act on them.

"Communists are that part of mankind which has recovered the power to live or die—to bear witness—for its faith.

"It is not new. It is, in fact, man's second oldest faith. Its vision is the vision of man without God. Its promise was whispered in the first days of creation under the tree of the knowledge of good and evil—'Ye shall be as Gods.'"

No. 76—December, 1976 Rudolph M. Unger

Chapter 77

Nearly four centuries after St. Pius V went to his eternal reward, God placed on the throne of Peter another Pius destined to be a giant of the Papacy.

He was chosen on March 2, 1939 by unanimous choice on the third ballot, less then eight hours after the conclave of cardinals had begun to vote. It was the quickest choice in history.

He was Cardinal Eugenio Pacelli who was to take the name Pius XII. He was to reign nearly twenty years and his rule began as the storm clouds fermented by the fury of hell were poised to pour forth fire and brimstone onto the earth.

The conflagration had already ensued by the time Pius XII, perhaps the most prolific writer in the history of the papacy, had issued his first encyclical—Summi Pontificatus—on October 20, 1939.

Entitled "Exhorting Unity In Opposing World Evils ", it portrayed Pius XII's view of the world on the brink of catastrophe and his analysis of what had brought it there. Excerpts from it follow.

"It is just forty years ago that our immortal predecessor, Leo XIII, consecrated mankind to Our Redeemer's Most Sacred Heart. We recall how, as a newly ordained priest just empowered to say, 'I will go in to the altar of God', we hailed the truly providential action of a pontiff so sure in his diagnosis of the open and hidden needs and sores of men.

"As we review, from the standpoint of eternity, those forty years we see the wisdom of the consecration to Christ The King of a mankind in a world in all too dire need of help and guidance, a world preoccupied with the worship of the ephemeral, a world which has lost its way and spent its forces in a vain search after earthly ideals.

"It is a world in which men in ever increasing numbers have cut themselves off from faith in Christ and from recognition and observance of His law.

"What age had greater need than ours of the graces of the Divine Heart Of Our Redeemer, Christ The King? What age has been, for all its technical and purely civic progress, more tormented than ours by spiritual emptiness and deep-felt interior poverty?

"Can there be, venerable brethren, a greater or more urgent duty than to preach the unsearchable riches of Christ to the men of our time? Can there be anything nobler than to unfurl the ensign of Christ The King before those who follow a false standard?

"Who among the soldiers of Christ does not feel himself spurred to a greater vigilance, to a more determined resistance, by the sight of the ever increasing host of Christ's enemies as he perceives them to—deny the values inherent in the belief of God and in Christ, perceives them to break God's commandments and substitute standards stripped of ethical content?

"Who could observe without profound grief the tragic harvest of such desertions among those who in days of calm and security were numbered among the followers of Christ, but who in the hour that called for endurance, for effort, for suffering, for a stout heart in face of hidden or open persecution, fell victims of cowardice, weakness and uncertainty?

"Those who, terror stricken before the sacrifices entailed by a profession of their Christian faith, could not steel themselves to drink the bitter chalice awaiting those faithful to Christ.

"In such dispositions of time and temperament, venerable brethren, may the approaching feast of Christ The King, on which this our first encyclical will reach you, be a day of grace and of thorough renewal and revival in the spirit of the Kingdom of Christ.

"May it be a day when the faithful of all peoples and all nations gather around the throne of the Eternal King, in adoration and reparation, and renew, now and forever, their oath of allegiance to Him and His law of truth and love.

"May it be a day on which the fire that Our Lord came to cast upon the earth will kindle with ever greater light and purity. May it be a day of grace for the lukewarm, for the weary, for the afflicted, that their hearts, which have become faint, may give proofs of interior renewal and regeneration of spirit.

"May it be a day of grace for those who have not known Christ or who have lost Him, a day when 'The light which enlightened every man that cometh into this world' may make clear to them the way of salvation.

"We place, with a heart full of confidence and hope, this first encyclical under the seal of Christ The King. We are consoled in these first months by the magnificent and tangible demonstration of the indissoluble unity of the Catholic Church rallying all the closer to the impregnable rock of Peter, to form around it a wall and a bulwark as the enemies of Christ become bolder.

"To all those not belonging to the visible body of the Catholic Church, we assure them that one thought only fills our minds—to imitate the example of the Good Shepherd in order to bring true happiness to all men 'That they may have life and may have it more abundantly.'

"We feel we owe no greater debt to our office and to our time than to testify to the truth with apostolic firmness. This duty necessarily entails the exposition and confutation of errors and human faults, for these must be made known before it is possible to tend and to heal them.

"'You shall know the truth and the truth shall make you free.' In the fulfillment of this, our duty, we shall not let ourselves be influenced by earthly considerations nor be held back by mistrust or opposition, by rebuffs or lack of appreciation of our words, nor yet by fear of misconceptions and misinterpretations.

"We shall fulfill our duty, animated ever with that paternal charity which, while it suffers from the evils which afflict our children, at the same time points out to them the remedy. We shall strive to imitate the Divine Model, The Good Shepherd, who is light as well as love, 'Doing the truth in charity.'

"At the head of the road which leads to the spiritual and moral bankruptcy of the present day stand the nefarious efforts of not a few to dethrone Christ and to abandon His law of truth and His law of love.

"In the recognition of the royal prerogatives of Christ and in the return of individuals and of society to the law of His truth and of His Love lies the only way to salvation.

"As we write these lines, venerable brethren, news comes to us that the dread tempest of war is already raging despite all our efforts to avert it. When we think of the wave of suffering that has come on countless people who, but yesterday, enjoyed in the environment of their homes some little degree of well being, we are tempted to lay down our pen.

"Our paternal heart is torn by anguish as we look ahead to all that will yet come forth from the baneful seed of violence and of hatred for which the sword today ploughs the blood drenched furrow.

"But precisely because of this apocalyptic foresight of disaster, imminent and remote, we feel we have a duty to raise with still greater insistence the eyes and hearts of those in whom there yet remains good will to—the one from whom alone comes the salvation of the world, to one whose almighty and merciful hand can alone calm this tempest.

"Perhaps—God grant it—one may hope that this hour of direst need may bring a change of outlook and sentiment to those many who have walked with blind faith along the path of popular modern errors, unconscious of the treacherous and insecure ground on which they trod.

"Perhaps the many who have not grasped the importance of the educational and pastoral mission of the church will now understand better her warnings.

"No defense of Christianity could be more effective than the present straits. From the immense vortex of error and Anti-Christian movements there has come forth the current crop of poignant disasters."

No. 77—January, 1977 Rudolph M. Unger

Chapter 78

"The present age, by adding new errors to the doctrinal aberrations of the past, has pushed these to extremes which lead inevitably to a drift towards chaos," wrote Pope Pius XII in his first encyclical in 1939.

"Before all else, it is certain that the radical and ultimate cause of the evils which we deplore in modern society is the denial and rejection of a universal norm of morality as well for individual and social life as for international relations.

"We mean the disregard, so common nowadays, and the forgetfulness of the natural law itself, which has its foundation in God, Almighty Creator and Father of all, supreme and absolve lawgiver, All Wise and Just Judge of human actions.

"When God is hated, every basis of morality is undermined, the voice of conscience is stilled or grows very faint, that voice which teaches even illiterate and uncivilized tribes that which is good and that which is bad.

"The denial of the fundamentals of morality has its origin, in Europe, in the abandonment of that Christian teaching of which the chair of Peter is the depository and exponent. That teaching had once given spiritual cohesion to a Europe which—educated, enobled and civilized by the cross—had reached such a degree of civil progress as to become the teacher of other peoples, of other continents.

"But, cut off from the infallible teaching authority of the church, not a few separated brethren have gone so far as to overthrow the central dogma of Christianity—the Divinity of The Saviour—and have hastened thereby the progress of spiritual decay.

"The consequence is that the moral values by which in other times public and private conduct was gauged have fallen into disuse. And the much vaunted civilization of society, which has accelerated the withdrawal of man, the family, and the state from the teaching of the church, has caused to reappear ever clearer, ever more distinct, ever more distressing the signs of a corrupt and corrupting paganism.

"Many perhaps, while abandoning the teaching of Christ, were not fully conscious of being led astray by a mirage of glittering phrases—which proclaimed such estrangement as an escape from the 'slavery' in which they were being before held.

"Nor did they then foresee the bitter consequences of bartering the truth that sets free for error which enslaves.

"They did not realize that, in renouncing the infinitely wise and paternal laws of God and the unifying and elevating doctrines of Christ's Love, that they were resigning themselves to the whim of a poor, fickle human wisdom.

"They spoke of progress when they were going back. Of being raised when they groveled. Of arriving at man's estate when they stooped to servility. They did not perceive the inability of all human effort to replace the law of Christ. 'They became vain in their thoughts.'

"With the weakening of faith in God and in Jesus Christ, and the darkening in men's minds of the light of moral principles, there disappeared the indispensable foundation of the stability and quiet of that internal and external, private and public order, which alone can support and safeguard the prosperity of states.

"It is true that even when Europe had a cohesion of brotherhood through identical ideals gathered from Christian preaching, she was not free of divisions, convulsions and wars which laid her waste. But perhaps they never felt the intense pessimism of today as to the possibility of settling them, for they had then an effective moral sense of the just and the unjust, of the lawful and unlawful, which, by restraining outbreaks of passion, left the way open to an honorable settlement.

"In our days, on the contrary, dissensions come not only from the surge of rebellious passion, but also from a deep spiritual crisis which has overthrown the sound principles of private and public morality.

"The aim of the church of Christ is a supernatural unity. She cannot and does not think of deprecating or disdaining the particular characteristics which each people, with jealous and intelligible pride, cherishes and retains as a precious heritage.

"She seeks a spiritual union and not the unity which is exclusively external, and superficial and by that very fact weak.

"The church hails with joy and follows with maternal blessing every method of guidance and care which aims at a wise and orderly evolution of particular forces and tendencies having their origin in the individual character of each race, provided that they are not opposed to the duties incumbent on men from their unity of origin and common destiny.

"She has repeatedly shown in her missionary enterprises that such a principle of action is the guiding star of her universal apostolate.

"All that in the usages and customs of the varied civilizations which is not inseparably bound up with religious errors will always be subject to kindly consideration and, when it is found possible, will be sponsored and developed.

"Those who enter the church, whatever be their origin or speech, must know that they have equal rights as children in the house of The Lord where the law of Christ and the peace of Christ prevail.

"In accordance with these principles of equality, the church devotes her care to forming cultured native clergy and gradually increasing the number of native bishops.

"Nor is there any fear lest the consciousness of universal brotherhood aroused by the teachings of Christianity and the spirit which it inspires, be in contrast with love of traditions or the glories of one's fatherland or impede the progress of prosperity or legitimate interests.

"For that same Christianity teaches that in the exercise of charity we must follow a God-Given order, yielding the place of honor in our affections and good works to those who are bound to us by special ties.

"Nay, the Divine Master Himself gives an example of this preference for His own country and fatherland, as He wept over the coming destruction of the holy city.

"But legitimate and well-ordered love of our native country should not make us close our eyes to the all embracing nature of Christian charity, which calls for consideration of others and their interests in the pacifying light of love.

"Such is the marvelous doctrine of love and peace which has been such an ennobling factor in the civil and religious progress of mankind.

"And the heralds who proclaimed it, moved by supernatural charity, not only tilled the land and cared for the sick, but above all they reclaimed, moulded, and raised life to divine heights, directing it toward the summit of sanctity in which everything is seen in the light of God.

"They have raised mansions and temples which show to what lofty and kindly heights the Christian ideal urges man, but above all, they have made of men—wise or ignorant, strong or weak—living temples of God and branches of the very vine which is Christ.

"They have handed on to future generations the treasures of ancient art and wisdom and have secured for them that inestimable gift of eternal wisdom which links men as brothers by the common recognition of a Supernatural Father.

"Venerable brethren, forgetfulness of the law of universal charity, of that charity which alone can consolidate peace by extinguishing hatred and softening envies and dissensions, is the source of very grave evils for peaceful relations between nations.

"But there is yet another error no less pernicious to the well being of nations. It is the error contained in those ideas which do not hesitate to divorce civil authority from every kind of dependence upon the Supreme Being and from every restraint of a higher law derived from God. Thus they accord the civil authority an unrestricted field of action that is at the mercy of the changeful tide of human will."

No. 78—February, 1977 Rudolph M. Unger

Chapter 79

"Once the authority of God and the sway of His law are denied, the civil authority as an inevitable result tends to attribute to itself that absolute autonomy which belongs exclusively to the Supreme Maker," wrote Pope Pius XII in his encyclical "Summi Pontificatus."

"It puts itself in the place of The Almighty and elevates the state or group into the last end of life, the supreme criterion of the moral and juridical order, and therefore forbids every appeal to the principle of natural reason and of the Christian conscience.

"Fortunately, false principles do not always exercise their full influence, especially when age-old Christian traditions, on which the people have been nurtured, remain still deeply, even if unconsciously, rooted in their hearts.

"Nonetheless, one must not forget the essential insufficiency and weakness of every principle of social life which rests upon a purely human foundation, is inspired by merely earthly motives, and relies for its force on the sanction of a purely external authority.

"Where the dependence of human right upon the divine is denied, where appeal is made only to some insecure idea of a merely human authority, and an autonomy is claimed which rests only upon a utilitarian morality, there human law itself justly forfeits in its more weighty application the moral force which is the essential condition for its acknowledgement and also for its demand of sacrifices.

"It is true that power based on such weak and unsteady foundations can attain at times, under chance circumstances, material successes apt to arouse wonder in superficial observers.

"But the moment comes when the inevitable law triumphs, which strikes down all that has been constructed upon a disproportion between the material and the outward and that of the inward value and its moral foundation. Such disproportion exists whenever public authority disregards or denies the Dominion of the Supreme Lawmaker.

"Indeed, as our great predecessor, Leo XIII, wisely taught in the encyclical "Immortale Dei", it was The Creator's will that civil

Sovereignty should regulate social life after the dictates of an order changeless in its universal principles: should facilitate the attainment in the temporal order by individuals of physical, intellectual and moral perfection; and should aid them to reach their supernatural end.

"It is for this natural perfection that society is designed by The Creator as a means.

"To consider the state as something ultimate to which everything else should be subordinated and directed cannot fall to harm the true and lasting prosperity of nations.

"This can happen either when unrestricted dominion comes to be conferred on the state as having a mandate from the nation, people, or even a social order, or when the state arrogates such dominion to itself as absolute master, despotically without any mandate whatsoever.

"If, in fact, the state lays claim to and directs private enterprises, these, ruled as they are by delicate and complicated internal principles which guarantee and assure the realization of their special aims, may be damaged to the detriment of the public good, by being wrenched from their natural surroundings, that is, from responsible private action.

"Further, there would be danger lest the primary and essential cell of society, the family, be considered from the narrow standpoint of national power, and lest it be forgotten that man and the family are anterior to the state and that The Creator has given to both of them powers and rights and has assigned them a mission and a charge.

"Before us stand out with painful clarity the dangers we fear will accrue to this and coming generations from the neglect or non-recognition, the minimizing and the gradual abolition of the rights peculiar to the family.

"Therefore we stand up as determined defenders of those rights. The stress and manifold errors of our times are tasted by none so bitterly as by that noble little cell, the family.

"True courage and heroism are often necessary to support the hardships of life, the daily weight of misery, growing want and restrictions on a scale never before experienced…Whoever has care of souls knows how the powers of disorder and destruction stand on the alert ready to make use of all these things for their dark designs…

"The charge laid by God on parents to provide for the material and spiritual good of their offspring and to procure for them a suitable training saturated with the true spirit of religion, cannot be wrested from them without grave violation of their rights...

"The crime of high treason against the 'King of Kings and the Lord of Lords' perpetrated by an education that is either indifferent or opposed to Christianity, the reversal of 'Suffer the little children to come unto Me' would bear most bitter fruits.

"Now what scandal is more permanently harmful to generation after generation, than a formation of youth which is misdirected towards a goal that alienates from Christ, 'The way and the truth and the life', and leads to open or hidden apostasy from Christ.

"That same Christ from whom they want to alienate the youthful generations of the present day and of the future, is the same Christ who has received from His Eternal Father all power in heaven and on earth.

"He holds in His omnipotent hand the destiny of states, of peoples and of nations. His it is to shorten or prolong life. His to grant increase, prosperity and greatness.

"A system of education that should not respect the family, protected by God's holy law, that should attack its foundations, bar to the young the way to Christ, to the saviour's fountains of life and joy; that should consider apostasy from Christ and the church as a proof of fidelity to the people or to the governing party's creed, is evil and will not stand.

"The idea which credits the state with unlimited authority is an error harmful to the internal life of nations, to their prosperity, and injures the relationship between peoples.

"Today all men are looking with terror into the abyss to which they have been brought by the errors and principles which we have mentioned. Gone are the proud illusions of limitless progress.

"What used to appear on the outside as order was nothing but an invasion of disorder—confusion in the principles of moral life. These principles, once divorced from the majesty of the Divine Law, have tainted every field of human activity.

"Safety does not come to peoples from external means. Forces that are to renew the face of the earth should proceed from within, from the spirit.

"They must rest, not on the quicksand of changeable and ephemeral standards, but on the unshakeable foundation, on the solid rock of Natural Law and of Divine Revelation.

"For true though it is that the evils from which mankind suffers today come in part from economic instability, it is not less true that their root is deeper and more intrinsic, belonging to the sphere of religious belief and moral convictions, which have been perverted by the progressive alienation of the peoples from that unity of doctrine, faith, customs, and morals which once was promoted by the tireless and beneficent work of the church.

"The re-education of mankind must be, above all things, spiritual and religious. It must proceed from Christ as from its indispensable foundation. It must be actuated by justice and crowned by charity.

"The accomplishment of this task of regeneration…Is an essential and maternal office of the church. Her preaching of the gospel, by which is inculcated to men truth, justice, and charity, and her endeavor to implant the gospel's precepts solidly in the mind and conscience of men is the most noble and most fruitful work for peace.

"Every Christian shares in this obligation. And if this means, in our day, having to face obstacles and oppositions as vast and deep and minutely organized as never before, that does not dispense a man from the frank, bold profession of our faith. Rather, it spurs one to stand fast in the conflict even at the price of the greatest sacrifices. Whoever lives by the spirit of Christ refuses to let himself be beaten down by difficulties."

No. 79—March, 1977 Rudolph M. Unger

Chapter 80

"A follower of Christ does not draw back before the difficulties of the moment—even in such an age as ours when the conflict between Christianity and Anti-Christianity grows intense—but rather he faces their severity with that love which flees no sacrifice, is stronger than death, and will not be quenched by the rushing waters of tribulation."

So wrote Pope Pius XII in his first encyclical "Summi Pontificatus."

"It gives us great joy to see in every region of the Catholic world evident signs of such a spirit which boldly faces the gigantic tasks of our age and which seeks to unite in fruitful harmony the first and essential duty of individual sanctification and apostolic activity for the spread of the kingdom of God.

"This cooperation of the laity with the hierarchy, clergy, and religious in consecrating themselves with full ardor to the works of the apostolate in order to bring back to Christ the masses of people who have been separated from him is inspiring.

"In promoting this participation by the laity in the apostolate, which is so important in our times, the family has a special mission, for it is the spirit of the family that exercises the most powerful influence on that of the rising generation.

"As long as the sacred flame of the faith burns on the domestic hearth and the parents forge and fashion the lives of their children in accordance with this faith, youth will be ever ready to acknowledge the royal prerogatives of the Redeemer and to oppose those who wish to exclude Him from society or to usurp His rights.

"When churches are closed, when the image of the Crucified is taken from the schools, the family remains the providential refuge of Christian life.

"What torrents of benefits would be showered on the world if men everywhere would concede to the church that liberty of action which is her sacred and indisputable right as teacher of justice and love!

"What calamities could be averted if the social and international forces working to establish peace would let themselves be permeated by the deep lessons of the gospel of love in their struggle against individual or collective egoism!

"We have no more ardent desire than this, that in the present difficulties that those who are in power may decide to allow the church a free course to work for the formation of the rising generation according to the principles of justice and peace.

"The church's mission to 'Re-Establish all things in Christ' is indispensable as never before now that sad experience teaches that external means and human provisions and political expedients of themselves bring no efficacious healing to the ills which affect mankind.

"Taught precisely by the sad failure of human expedients to stave off the tempest that threatens to sweep civilization away, many turn their gaze with renewed hope to the church, the rock of truth and of charity, to that chair of Peter from which they feel can be restored to mankind that unity of religious teaching and of the moral code which of old gave consistency to pacific international relations.

"Unity, the hope of so many noble minds separated from us, who yet in their hunger and thirst for justice and peace turn their eyes to the See of Peter and from it await guidance and counsel!

"These last are recognizing in the Catholic church principles of belief and life that have stood the test of two thousand years.

"And we affirm that the church, which spreads its maternal arms towards this world does so not to dominate but to serve. She does not claim to take the place of other legitimate authorities in their proper spheres.

"The church preaches and inculcates obedience and respect for earthly authority which derives from God its whole origin and holds to the teaching of her Divine Master who said—'Render therefore to Caesar the things that are Caesar's.' She has no desire to usurp. She does not suppress human energies but lifts them up to all that is noble and forms characters which do not compromise with conscience.

"Nor does she who civilizes the nations ever retard the civil progress of mankind, at which on the contrary she is pleased and glad with a mother's pride.

"The end of her activity was admirably expressed by the angels when they sang 'Glory to God in the highest and on earth peace to men of good will.'

"This peace, which the world cannot give...History, wisely called by a great Roman, 'the teacher of life', has proved for close on to two thousand years how true is the word of scripture that he will not have peace who resists God.

"For Christ alone is the 'corner stone' on which man and society can find stability and salvation.

"On this corner stone the church is built and hence against her the adversary can never prevail—'the gates of hell shall not prevail.'

"Venerable brethren, the hour when this our first encyclical reaches you is in many respects a real 'hour of darkness' in which the spirit of violence and of discord brings indescribable suffering on mankind. The nations swept into the tragic whirlpool of war are perhaps as yet only at the 'beginnings of sorrows.'

"In the midst of this world which today presents such a sharp contrast to 'the Peace of Christ', the church and her faithful are in times and in years of trial such as have rarely been known in her history of struggle and suffering.

"But in such times especially, he who remains firm in his faith and strong at heart knows that Christ the King is never so near as in the hour of trial—which is the hour for fidelity.

"With a heart torn by the suffering and afflictions of so many of her sons, but with the courage and the stability that comes from the promises of Our Lord, the spouse of Christ goes to meet the gathering storms.

"This she knows, that the truth which she preaches, the charity which she teaches and practices, will be the indispensable counselors and aids to men of good will in the reconstruction of a new world based on justice and love.

"The 'Catholic church, the city of God, whose king is truth, whose law is love and whose measure eternity' preaching fearlessly the whole truth of Christ and toiling as the love of Christ demands with the zeal of a mother, stands as a blessed vision of peace above the storm of error and passion awaiting the moment when the all powerful hand of Christ the

King shall quiet the tempest and banish the spirits of discord which have provoked it.

"Trusting in God Almighty, to Him we daily pray 'In the shadow of thy wings will I hope, until iniquity pass away.' God can do all things. As well as the happiness and the fortunes of nations, He holds in His hands human counsels and sweetly turns them in whatever direction he wills. Even obstacles are for His Omnipotence means to mould affairs and events and to direct minds and free wills to His all high purposes.

"Pray then, venerable brethren, pray without ceasing, especially when you offer the Divine Sacrifice of love. Do you, too, pray you whose courageous profession of the faith entails today hard, painful and not rarely heroic sacrifices. Pray you, suffering and agonizing members of the church.

"Pray to Him 'who lifteth up all that fall' that He in His mercy may shorten the days of trial and that thus the words of the psalmist may be verified—'Then they cried to the Lord in their affliction and He delivered them out of their distresses.'

"And you, white legions of children so loved and dear to Jesus, when you receive Holy Communion raise up your simple and innocent prayers and unite them with the universal church. Pray everyone, pray uninterruptedly, 'Pray without ceasing.'

"'Remember, O Lord, Thy church, to free her from all evil and to perfect her in Thy love, and sanctify and collect her from the four winds into Thy kingdom which Thou hast prepared for her, because Thine is the power and the glory forever.'

"Given at Castel Gandolfo, near Rome, on the 20th day of October, in the year of Our Lord 1939, the first of our pontificate. Pope Pius XII."

No. 80—April, 1977 Rudolph M. Unger

Chapter 81

Most of the giants of the papacy in modern times have borne the name Pius.

In the last 131 years, beginning with Pius IX in 1846, four of them reigned a total of 79 years.

Preceding Pius XII to the throne of Peter was Achille Ratti, Pius XI, who ruled for 17 years, from 1922 to 1939, those horrendous years that bridged World wars I and II.

In March, 1937, two years before his death and two and one-half years before his successor wrote his first encyclical, "Summi Pontificatus" in "Exhorting Unity In Opposing World Evils", Pius XI in his encyclical "Divini Redemptoris" zeroed in on the most concentrated, well organized, and consummate of these evils—Atheistic Communism.

It was in this between the wars period that communism solidified its base of operation in Russia and from there spread its tentacles throughout the world. World War II enabled it to catapulte itself into a world wide power.

So powerful has it become, that in the past two decades the spiritual and secular leadership of western civilization, in fear and trembling, has sought to find some sort of accommodation with it.

This defeatist mentality was well described by Whittaker Chambers in his "Witness":—

"Their foremost belief was that peace could be preserved, World War III could be averted only by conciliating the Soviet Union. For this no price was too high to pay, including the price of willful historical delusion. Like most people who have substituted the habit of delusion for reality, they became hysterical when the root of their delusion was touched and reacted with a violence that completely belied the openness of mind which they prescribed for others."

These leaders have forgotten what Chambers sought to remind them of—"Evil is not something that can be condescended to, waved aside, or smiled at. Evil can only be fought."

This delusion of leadership was not always so. For proof of this, let us go back to Pius XI's "Divini Redemptoris" forty years ago.

"The promise of a redeemer brightens the first pages of the history of mankind. It was this hope that accompanied the human race on its weary journey, until in the fullness of time the expected savior came to begin a new universal civilization, the Christian civilization, far superior even to that which up to this time had been laboriously achieved by certain more privileged nations.

"Nevertheless, the struggle between good and evil remained in the world as a sad legacy of the original fall. Nor has the ancient tempter ever ceased to deceive mankind with false promises.

"It is on this account that one convulsion following upon another has marked the passage of the centuries, down to the revolution of our days.

"This modern revolution, it may be said, has actually broken out or threatens everywhere, and it exceeds in amplitude and violence anything yet experienced in the preceding persecutions launched against the church.

"Entire peoples find themselves in danger of falling back into a barbarism worse than that which oppressed the greater part of the world at the coming of The Redeemer.

"This all too imminent danger, venerable brethren, as you have already surmised, is Bolshevistic and Atheistic Communism, which aims at upsetting the social order and at undermining the very foundations of Christian civilization."

So began the former Archbishop of Milan's portrayal of the modern face of Lucifier. And what was his response to it? Watch and mark it well!

"In the face of such a threat the Catholic church could not and does not remain silent.

"This Apostolic See, above all, has not refrained from raising its voice, for it knows that its proper and special mission is to defend truth, justice and all those eternal values which communism ignores or attacks.

"Ever since the days when groups of 'Intellectuals' were formed in arrogant attempt to free civilization from the bonds of morality and religion, our predecessors overtly and explicitly drew the attention of the world to the consequences of the de-Christianization of human society.

"With reference to communism, our venerable predecessor, Pius IX, of holy memory, as early as 1846 pronounced a solemn condemnation, which he confirmed in the words of the 'Syllabus' directed against 'That infamous doctrine of so-called communism which is absolutely contrary to the natural law itself, and if once adopted would utterly destroy the rights, property and possessions of all men, and even society itself.'

"With clear intuition he pointed out that the atheistic movements existing among the masses of the machine age had their origin in that school of philosophy which for centuries had sought to divorce science from the life of the faith and the church.

"During our pontificate we, too, have frequently and with urgent insistence denounced the current trend to atheism which is alarmingly on the increase.

"In 1924, when our relief mission returned from the Soviet Union, we condemned communism in a special allocution which we addressed to the whole world.

"In our encyclicals—'Miserentissimus Redemptor', 'Quadragesimo Anno,' 'Caritate Christi,' 'Acerba Animi,' 'Dilectissimo Nobis,'—We raised a solemn protest against the persecutions unleashed in Russia, in Mexico, and now in Spain.

"In fact, the most persistent enemies of the church who from Moscow are directing the struggle against Christian civilization, themselves bear witness, by their unceasing attacks in word and act, that even to this hour the papacy has continued faithfully to protect the sanctuary of the Christian Religion, and that it has called public attention to the perils of communism more frequently and more effectively than any other public authority on earth.

"To our great satisfaction, venerable brethren, you have by means of individual and even joint pastoral letters, accurately transmitted and explained to the faithful these admonitions.

"Yet, despite our frequent and paternal warnings, the peril only grows greater from day to day because of the pressure exerted by clever agitators.

"Therefore we believe it to be our duty to raise our voice once more, in a still more solemn missive, in accord with the tradition of this Apostolic See, the teacher of truth, and in accord with the desire of the whole

Catholic world, which makes the appearance of such a document but natural.

"We trust that the echo of our voice will reach every mind free from prejudice and every heart sincerely desirous of the good of mankind. We wish this the more so because our words are now receiving sorry confirmation from the spectacle of the bitter fruits of subversive ideas, which we foresaw and foretold. And which are in fact multiplying fearfully in the countries already stricken, or threatening every other country of the world.

"Hence we wish to expose once more the principles of Atheistic Communism as they are manifested chiefly in bolshevism.

"We wish also to indicate its method of action and to contrast with its false principles the clear doctrine of the church, in order to inculcate anew and with greater insistence the means by which the Christian Civilization, the truth Civitas Humana, can be saved from the satanic scourge, and not merely saved, but better developed for the well being of human society.

"The communism of today, more emphatically than similar movements in the past, conceals in itself a false messianic idea. A pseudo-ideal of justice, of equality and fraternity in labor impregnates all its doctrine and activity with a deceptive mysticism, which communicates a zealous and contagious enthusiasm to the multitudes entrapped by its delusive promises. This pseudo-ideal is even boastfully advanced as if it were responsible for economic progress, when in fact the true causes of that progress are quite different."

No. 81—May, 1977 Rudolph M. Unger

Chapter 82

"The doctrine of modern communism, which is often concealed under the most seductive trappings, is in substance based on the principles of dialectical and historical materialism previously advocated by Marx, of which the theoreticians of bolshevism claim to possess the only genuine interpretation."

So began Pope Pius XI in his explanation of atheistic communism in his encyclical "Divini Redemptoris."

"According to this doctrine, there is in the world only one reality—matter—the blind forces of which evolve into plant, animal, and man. Even human society is nothing but a phenomenon and form of matter, evolving in the same manner.

"By a law of inexorable necessity and through a perpetual conflict of forces, matter moves toward the final synthesis of a classless society.

"In such a doctrine, as is evident, there is no room for the idea of God. There is no difference between spirit and matter, between soul and body. There is neither survival of the soul after death nor any hope in a future life.

"Insisting on the dialectical aspect of their materialism, the communists claim that the conflict which carries the world toward its final synthesis can be accelerated by man. Hence they endeavor to sharpen the antagonisms which arise between the various classes of society.

"Thus the class struggle with its consequent violent hate and destruction takes on the aspect of a crusade for the progress of humanity. On the other hand, all other forces whatever, as long as they resist such systematic violence, must be annihilated as hostile to the human race.

"Communism, moreover, strips man of his liberty, robs human personality of all its dignity, and removes all the moral restraints that check the eruptions of blind impulse.

"There is no recognition of any right of the individual in his relations to the collectivity. No natural right is accorded to human personality, which is a mere cogwheel in the communist system.

"In man's relations with other individuals, besides, communists hold the principle of absolute equality, rejecting all hierarchy and divinely constituted authority, including the authority of parents. What men call authority and subordination is derived from the community as its first and only font.

"Nor is the individual granted any property rights over material goods or the means of production, for inasmuch as these are the source of further wealth, their possession would give one man power over another. Precisely on this score, all forms of private property must be eradicated, for they are at the origin of all economic enslavement.

"Refusing to human life any sacred or spiritual character, such a doctrine logically makes of marriage and the family a purely artificial and civil institution, the outcome of a specific economic system.

"There exists no matrimonial bond of a juridico-moral nature that is not subject to the whim of the individual or of the collectivity. Naturally, therefore, the notion of an indissoluble marriage tie is scouted.

"Communism is particularly characterized by the rejection of any link that binds woman to the family and the home, and her emancipation is proclaimed as a basic principle.

"She is withdrawn from her family and the care of her children, to be thrust instead into public life and collective production under the same conditions as man. The care of home and children then devolves upon the collectivity.

"Finally, the right of education is denied to parents, for it is conceived as the exclusive prerogative of the community, in whose name and by whose mandate alone parents may exercise this right.

"What would be the condition of a human society based on such materialistic tenets? It would be a collectivity with no other hierarchy than that of the economic system. It would have only one mission—the production of material goods by means of collective labor so that the goods of this world might be enjoyed in a paradise where each would 'give according to his powers' and would receive 'according to his needs.'

"Communism recognizes in the collectivity the right, or rather, unlimited discretion, to draft individuals for the labor of the collectivity with no regard for their personal welfare so that even violence could be legitimately exercised to dragoon the recalcitrant against their wills.

"In the communistic commonwealth, morality and law would be nothing but a derivation of the existing economic order, purely earthly in origin and unstable in character. In a word, the communists claim to inaugurate a new era and a new civilization which is the result of blind evolutionary forces culminating in a humanity without God.

"When all men have finally acquired the collectivist mentality, in this Utopia of a really classless society, the political state—which is now conceived by communists merely as the instrument by which the proletariat is oppressed by the capitalists—will have lost all reason for its existence and will 'Wither Away.'

"However, until that happy consummation is realized, the state and the powers of the state furnish communism with the most efficacious and most extensive means for the achievement of its goal.

"Such, venerable brethren, is the new gospel which Bolshevistic and Atheistic Communism offers the world as the glad tidings of deliverance and salvation!

"It is a system full of errors and sophisms. It is in opposition both to reason and to Divine Revelation. It subverts the social order, because it means the destruction of its foundations, because it ignores the true origin and purpose of the state, because it denies the rights, dignity and liberty of human personality.

"How is it possible that such a system, long since rejected scientifically and now proved erroneous by experience, how is it, we ask, that such a system could spread so rapidly in all parts of the world?

"The explanation lies in the fact that too few have been able to grasp the nature of communism.

"The majority instead succumb to its deception, skillfully concealed by the most extravagant promises. By pretending to desire only the betterment of the condition of the working classes, by urging the removal of very real abuses chargeable to the liberalistic economic order, and by demanding a more equitable distribution of this world's goods (objects entirely and undoubtedly legitimate) the communist takes advantage of the present worldwide economic crisis to draw into the sphere of its influence even those sections of the populace which on principle reject all forms of materialism and terrorism.

"And as every error contains its element of truth, the partial truths to which we have referred are astutely presented according to the needs of time and place, to conceal, when convenient, the repulsive crudity and inhumanity of communistic principles and tactics.

"Thus the communist ideal wins over many of the better minded members of the community. These in turn become the apostles of the movement among the younger intelligentisa who are still too immature to recognize the intrinsic errors of the system.

"The preachers of communism are also proficient in exploiting racial antagonisms and political divisions and oppositions. They take advantage of the lack of orientation characteristic of modern agnostic science in order to burrow into universities, where they bolster up the principles of their doctrine with pseudo-scientific arguments.

"The explanation for the rapid diffusion of the communistic ideas also is to be found in a propaganda so truly diabolical that the world has perhaps never witnessed its like before. It is directed from one common center. It makes use of pamphlets and reviews, of cinema, theater and radio, of schools, and even universities. Little by little it penetrates minds and hearts.

"Another factor in communism's diffusion is the conspiracy of silence on the part of a large section of the non-catholic press of the world. How can a press usually eager to exploit even the little daily incidents of life remain so silent so long over the horrors perpetrated by the Marxists? This is due in part to short-sighted political policy."

No. 82—June 1977 Rudolph M. Unger

Chapter 83

"Where communism has been able to assert its power—and here we are thinking with special affection of the people of Russia and Mexico—it has striven by every possible means, as its champions openly boast, to destroy Christian civilization and the Christian religion by banishing every remembrance of them from the hearts of men, especially of the young."

So continued Pope Pius XI in his straightforward, unequivocal, unambiguous exposure and condemnation of atheistic communism in his encyclical "Divini Redemptoris" forty years ago.

"Bishops and priests exiled, condemned to forced labor, shot and done to death in inhuman fashion. Laymen suspected of defending their religion vexed, persecuted, dragged off to trial and thrown into prison.

"Even where the scourge of communism has not yet had time enough to exercise to the full its logical effect, as witness our beloved Spain, it has found compensation in the fiercer violence of its attack.

"Not only this or that church or isolated monastery sacked, but as far as possible every church and every monastery destroyed, every vestige of Christian religion eradicated.

"The fury of communism has not confined itself to the indiscriminate slaughter of bishops, of thousands of priests and religious of both sexes. It searches out above all those who have been devoting their lives to the welfare of the working classes and the poor.

"But the majority of its victims have been laymen of all conditions and classes, masses of them slain almost daily for no other offense than the fact that they are good Christians or at least opposed to atheistic communism.

"And this fearful destruction has been carried out with a hatred and a savage barbarity one would not have believed possible in our age. No man of good sense—nor any statesman conscious of his responsibility—can fall to shudder at the thought that what is happening today in Spain may perhaps be repeated tomorrow in other civilized countries.

"Nor can it be said that these atrocities are a transitory phenomenon. No, they are the natural fruit of a system which lacks all inner restraint.

Tear the very idea of God from the hearts of men and they are necessarily urged by their passions to the most atrocious barbarity.

"This, unfortunately, is what we now behold. For the first time in history we are witnessing a struggle, cold-blooded in purpose and mapped out to the last detail, between man and 'All that is called God.'

"Communism is by its nature anti-religious. It considers religion as 'The Opiate of the people' because the principles of religion which speak of a life beyond the grave dissuade the proletariat from the dream of a Soviet paradise which is of this world.

"But the law of nature and its Author cannot be flouted with impunity . Communism has not been able, and will not be able, to achieve its objectives even in the merely economic sphere.

"In spite of slavery imposed on millions of men, communism has not reached its promised goal. After all, even the sphere of economics needs some morality, some moral sense of responsibility, which can find no place in a system so thoroughly materialistic as communism.

"Terrorism is the only possible substitute and it is terrorism that reigns today in Russia where former comrades in revolution are exterminating each other.

"In making these observations it is no part of our intention to condemn en-masse the peoples of the Soviet Union. For them we cherish the warmest paternal affection. We are well aware that not a few of them groan beneath the yoke imposed on them by men who in very large part are strangers to the real interests of their country.

"We recognize that many others were deceived by its fallacious hopes. We blame only the system with its authors and abettors who considered Russia the best prepared field for experimenting with a plan elaborated decades ago and who from there continue to spread it from one end of the world to the other.

"We have exposed the errors and the violent, deceptive tactics of Bolshevistic and Atheistic Communism. It is now time to contrast with it the true notion of the 'Civitas Humana' or human society as taught by reason and revelation through the mouth of the church, 'Magistra Gentium.'

"Above all other reality, there exists one supreme being—God, the omnipotent creator of all things, the all wise and just judge of all men.

"This supreme reality, God, is the absolute condemnation of the impudent falsehoods of communism. In truth, it is not because men believe in God that he exists. Rather because he exists do all men whose eyes are not deliberately closed to the truth believe in him and pray to him."

"Man has a spiritual and immortal soul. He is a person, marvelously endowed by his creator with gifts of body and mind. He is a true 'Microcosm" as the ancients said, a world in miniature, with a value far surpassing that of the vast inanimate cosmos.

"God alone is his last end, in this life and the next. By sanctifying grace he is raised to the dignity of a son of God and incorporated into the kingdom of God in the mystical body of Christ.

"In consequence, he has been endowed by God with many and varied prerogatives—the right to life, to bodily integrity, to the necessary means of existence, the right to tend toward his ultimate goal in the path marked out for him by God, the right of association, and the right to possess and use property.

"God has likewise destined man for civil society according to the dictates of his very nature. In the plan of the creator, society is a natural means which man can and must use to reach his destined end.

"Society is for man and not vice versa. Only man, the human person, and not society in any form is endowed with reason and a morally free will.

"St. Paul wrote, 'All things are yours, and you are Christ's, and Christ is God's.' While communism impoverishes human personality by inverting the terms of the relation of man to society, to what lofty heights is man not elevated by reason and revelation!

"The principles concerning the social-economic order have been expounded in Leo XIII's 'Rerum Novarum' on the question of labor. Our own encyclical 'Quadragesimo Anno' on the 'Reconstruction Of The Social Order' adapted these principles to present needs.

"Then, insisting anew on the age old doctrine of the church concerning the individual and social character of private property, we explained clearly the right and dignity of labor, the relations of mutual aid and collaboration which should exist between those who possess capital and those who work.

"We have shown that the means of saving the world of today from the lamentable ruin into which amoral liberalism has plunged us, are neither the class struggle nor terror, nor yet the autocratic abuse of state power, but rather the infusion of social justice and the sentiment of Christian love into the social-economic order.

"We have indicated how a sound prosperity is to be restored according to the true principles of a sane corporative system which respects the proper hierarchic structure of society. And how all the occupational groups should be fused into a harmonious unity inspired by the principle of the common good.

"And the genuine and chief function of public and civil authority consists precisely in the efficacious furthering of this harmony and coordination of all social forces.

"Catholic doctrine vindicates to the state the dignity and authority of a vigilant and provident defender of those divine and human rights on which the sacred scriptures and the fathers of the church insist so often.

"It is not true that all have equal rights in civil society. It is not true that there exists no lawful social hierarchy.

"The enslavement of man despoiled of his rights, the denial of a transcendental origin of the state and its authority, the horrible abuse of public power in the service of a collectivistic terrorism, are the very contrary of the will of the creator who originated both man and civil society and mutually ordained them one to another."

No. 83—July, 1977 Rudolph M. Unger

Chapter 84

"The church seeks true peace and true happiness for men, even here below as far as is possible, in preparation for the happiness of heaven—but for men of good will—as the angels at Bethlehem promised.

"The church does not separate a proper regard for the temporal welfare from solicitude for the eternal. If she subordinates the former to the latter, according to the words of her Divine Founder, 'Seek ye first the Kingdom of God and his justice, and all these things shall be added unto you;' She is nevertheless far from unconcerned with human affairs and fosters and promotes civil progress and material advancement in a sensible and efficacious manner.

"Her teaching on the relationship between man and society maintains an equilibrium of truth and justice, bringing into harmony the rights and duties of all parties.

"Thus authority is reconciled with liberty, the dignity of the individual with that of the state, the human personality of the subject with the divine delegation of the superior...Striking a balance between the due dependence and well ordered love of a man for himself, his family, and country, and his love of other families and other peoples, founded on the Love of God, the Father of all, their First Principle and Last End."

So wrote Pius XI in "Divini Redemptoris" and he went on to say that:

"As in all the storm periods of the history of the church, the fundamental remedy today lies in a sincere renewal of private and public life according to the principles of the gospel by all those in the fold of Christ, so that they may be in truth the salt of the earth to preserve human society from total corruption.

"We see consoling signs of this spiritual renewal on all sides. Not only in so many singularly chosen souls who have been elevated to the sublime height of sanctity, and in so many others who with generous hearts are making their way toward the same luminous goal, but also in the new flowering of a deep and practical piety in all classes of society.

"Nevertheless, we cannot deny that there is still much to be done in the way of spiritual renovation. Even in Catholic countries there are still too many who are Catholics hardly more than in name.

"The Catholic who does not live really and sincerely according to the faith he professes will not long be master of himself in these days when the winds of strife and persecution blow so fiercely, but will be swept away defenseless in this new deluge which threatens the world.

"And here we wish to insist more particularly on two teachings of Our Lord which have special bearing on the present condition of the human race—detachment from earthly goods and the precept of charity.

"'Blessed are the poor in spirit' were the first words that fell from His lips in The Sermon On The Mount. This lesson is more than ever necessary in these days of materialism athirst for the goods and pleasures of this earth.

"All Christians, rich or poor, must keep their eye fixed on heaven, remembering that 'We have not here a lasting city, but we seek one that is to come.'

"Not only the rich, who have a special obligation to share their good fortune, but the poor too, while seeking, according to the laws of justice and charity, to better their condition, should always remain 'poor in spirit,' and hold spiritual goods in higher esteem than earthly property and pleasures.

"Still more important is the need for that Christian Charity, 'Patient and kind', which perseveringly practices the spiritual and corporal works of mercy, even to the point of sacrifice. Its faithful observance will pour into the heart an inner peace which the world knows not.

"And as a most efficacious remedy we recommend fostering and intensifying the spirit of prayer joined with penance. The evil which torments the world today can be conquered only by a worldwide holy crusade of prayer and penance.

"We ask especially the contemplative orders, men and women, to redouble their prayers and sacrifices to obtain from heaven efficacious aid for the church in the present struggle.

"Let them implore also the powerful intercession of the Immaculate Virgin, who, having crushed the head of the serpent of old, remains the sure protectress and invincible 'Help of Christians.'

"To save the world, Christ chose priests as the first line ministers and messengers of His gospel. Theirs is the duty of keeping alight in the world the torch of faith and of filling the hearts of the faithful with that supernatural trust which has aided the church to fight and win so many other battles in Christ's name. 'This is the victory which overcometh the world—our faith!'

"We also extend our paternal invitation to our beloved sons among the laity who are doing battle in the ranks of Catholic action, whose object is to spread the kingdom of Jesus Christ.

"We must warn against the insidious deceits with which communists endeavor, all too successfully, to attract even men of good faith.

"Aware of the universal desire for peace, the leaders of communism pretend to be the most zealous promoters and propagandists in the movement for world amity. Yet at the same time, they stir up class warfare which causes rivers of blood to flow, and have recourse to unlimited armaments.

"Under various names which do not suggest communism, they establish organizations and periodicals with the sole purpose of carrying their ideas into quarters otherwise inaccessible.

"They try perfidiously to worm their way even into professedly Catholic and religious organizations. Again, without receding an inch from their subversive principles, they invite Catholics to collaborate with them in the realms of so-called humanitarianism and charity, and at times even make proposals that are in perfect harmony with the Christian spirit and the doctrine of the church.

"Elsewhere they carry their hypocrisy so far as to encourage the belief that communism, in countries where faith and culture are more strongly entrenched, will assume another and much milder form. It will not interfere with the practice of religion. It will respect liberty of conscience. There are even some who refer to certain changes recently introduced into soviet legislation as a proof that communism is about to abandon its program of war against God.

"<u>See to it, venerable brethren, that the faithful do not allow themselves to be deceived!</u> Communism is intrinsically wrong, and no one who would save Christian civilization may collaborate with it in any undertaking whatsoever.

"Those who permit themselves to be deceived into lending their aid toward the triumph of communism in their own country will be the first to fall victims of their error.

"And the greater the antiquity and grandeur of the Christian Civilization in the regions where communism successfully penetrates, so much more devastating will be the hatred displayed by the Godless.

"This means that all diligence should be exercised by states to prevent within their territories the ravages of an Anti-God campaign which shakes society to its very foundation. For there can be no authority on earth unless the authority of God is recognized.

"How can any contract be maintained, what value can any treaty have, in which every guarantee of conscience is lacking? How can there be talk of guarantees of conscience when all faith in God and all fear of God have vanished? Take away this basis and with it all moral law falls and there is no remedy left to stop the gradual but inevitable destruction of peoples, families, the state, civilization itself.

"The evil we must combat today is at its origin primarily an evil of the spiritual order. The church must be free to combat it. Those who would ban religion from education and public life and rely on purely political and economic means to combat communism are in the grip of a dangerous error. Neither can control a movement whose roots lie in materialism."

No. 84—August, 1977 Rudolph M. Unger

Chapter 85

Pope Pius XI warned against not only the enemy who attacks from without but also of the enemy who burrows from within.

In our age, another false reformation, parading under the banner of renewal, has blossomed forth inside the church in the guise of a false ecumenism which is based upon a faulty conception of peace, unity, and charity.

Nearly fifty years ago, on January 6, 1928, Pope Pius XI took aim at this cunning aberration in his encyclical "Mortalium Animos" on the "Promotion Of True Religious Unity."

"The will to strengthen and diffuse for the common good of human society that brotherhood in which we are all closely united by the bonds of a common nature and origin has never perhaps so taken hold of men's minds as in our times," began the pontiff.

"Some seem to draw from this reason to hope that without great difficulty it may come about that all peoples, no matter how different their religions, will stand fraternally together in the profession of a few doctrines which will serve as a kind of common foundation for the spiritual life.

"They are accustomed, therefore, to call congresses which are attended by many and they invite there, indiscriminately, to decide the question—infidels of all kinds as well as Christians and even those who have miserably apostatized from Christ or who intransigently and tenaciously deny the Divinity of His Person and His Mission.

"Certainly such movements as these cannot gain the approval of Catholics. They are founded upon the false opinions of those who say that, since all religions equally signify the native inborn feeling in us all—through which we are borne toward God and humbly recognize His rule—therefore, all religions are more or less good and praiseworthy.

"The followers of this theory are not only deceived and mistaken but, since they repudiate the true religion by attacking it in its very essence, they move step by step to naturalism and atheism.

"Anyone who gives assent to such theories and undertakings utterly abandons the divinely revealed religion.

"When the question of promoting unity among Christians is under consideration, many are easily deceived by the semblance of good. Is it not right, they ask repeatedly, and indeed is it not the duty of all who call upon Christ's name to cease mutual recriminations and join together in ties of mutual charity?

"Would that all Christians were one, they add, so that they might drive out the evil of irreligion, which every day spreads more widely and threatens to overturn the gospel.

"These and like arguments are brought forward and amplified by those who call themselves pan-Christians. No longer are they confined to small and scattered groups, but they grow by strong phalanxes and unite themselves in widespread organizations which, although their members are of different faiths, are directed for the most part by non-Catholics.

"The work itself is advanced with such zeal that it has gained a great variety of followers and has even ensnared the minds of Catholics with the beguiling hope of attaining a union that would seem to meet the mind of holy mother church, to whom nothing is more hallowed than the recall and the return of her wandering children to her bosom.

"Yet beneath the enticing words there lies concealed an error so great that it would destroy utterly the foundations of the Catholic faith.

"Moved by the consciousness of our apostolic office to guard the flock of the Lord from error, we invoke your zeal, venerable brethren, to ward off this evil.

"Precisely so that we might rightly fulfill both our duties for the glory of God and for our own salvation, the only begotten Son of God founded his church upon earth.

"They, therefore, who profess themselves Christians cannot but believe in Christ's establishment of one church and only one.

"A great many deny that Christ's church ought to be visible—at least in a sense that it should stand forth as one body of faithful united in one identical doctrine and under one single authority and rule.

"On the contrary, they understand by a visible church nothing but a society formed by various Christian communities, even though these adhere to different and even mutually contradictory doctrines.

"Instead, Christ Our Lord founded His church as a perfect society, external of its own nature and perceived by the senses, which would pursue for all time the task of saving mankind through the guidance of one head, through being taught by a living voice and through the dispensation of the sacraments, as fountains of the grace of heaven.

"It has been commanded to lead to eternal salvation all men, to exist not only today and always, but, still more, to be the same as it was in the apostolic ages, unless we should wish to utter the absurdity that Christ Our Lord either was not adequate to His purpose or had erred when He asserted that 'The gates of hell shall not prevail against it.'

"And here there is presented the opportunity of singling out and removing a falsity upon which, it seems, this whole question hinges, and from which is drawn the multiple effort of those non-Catholics who strive for the confederation of the Christian Churches.

"They contend that the unity of faith and governance which is the sign of the true and one church of Christ has almost never existed up to this time and does not exist today.

"They say, moreover, that the church by its very nature is divided into parts, that it consists of many churches or particular communities which are separated among themselves, and although they have certain points of doctrine in common, they differ in others; and that at most the church was the one church and only church between the apostolic era and the first ecumenical councils.

"Therefore, they say, the controversies and old differences of opinion which to this day divide the Christian name, should be put aside and, with the remaining doctrines, there should be formulated and proposed a common rule of faith in which all can believe and feel themselves brothers.

"United by some sort of universal covenant, the multitude of churches, or communities, will then be in a position to oppose fruitfully the progress of unbelief, they explain.

"There are, however, some among them who assume and concede that Protestantism has rejected very inadvisedly certain articles of faith and certain rites of external worship that are fully acceptable and even useful, which the Roman church still preserves.

"But they add immediately that the church has corrupted the early religion by adding to it and by proposing for belief certain doctrines that are not only foreign to but are opposed to the gospel, among which they bring forward chiefly that of the primacy of jurisdiction assigned to Peter and his successors of the Roman See.

"Among them are a few who indulge the Roman pontiff with a primacy of honor or a certain jurisdiction and power which, however, they think is derived not from divine right, but in a certain manner from the consent of the faithful.

"Others have even advanced so far as to wish the pope himself to preside over their variegated conferences.

"If, however, it is easy to find many non-Catholics often preaching of brotherly communion in Christ Jesus, you will indeed find none to whose mind it would occur to submit themselves and to obey the Vicar of Christ either as teacher or as ruler of the church.

"Meanwhile they affirm that they would gladly treat with the Roman Church, though upon the basis of equality of rights and as equals. If they could so treat, they do not seem to doubt but that an agreement might be reached through which they would not be compelled to give up those opinions which are thus far the cause of their having wandered outside the one fold of Christ.

"On such conditions it is clear that the Apostolic See cannot in any way participate in their reunions and why Catholics cannot grant aid to such efforts.

"If they should do so, they would give authority to a false Christian religion alien to the one church of Christ. Could we suffer the divinely revealed truth to be brought down to the bargaining level? For it is the safeguarding of revealed truth that now is at stake."

No. 85—September, 1977 Rudolph M. Unger

Chapter 86

"When the only begotten Son of God commanded his legates to teach all nations, he bound all men with the duty to believe what was announced to them by 'Witnesses preordained by God.'

"He attached to His command the sanction—'He that believeth and is baptized shall be saved. But he that believeth not shall be condemned.'

"Now this double commandment of Christ, which must be observed, to teach and to believe so as to attain eternal salvation, cannot even be understood if the church does not propose the evangelical doctrine clear and entire and if, in the teaching of it, it is not free from all danger of error.

"How far, indeed, do they wander from the way who think that a deposit of truth exists on earth but that one must seek it with such tiring labor and lengthy studies and disputes that hardly is the life of a man long enough to find and master it.

"As if the most kind God had spoken—through the prophets and His only begotten Son—so that a few only, and those already bowed down in years, might learn the truth that he has revealed through them, and not to give a teaching of faith and morals through which man would be ruled throughout the entire course of his life."

So wrote Pope Pius XI in his encyclical "Mortalium Animos" on the "Promotion Of True Religious Unity." He went on:

"It might appear that the Pan-Christians, engaged in trying to confederate the churches, are pursuing the noble idea of increasing charity among all Christians. Yet how could charity harm faith?

"All remember how John, the very apostle of charity, who always inculcated in his disciples the new commandment of 'Love ye one another' had wholly forbidden them to have relations with those who did not profess entire and uncorrupted the teachings of Christ.

"'If any man cometh to you and bring not this doctrine, receive him not into your house nor say to him, God speed you' (II John 10). Since charity is founded in whole and sincere faith, the disciples of Christ must be united by the bond of unity in faith and by it as the chief bond.

"How could a Christian covenant be imagined in which they who entered it could, in matters of faith, each retain, although contrary to those of others, their own opinions and judgments? Through what agreement could men of opposite opinions become one and the same society of the faithful?

"How, for example, they who affirm that sacred tradition is a true source of revelation and they who deny it?

"They who hold that an ecclesiastical hierarchy formed of bishops, priests, and ministers is divinely constituted and they who assert that little by little it came into being to suit the conditions of time and events?

"They who adore Christ really present in the Most Holy Eucharist by that wonderful change of bread and wine called transubstantiation and they who say that the Body of Christ is present there only through faith or through the sign and virtue of the sacrament? They who hold that in the Eucharist there is both sacrifice and sacrament and they who say it is only a remembrance of the last supper?

"When some will hold that it is good humbly to invoke the saints reigning with Christ—above all Mary, Mother of God—and to venerate their images, and they who contend that such a form of homage is wrong because it draws from the honor due Jesus Christ, 'The one Mediator of God and men'?

"In such great differences of opinion we do not know how a road may be paved to the unity of the church save only through one teaching authority, one sole law of belief, and one sole faith among Christians.

"Moreover, we know how easy is the path from denial of this to the neglect of religion, or indifferentism, and to modernism, which holds the very same error, namely—dogmatic truth is not absolute but relative. It is proportionate to the various 'Needs' of times and places and to the various tendencies of the mind, since dogmatic truth is not contained in unchanging revelation, but is such that it accommodates itself to the life of men.

"Therefore it is clear why the Apostolic See has never permitted its children to take part in these congresses. The unity of Christians cannot be otherwise obtained than by securing the return of the separated to the one true church from which they once, unhappily, withdrew.

"To the one true church of Christ that stands forth before all and that, by the will of its Founder, will remain forever the same as when He Himself established it for the salvation of all mankind.

"The mystical spouse of Christ has, in the course of the centuries, remained unspotted, nor can it ever be contaminated.

"St. Cyprian says—'The spouse of Christ cannot commit adultery. She is incorrupt and modest, she knows one house, she guards with chaste modesty the holiness of one room.'

"The same Holy Martyr marveled, and with reason, how anyone could think that 'The unity which proceeds from the stability of God and is bound together by the sacraments of heaven could be torn asunder in the church or separated by the wills of the discordant.'

"Since the Mystical Body Of Christ, the church, is a unity it would be false and foolish to say that Christ's Mystical Body could be composed of separated and scattered members. Whoever, therefore, is not united with it is not a member of it, nor does he communicate with its head who is Christ.

"No one is found in the one church of Christ and no one perseveres in it unless he acknowledges and accepts obediently the supreme authority of St. Peter and his legitimate successors. Did not the very ancestors of those who are entangled in the errors of Photius and the Protestants obey the Roman bishop as the high shepherd of souls?

"Children did, alas, abandon their father's house, but the house did not, therefore, fall in ruins, supported as it was by the unceasing help of God.

"Let them return, then, to the common father of all. He has forgotten the unjust wrongs inflicted upon the Holy See and will receive them most lovingly.

"If, as they often say, they desire to be united with us and ours, why do they not hasten to return to the church, 'The mother and mistress of all the followers of Christ?'

"Let them listen to Lactanius crying—'It is only the Catholic church that retains the true worship. It is the fountain of truth, it is the household of faith, it is the Temple of God. If anyone does not enter it or if anyone departs from it, he is a stranger to the hope of life and salvation.'

"Let these separated children return to the Apostolic See, consecrated with the blood of Peter and Paul, to this See, 'The root and matrix of the Catholic church'.

"Not indeed with the idea or hope that 'The church of the Living God, the pillar and ground of truth' will abandon the integrity of the faith and bear their errors, but to subject themselves to its teaching authority and truth.

"Would that it be granted to us to embrace with the heart of a father the children over whom we mourn, separated by an evil discord from us.

"May God Our Saviour 'Who will have all men to be saved and to come to the knowledge of the truth' hearken to our ardent prayer and vouchsafe to call back all wanderers to the unity of the church!

"In behalf of which lofty intention, we invoke the intercession of the Blessed Virgin Mary, Mother of Divine Grace, conqueror of all heresies and Help Of Christians, that soon may dawn that longed for day when all will hear the voice of her Divine Son 'Keeping the unity of the spirit in the bond of peace.'

"You know well, venerable brethren, how we desire their return. And we wish all our children to know it and not only they of the Catholic World, but all who are separated from us.

"If they will ask in humble prayer the Grace of God, there is no doubt but that they will come to recognize the one true church of Jesus Christ and enter it, United with us in perfect charity."

"O God, our refuge and strength, graciously look upon thy people who cry to thee and through the intercession of Mary, Mother of God, Joseph, Peter and Paul, and of all the saints, in thy mercy and kindness hear our prayers for the conversion of sinners and the liberty and exaltation of Holy Mother church. Through Christ our Lord. Amen."

No. 86—October, 1977 Rudolph M. Unger

Chapter 87

In the fall of last year the conservative Catholic publication "The Remnant" carried a penetrating article which had run a few weeks earlier in the "London Daily Telegraph."

Written by Gerald Warner, it carried the headline, "What Is The Crime In The Old Mass?" It echoed what the writer of this newsletter had written Pope Paul in May, 1974 upon the banning of the last Latin Tridentine Mass in the Chicago Archdiocese. That letter was reproduced in the December, 1975 issue of this newsletter.

Warner began—and I know not if he is Catholic or not –

"'With burning sorrow' (Mit Brennender Sorge) Pope Pius XI denounced the Anti-Christian excesses of Nazi Germany. The phase seems peculiarly apt to describe one's reaction to the present clumsy, authoritarian repression of liturgical conservatives within the Catholic Church.

"Even those who take little interest in religious affairs must have felt a faint unease on reading of the Vatican's move against Archbishop Marcel Lefebvre, Father Oswald Baker and other supporters of the Tridentine mass. For the first time since the Second Vatican Council the bogy of excommunication is being brandished with as much nonchalance as an ecumenical document.

"Even at the time of the debate on artificial contraception, provoked by 'Humanae Vitae', such dire sanctions were not invoked as are now threatened against Roman Catholics whom most people would regard as pillars of Orthodoxy. Observers with long experience of Vatican politics are bemused by the ferocity of this Vendetta against men and women who in all other respects are fanatically loyal to the Holy See.

"The overriding question is—Why? Why has the Tridentine mass been singled out for extirpation, root and branch?

"Though the prayers are somewhat different from the new normative mass, no one has ever suggested that the Tridentine rite is theologically suspect. For centuries the Tridentine mass was the almost exclusive vehicle of worship in the western Roman church. If it has shepherded millions of Catholics to salvation in the past, what harm can it do now?

"Yet when Father Baker recently celebrated a Tridentine Mass the Bishop of Hexham and Newcastle went to the extraordinary lengths of issuing a pastoral letter to be read throughout the diocese, forbidding Catholics to attend. In these ecumenical times, is it credible that his lordship would have issued a similar prohibition against attending an Anglican or Methodist or Presbyterian service?

"It should also be borne in mind that the Tridentine/Mass, according to Catholic theology, is a valid reenactment of the sacrifice of Calvary, effecting transubstantiation, a claim which no one would advance for those Protestant services in which the hierarchy encourages the laity to participate.

"It might also be said that the liturgy celebrated by the Uniate (Eastern Catholic) rites differs more radically from the normative mass than does the Tridentine Rite. Yet past Popes have come to a wise accommodation with the eastern rites in communion with Rome. Why can a similar arrangement not be attempted with the Tridentine rite?

"Yet the incredible fact is that it has been seriously proposed to employ the weapon of excommunication against men and women who have not trespassed against the laws of the Roman Catholic Church in any article of faith or dogma, who have committed no heresy.

"The very prelates who are presently preparing this sentence of spiritual death were to be observed within the last decade celebrating the Tridentine Mass with every circumstance of reverence.

"If this inhuman sentence is passed, it will represent one of the most merciless acts of the papacy in its 2,000 years history.

"Of course, it is easy to dismiss the supporters of the Tridentine Mass as cranks who have been bypassed by progress. In an age when men walk on the moon, who can feel sympathy with a reactionary clique whose inspiration derives from a Latin Incantation whispered over a chalice?

"A minority persecuted on grounds of conscience, however, must always have a claim on public respect. Probably nobody outside the Catholic church can imagine the anguish endured by believers threatened with the anathema of Rome.

"Nor would any believing Catholic deny that there must be a Magisterium in the church, an ultimate repository of authority capable of invoking awful sanctions in extreme cases of heresy or blasphemy.

"Yet by no stretch of the imagination could the liturgical conservatives be termed heretical or blasphemous. So we return to the fundamental question—why such drastic measures in this case?

"On consideration, it is difficult to escape the conclusion that the Vatican bureaucrats bent on reasserting papal authority in the face of many recent challenges, and notoriously disposed to invoke the Pope's name as a sanction for their own arbitrary initiatives, have opted for a soft target.

"Where Dutch radicals would scoff at Anathema, liturgical conservatives will shudder. So, the Vatican 'Apparatchniki' reason, the spectacle of Tridentinists making Canossa-Style submission to Rome will be a salutary warning to unruly elements in the church.

"Where they have possibly miscalculated is that the target may not be as soft as they imagine. The latest opinion poll shows twenty-eight percent of the French Catholics supporting Archbishop Lefebvre, twenty-four percent supporting the Pope, and the remainder undecided.

"It is difficult to believe that the Pope, who enjoys the love and respect of all parties involved can be fully informed about the situation. Surely he cannot propose to cut off one of the elite elements of his church. It is a shortsighted Caesar who liquidates his praetorian guard.

"There would seem to be only two immediate remedies to avert a tragic schism created quite unnecessarily. One lies outside the Catholic Church. If ecumenical churchmen of other denominations will make toleration for the Tridentine Faction a precondition for further consultations, Rome cannot ignore such a sanction.

"In any case, can Anglicans grasp a hand that has intolerantly struck down its own dissidents while professing a liberal attitude to other Christians?

"The Catholic church has opened its doors to Protestant visitors. It cannot now leave them in the drawing room and retire discreetly, like a Victorian father, to thrash a recalcitrant child and then return smiling sociably.

"The other remedy is in the hands of radical Roman Catholics. For a decade they have expressed abhorrence of heavy handed authoritarianism within the church, usually when it was directed against themselves. Let them now prove their consistency by protesting against the persecution of liturgical conservatives.

"If the most respected progressive churchman, Cardinal Suenens, were to intervene on behalf of his fellow pastor, Archbishop Lefebvre, there would be the beginnings of a more united church.

"The radicals appear to have triumphed. Will there be magnanimity in victory?

"So, more than ten years on, this is the squalid ending to the high hopes of 'Aggiornamento'.

"Whatever happens, few objective observers would assess the Catholic Church as an influential force for the remainder of this century. It is all a far cry from the optimism of John XXIII."

"A Christianity which keeps a grip on itself, refuses every compromise with the world, takes the commands of God and the church seriously, preserves its Love of God and of men in all its freshness, such a Christianity can and will be a model and a guide to a world which is sick to death and clamors for directions lest it be condemned to a catastrophe that would baffle the imagination...The cross of Christ, though it has become to many a stumbling block and foolishness, remains for the believer the holy sign of his redemption, the emblem of moral strength and greatness. We live in its shadow and die in its embrace. It will stand on our grave as a pledge of our faith and our hope in the eternal light." Pope Pius XI in "Mit Brennender Sorge."

"When Christianity comes to terms with the world, it will be the end of Christianity." Gilbert K. Chesterton

No. 87—November, 1977 Rudolph M. Unger

Chapter 88

A year ago the following article was written by Walter L. Matt, editor of "The Remnant", the Catholic conservative newspaper.

"Looking about at the sad state of affairs in which the world is, with barbarism and savagery more and more palpably manifest almost everywhere, I find myself thinking back to the days· more than a dozen years ago, when my good father, Lord rest him, after more than sixty years of unremitting toil and struggle as a Catholic lay publisher and journalist, sat down at his desk and committed to paper what was to be one of his last weekly 'Rundschaus', or analyses of world events and trends.

"His article, 'The Light That Shineth In the Darkness' appeared in the Christmas issue of 'The Wanderer.' I find today that 'The light' of which my father wrote is perhaps even more urgently needed than in those days, what with the world situation and more specifically, the church situation, having deteriorated well beyond what it was in 1963.

"I would like, therefore, to reiterate some of my good father's parting thoughts, so to speak, and let my readers judge for themselves whether or not they are still appropriate and timely today. He wrote:

'Leafing through the newspaper clippings stacked up on my desk and noting the continuing message of world unrest and upheaval which they reflect, we find our thoughts straying back to an ancient dictum. Like a sonorous bell ringing through our mind from long ages past, comes the solemn message of St. John's revealing gospel—'And the light Shineth in darkness and the darkness did not comprehend it.'

'Truly, today too, the light shineth in darkness and the darkness does not comprehend it! For what else is it save a cold and dreary darkness in which we continue to view the endless officious debating and deadlocking of the leaders of nations, and of the less important but even more pompous and self-assured politicians whose congenial immaturity and lack of principle makes them incapable, even at this late date, of recognizing the growing arrogance and derisive cynicism of the bolshevists, whose lips speak peace but whose hearts are full of hate and contempt for all that remains of a once proud Christendom?

'And what else is it we see in our public and private life today in America? Have we not seen signs in recent weeks and months of God's light, like a sudden, all transforming warning beacon, stabbing the murky darkness of crime and corruption all around us and reminding us that the road we have been traveling in recent decades is a dead end road and that violence and bloody revolution is the ultimate end result for any nation or people which, ignoring the tell tale signs of the times, continues its frenzied pell-mell course of selfish personal aggrandizement, wealth, power, sensuous pleasure, whilst forgetting in large measure the values and responsibilities in life that make for man's only real and lasting freedom and happiness?

'Whether on the international diplomatic front or in our everyday social and political affairs right here at home, in both instances what is lacking is the life-giving Divine sun which a vain glorious and deluded human pride obstinately continues to reject as outmoded and therefore superfluous.

'The origins of this rejection, which have resulted in modern society's frightful loss, were in its beguilement with 18th century liberalism and secularism, misnamed 'Enlightenment.'

'This led it to dispense in public affairs with the light of faith and divinely ordained order and led it instead to shape things in accordance with its own 'Enlightenment.'

'Thus came to pass once again what had happened before—'He came unto his own and his own received him not.' Thus it came to pass that governments and nations wandered in the darkness.

'In spite of all material progress there is no real advance onward and upward. The 'Four Freedoms' proclaimed by Franklin D. Roosevelt as the glorious goal of our humanitarian age are in large measure still a mirage and a catch phrase. Especially the 'Freedom From Fear' has been turned into its exact reverse—men have become slaves of fear as they seldom have before.

'Fear, uncertainties and insecurities rest heavily upon the political and economic life of all countries, including the United States which, up to a few decades ago, was a secure haven of freedom, the envy of the world, the land of almost unlimited possibilities for peaceful, prosperous existence.

'The most disastrous ersatz which has come from the witches' kettle of materialism is that syrupy humanitarianism (or humanism) which is peddled as a substitute for Christian truths and precepts. It is a concoction of aesthetic and emotional sentiments, an outward show of decency (if it does not conflict too uncomfortably with human frailties and concupiscence), 'practical' realism unhampered by 'dogmatism', and a strong admixture of skepticism and agnosticism, if not outright atheism.

'Because the west, particularly in its governments, has lost the ability to accept the blessed message of Bethlehem with the confidence and strength of simple shepherds and to look up to the star with the same fervid faith of the wise men, it is indeed lost in the darkness of towering problems and knows no better solutions than 'accommodation' and compromise and detente vis-à-vis the Kremlin dictators!

'The latter, of course, are only too aware of the fact that the Christian Occident is no longer a real unity, that it has been weakened by false philosophies. Thus the struggle between west and east continues in the darkness of fears and doubts and the wily muscovities, while avoiding a showdown, hope to tire out and enervate the west. Truly, the light still shineth in the darkness, but the darkness refuses to comprehend it.'

"Sadly enough, since my father penned that testament, the world situation has not improved. On the contrary, we have become more of a house divided. Our once Christian west stands ravaged and desolate with Herod's slaughter of the innocents now sanctioned by a so-called high court, which rejects God's commandments, and by a society too sick to withstand its present drift toward self-destruction. Even for many Catholics, the right to life has become a debatable issue with neither the word of the pope or of God himself allowed to determine the outcome!

"And the church? What has become of our beloved old church? In a world already dangerously tottering and threatening to fall into ruin—Where is the refuge or rock of unchanging tradition and principle, where is the rock that is eternal in Christ Jesus, the rock that is everlastingly anchored in God, the rock that must always refuse somehow to be swept along by the cross currents of earthly caprice and opinion which eddy and swirl around it?

"The atomization of society which began with the ill-starred 'Reformation' of the 16th century and was further fragmented by the ‘reforms’ of 18th century ‘Enlightenment’ has not yet run its full downhill course, even now.

“In fact, the catastrophic cleavage, brought into the open by that singular bone of contention called Vatican II, has even ‘the people of God’ wrangling and bickering and quarreling. Instead of more closely uniting and renewing us in Christ Jesus, there is now greater discord and division, even in ‘the household of faith’, than ever before.

“Instead of a Novus Ordo round which the faithful might rally, there are now as many new ordos or ‘liturgies’ or even ‘creeds’ as there are priests and people. Universality and oneness have given way to everyone ‘doing their own thing.’ ‘The people of God’ are divided, confused, askance, and afraid.

“Still, ‘The Light Shineth In the Darkness.’ There still is and always will be Bethlehem and Christmas, when the Word Became Flesh, when men of good will were redeemed, no matter how many there were and still are who ‘receive Him not’ and love him not.

“And for those of good will, there is faith, there is hope, there is happiness. As for the world that received Him not and seems never to learn from the lessons of history, it is condemned to repetition of past mistakes, to frustration and futility.

“O blessed night, from whose bosom came forth the light of lights, the Lord of Lords, the King of Kings, may thy light lead us through the gloom of the new paganism and barbarism, and comfort and sustain and save us from despondency and sin! Grant this, O Infant Lord, we plead!”

No. 88—December, 1977 Rudolph M. Unger

Remembrances

God Is. He Is Good. He Loves You.
The Awesome God Is A Gentle Father.
God's Love Is Greater Than Our Need.
That Which Works The Will Of God is Good And Nothing Else.
Man Has Meaning Only In The Context of God.
God Loves Us More Than We Love Ourselves.
Lord—My Faith, My Hope, My Charity, My All!
Lord, Help Me This Day To Do My Reasonable Best And Leave In Your Hands The Rest.
Happiness Is The Fruit of Good Will.
Joy And Peace Do Not Come Where Sin Is.
If Love Is Not Led By Truth It Will End In Hell.
Action Not Preceded By Thought And Prayer Will End In Disaster.
The Lord Waits At The End Of The Road.
Life Is An Act Of Faith.
Life Is A Promise Of Things To Come.
Prayer Is The Highest Activity.
Yea! My Lord Is A Wonderous One!
Blessed Be The Lord Of The Daisies!
Charity, Justice And Truth Are Inseparably Intertwined In The Wisdom Of God.
God Said "Love One Another" Not "Coerce One Another."
Man's Salvation Does Not Lie In Humanity, But In Divinity.
Christianity Is Not Soft Headed.
Christianity Is Not A Country Club.
Bending To The World Never Proves Fruitful For The Souls of God's Children.
Men Were Not Created To Be Wards Of The State, But To Be Free Sons Of God.
Where There Is Not Liberty, There Is Not Love, There Is Not God.
The Lord Did Not Make Man The Lord of Man.
The Arrogant Will Of Man Does Not Work The Just Will Of God.

Within Each Man's Will Lies Heaven Or Hell.
The Road To Hell Is Paved With Compromises.
Seek Refuge In The Truth, There You Will Find Freedom.
The Challenge Of Man Does Not Change From Age To Age.
That Challenge Is To Be Good.
Hold Fast To What Is Good And True And Beautiful. No Matter What. And Die Rather Than Surrender Them.
If You Feel There Is But A Speck Of Good In Your Life Or Your Memory, Hold Fast To It. It Will See You Through To The End.
Beware Of Men Who Do Malice To Truth and Justice In The Name of Charity.
He Who Strangles Liberty, Murders Justice and Is The Foe Of Charity.
Where There Is Force There Is Not Faith, Not Virtue, Not Charity.
The Powerful State Is The Mortal Enemy Of Individual Liberty.
The Question Is—Shall Man Serve Government or Shall Government Serve Man?
Socialism Promises What Capitalism Delivers and Socialism Then Seeks To Confiscate.
The Bigger You Make Government, The Smaller You Make Man.
Beware Of The Corruption of Contemporanity.
In Life There Are Those Who Give and There Are Those Who Take.
Man's Great Error Is To Mistake His Means For His End.
The "Ayes" Of Many Men Do Not Make A Wrong Right.
As License Grows Liberty Dies.
The 18th Century Was Concerned Primarily With The Spirit Of Man.The 20th With The Body.
Beware The Unprincipled.
The Measure Of Love Is Sacrifice.
The Joy Of Life Is Sharing.
He Who Cannot Share Is The Poorest Of The Poor.
Love Is Long In Learning. Love Is Long In Coming.
If You Love, You Will Suffer. The Greater, The Closer The Love; The Deeper, More Poignant The Pain.
To Love And Not Be Loved. Is There A Greater Pain Than That?
Everybody Is Somebody. Everybody Wants To Be Somebody.
A Little Honest Praise Goes A Long Way.

A Modest Woman Is Always In Good Taste.
What Do I Seek? I Seek "The Peace That Surpasses All Understanding."
"I Know Nothing Of Tomorrow, But That The Love Of God Will Rise Before The Sun." (Unknown)
"In The Family, As In The State, The Best Source Of Wealth Is Economy." (Cicero)
"Man Is So Lost In The Night Time Of Peace That He Fails To Recognize The Dawn Of Destruction." (Langley)
"They Tried To Turn Us Into Machines…But All My Life I've Fought To Be A Person." (Simas Kudirka)
"The Miracle Is Not That Man Has Walked Upon The Moon.
But That The Son Of God Has Walked Upon The Earth."
(Angela Bryce)